Performance at the Limit

The world of Formula 1® is a powerful mirror to the world of management, where high performance relies on strong leadership, clear goals, selfless teamwork, innovation through constant learning and a winning culture. *Performance at the Limit: Business Lessons from Formula 1® Motor Racing* uses the case of Formula 1® to demonstrate how businesses can achieve optimal performance in highly competitive and dynamic environments. This third edition has been extensively updated, including a powerful new framework, the Performance Pyramid, recent interviews with leading figures in the industry and a wide range of lessons for improved business practice. It is an invaluable guide for managers and students of business alike.

MARK JENKINS is Professor of Business Strategy at Cranfield School of Management. He has twenty-eight years' experience as a teacher, researcher and consultant in the areas of competitive strategy and innovation. He has undertaken research on the performance of Formula 1 teams since 1997.

KEN PASTERNAK has lived in six countries and worked with executives from over 100 different cultures. Building on his management and banking experiences at Citibank and the European Bank for Reconstruction and Development, he delivers executive development seminars covering leadership, teamwork and multicultural communication. He is based in both Finland and the USA.

RICHARD WEST has held senior commercial roles with the McLaren, Williams and Arrows Formula 1 teams and the Jaguar Sports Car team. Having raised in excess of $165 million in commercial sponsorship, today he works as an international keynote speaker and runs high-performance management training programmes across a broad range of business sectors throughout the world.

Performance at the Limit

Business Lessons from Formula 1® Motor Racing

Third Edition

MARK JENKINS

KEN PASTERNAK

RICHARD WEST

CAMBRIDGE
UNIVERSITY PRESS

CAMBRIDGE
UNIVERSITY PRESS

University Printing House, Cambridge CB2 8BS, United Kingdom

Cambridge University Press is part of the University of Cambridge.

It furthers the University's mission by disseminating knowledge in the pursuit of education, learning and research at the highest international levels of excellence.

www.cambridge.org
Information on this title: www.cambridge.org/9781107136120

© Mark Jenkins, Ken Pasternak and Richard West 2016

First edition published 2005
Second edition 2009
Reprinted 2012
Third edition 2016

A catalogue record for this publication is available from the British Library

ISBN 978-1-107-13612-0 Hardback

Cambridge University Press has no responsibility for the persistence or accuracy of URLs for external or third-party internet websites referred to in this publication, and does not guarantee that any content on such websites is, or will remain, accurate or appropriate.

Contents

Plates

Figures

Tables

Foreword

As a three-time World Champion driver, founder of two international airlines and non-executive Chairman of the Mercedes Formula One Team since late 2012, I have experienced many challenges in my life, but nothing is as exciting and relentlessly demanding as keeping a focus on winning in the ultra-competitive world of Formula One. It is not just a sport but also a business. The teams must always be at the top of their game because if their competitiveness is compromised, so is their commercial success.

This book looks deep inside the world of Formula One and provides the reader with a frank and uncompromising look at what it takes for a Formula One team to maintain its competitive position. Many of these lessons are relevant to businesses that want to develop and maintain their edge in the global marketplace.

This is the third edition that the authors have produced and, through their knowledge and access to the sport's principal players, leaders, suppliers and commercial partners, they have found further insights into what it takes to attain and, very importantly, maintain a competitive position, both on the track and in the business world today.

NIKI LAUDA
Non-Executive Chairman
Mercedes AMG Petronas Formula One Team

Acknowledgements

Having now published editions in English and Japanese in 2005 and 2009, and in 2011 as a special South Asian edition, it is our sincere wish to thank all of the people who have contributed to those earlier books and who once again have added their latest insights into the business world of Formula 1 Motor Racing, along with a number of new highly influential individuals whose contributions we are most grateful for.

Formula 1, both as a sport and as a business, requires huge commitment and unrelenting efforts from all involved. Despite these pressures, everyone we have spoken to has given freely their time, experience and knowledge, and for this we thank them one and all.

We trust that the reader will bear with us in recognising people by name, as without their time and contributions the previous editions of *Performance at the Limit* and this latest book would never have been written.

Firstly, and without whom our research and interviews could not have been undertaken so thoroughly, our sincere thanks go to Formula 1 supremo Bernie Ecclestone for allowing us unrestricted access to Round 11 of the FIA Formula 1 World Championship, the 2015 Formula 1® Shell Belgian Grand Prix at Spa-Francorchamps in August.

As with all earlier editions, his positive response to our request enabled us to meet and talk with many of the great names and characters in the sport and business of Grand Prix racing, with many of our detailed interviews taking place over that weekend.

Equally, this new edition would not have been published without the continued commitment of our publisher, Cambridge University Press, and our relationship manager Paula Parish. We would like to thank Matthew Bastock, Adam Hooper and Jeevitha Baskaran for their help with the production process. We are indebted to Michelle Atherton for transcribing our (often noisy) interviews and to Robert Swanson for preparing the index.

While the teams and individuals we approached for interviews, materials and key information all deserve our gratitude, our thanks in particular must go to the Mercedes AMG Petronas Formula One Team, which granted us access to their staff, photo library and motorhome facilities for the weekend at Spa and also provided us with access to Head of Mercedes-Benz Motorsport Toto Wolff for a truly insightful interview – thanks also to Tobias Kappeler for his help in talking to Toto. We were also able to spend some time in the company of three-time world Drivers' Champion and team non-executive Chairman Niki Lauda, who in his inimitable style gave us a number of direct and valuable answers. Niki also kindly provided the foreword for this third edition for which we are truly honoured.

Staying with Mercedes, Executive Technical Director Paddy Lowe shared with us many of his thoughts on process, and we are most grateful to him for his openness.

All of the input from Mercedes was coordinated through their Head of Communications Bradley Lord, to whom we offer our grateful thanks for his patience and commitment to help us with this project.

The Williams Martini Racing organisation as ever did not disappoint. We were able to spend considerable time with Group CEO Mike O'Driscoll, Deputy Team Principal Claire Williams and Chief Technical Officer Pat Symonds, and to look closely at the Williams revival that once again sees them as a front-running team. Thanks to Julia Tilling and Jen Williams for their help with setting up these interviews. We also benefited from a meeting with Williams shareholder Brad Hollinger, who shared with us his passion for F1, the Williams team and why he became a shareholder of one of Formula 1's most successful entrants. Further insights to Williams and women in motor sport were generously provided by reserve and test driver Susie Wolff.

McLaren Honda's racing director, Eric Boullier, was gracious with both his time and honesty at a time when McLaren was rebuilding its on-track fortunes, and Christian Horner, team principal of Infiniti Red Bull Racing, gave us valuable time and information in our quest for leading content. Thanks are also due to Sylvia Hoffer-Frangipane and Matt Bishop for their help in providing access to McLaren, and for Nicole Carling and Nikki Vasiliadis for Red Bull Racing.

From an organisational perspective we spoke with FIA Race Director Charlie Whiting, the man charged with ensuring safe race starts and dealing with on-track safety issues, and from the back end of the grid we appreciated the time and insights provided to us by Graeme Lowdon of the Marrusia/Manor Team.

With investment and sponsorship playing a critical role in the sport, a session with Just Marketing International (JMI) founder Zak Brown provided valuable insights, and Nick Chester, technical director of the Lotus F1 team, also provided us with an interesting interview and great insights on the pit-stop process. Thanks also to Chloe Todd of JMI and Clarisse Hoffmann of Lotus for both of their contributions.

With so much continued talk around engine supply and performance, Andy Cowell, managing director at the Mercedes engine division at Brixworth, guided us through the complex world of F1 power plants, and chance meetings with behind-the-scenes men of the stature of ex-Philip Morris man John Hogan gave us yet more valuable insights.

From a key transmission suppliers perspective we spoke with Xtrac chairman Peter Digby, and gained some very entertaining and valuable insights from three of the sport's leading scribes, David Tremayne, Joe Saward and Kevin Eason of *The Times* newspaper.

With the arrival of the new Hass F1 Team in 2016, our thanks go to long-serving motor racing stalwart Tony Dowe, currently serving with Walkinshaw Performance in Australia. Tony kindly arranged contact between us and Haas Team Principal Guenther Steiner. Also, thanks to Nigel Geach and Steve Troon at Repucom for updated information on F1 audiences in the USA.

To former Grand Prix driver and Le Mans winner and now TV commentator Martin Brundle, we offer our sincere thanks. Concise and to the point, Martin can always be counted upon for a true insight into the comings and goings of the F1 industry, and we also traded information with Le Mans winner and former F1 driver Allan McNish, both of whom were generous with their time.

Former Philip Morris press officer and now international media syndicator Agnes Carlier provided us with invaluable assistance in meeting and interviewing the Sauber F1 team's team principal, Monisha Kaltenborn, for which we also thank Robert Höpoltseder, who throughout the build-up to Spa provided us with assistance in a number of areas.

Thanks go to Andrew Lezala, CEO of Metro Trains Melbourne PTY, who over a number of years as a huge Formula 1 fan has utilised many of the *Performance at the Limit* lessons in building better practices and safety within businesses under his control, and who in a brief and frank exposé revealed how he was able to save £64 million in a single year by applying F1 philosophy to his engineering teams in the rail industry.

Lynden Swainston and her team at LSA rose to the challenge of sourcing quality accommodation for us in the centre of Spa, and to Marie and Georges for their great hospitality at La Vigie Spa. We were fortunate in meeting Willem Dinger, Unilever's global F1 manager working closely with the Williams team, who kindly helped us with access support at the Spa circuit.

Since commencing on our publishing journey with *Performance at the Limit* and now this latest book, we have benefitted in earlier editions from inputs from some who have moved on to new careers and roles, some who have sadly passed away and others who have moved teams and business roles; however, it would be remiss not to thank notable people such as Sir Jackie Stewart, Sir John Allison, John Barnard, Paul Edwards, Bernard Ferguson, (now Sir) Patrick Head, Eddie Jordan, Paul Jordan, Paolo Martinelli, Raoul Pinnell, David Richards, Dickie Stanford, Paul Stoddart, Jean Todt, John (Boy) Walton, Alex Burns, Sir Frank Williams and Hiroshi Yasukawa. Their words are in some cases still quoted and for those who are not, we still recognise their earlier contributions and the value of their comments to our earlier research process.

We hope and trust we have correctly identified everyone's inputs and contributions; however, last and most definitely not least, our thanks go to our ever supportive wives, Sandra, Harriet and Denise, who also give their continual commitment in terms of understanding the long hours of discussion, research, writing and production that a book such as this requires, and of course taking account of the visits to race tracks, team facilities or interview sessions that made creating this third edition of our book such a pleasure.

Mark Jenkins, Ken Pasternak and Richard West
Ampthill, Helsinki and Dartford 2016

Note on the reference system

A numbered list of all sources used is given in the References section at the end of the book. Where these sources are quoted from or referred to in the main text, a superscript numeral cross-refers to the relevant numbered source.

1 Overview and Formula 1 experience

The Grand Prix experience

Since researching and publishing the original 2005 edition of *Performance at the Limit – Business Lessons from Formula 1 Motor Racing*, the authors have had the continued privilege of attending a number of Grand Prix races.

Personal attendances at some of the world's most outstanding venues in Melbourne, Shanghai, Monaco, Imola, Spa-Francorchamps, Barcelona and Silverstone have left many lasting impressions and have allowed us the opportunity to interview many of Formula 1's leading team principals, drivers, sponsors, manufacturers and the sport's key movers and shakers.

For this edition, we were once again delighted to be granted full paddock access by the sport's long-term architect and leader, Bernie Ecclestone. By allowing us that access he has enabled us to work closely with a range of key people central to one of the world's greatest sporting arenas and businesses, Formula 1. This has allowed us to observe first-hand the many changes that the sport has undergone since our last collective visit to Barcelona in 2008, and with fresh information we have again recorded how, in a highly competitive business world, Formula 1 continually provides examples of innovation, teamwork, leadership and phenomenal rates of learning and improvement.

The ability to gain access to the inner sanctum of Formula 1 can never be underestimated, and as we have stated in previous editions, there are in reality two types of Grand Prix world: the outer public areas and the inner team areas.

The outer world is comprised of the public grandstands, vending and merchandising areas, programme sellers, camp sites, huge parking areas and the hundreds of thousands of passionate racing fans that flock to the races over the three-day periods of each weekend of racing.

The inner world of the circuit is comprised of the central paddock area, where access is strictly controlled by a highly desired credit card–sized pass worn around the neck on a lanyard. The pass carries the name and a photo ID of the person wearing it and it allows access to specifically accredited areas via a microchip sealed within it. Access is gained through the electronic pass readers at the paddock entry/exit points.

Once swiped in, the wearer of the FOM (Formula One Management) issued pass is now within the inner world of Formula 1 motor racing. This is a world reserved for the drivers and their managers, team members, sponsors, media and VIP guests, and is where, up to twenty-one times each year, the Grand Prix paddock becomes an extension of the world's corporate boardrooms. It is a place where deals are won and lost; politics and policy are played out; and where the world's sporting power brokers, investment bankers and capital venture firms meet and do business. Once referred to as 'The Piranha Club' by McLaren CEO Ron Dennis, it is not a place for the faint-hearted when it comes to business, for at times it is almost gladiatorial.

For the authors, the race of choice for the many interviews that were to be undertaken was the iconic Spa-Francorchamps race track in Belgium, with the event being run over the three days of the 21–23 August 2015 weekend.

This is the first race in the Championship held after the compulsory summer break period when the F1 teams are committed to taking time off in order to allow their staff to have a short period of holiday and rest, prior to recommencing on track battles at Spa for the remainder of the season. This race track is without doubt one of the most challenging and popular races in the Formula 1 calendar and one that the teams enjoy visiting immensely.

The original Spa motor racing circuit was built in 1921 and was first used for car racing in 1924, with the first Grand Prix held in 1925.

The race in that inaugural car racing year was won by Antonio Ascari in a factory 'works' Alfa. Sadly, Ascari died later that same year when racing at the French Grand Prix at a time when driver fatality was a regular occurrence.

Throughout its long and famous history, Spa has undergone many changes and is well known for its unpredictable weather. At one point in its past, twenty consecutive races were held in rainy conditions. Its location in the Ardennes region means the circuit can be dry in one

	Driver	Entrant	Time
1	L. Hamilton	Mercedes AMG Petronas F1 Team	01:47.197
2	N. Rosberg	Mercedes AMG Petronas F1 Team	01:47.655
3	V. Bottas	Williams Martini Racing	01:48.537
4	S. Perez	Sahara Force India F1 Team	01:48.599
5	D. Ricciardo	Infiniti Red Bull Racing	01:48.639
6	F. Massa	Williams Martini Racing	01:48.685
7	P. Maldonado	Lotus F1 Team	01:48.754
8	S. Vettel	Scuderia Ferrari	01:48.825
9	R. Grosjean*	Lotus F1 Team	01:48.561
10	C. Sainz	Scuderia Toro Rosso	01:49.771
11	N. Hulkenberg	Sahara Force India F1 Team	01:49.121
12	D. Kvyat	Infiniti Red Bull Racing	01:49.228
13	M. Ericsson	Sauber F1 Team	01:49.586
14	F. Nasr	Sauber F1 Team	01:49.592
15	W. Stevens	Manor Marussia F1 Team	01:52.948
16	K. Raikkonen*	Scuderia Ferrari	
17	R. Mehri	Manor Marussia F1 Team	01:53.099
18	M. Verstappen*	Scuderia Toro Rosso	
19	J. Button*	McLaren Honda	01:50.978
20	F. Alonso*	McLaren Honda	01:51.420

* Grid penalities incurred

Figure 1 Starting grid 2015 Formula 1® Shell Belgian Grand Prix

place and wet in another with fog and rain hanging in between the millions of trees that inhabit the area, and therefore it challenges drivers, mechanics and teams to come up with the best engineering solutions possible for the weekend, and with the added pressures of continually having to change the set-up of the race cars, which due to their complexity have a great many changeable parameters which can be altered to maximise their on-track performance.

It is a place where continuous improvement is a must and decisions need to be taken quickly if the teams of mechanics are to undertake their jobs efficiently and within the short time windows available to them each day. Unlike other, more glamourous locations such as Monaco and Singapore, the drivers, teams, guests and supporting staff required to run a Grand Prix find themselves living not in high-rise spacious apartments and luxury five-star hotels, but smaller family-run hostels and private dwellings, all of which adds to the unique atmosphere of this incredible venue.

The track itself provides some of the most challenging and high-speed corners in motor racing and pushes the drivers to the limits of their abilities. The famous Eau Rouge left-to-right hand flick and the super-fast entry and exit speeds always thrill the large crowds that attend, many of whom camp out for four days in the forests that surround this iconic motor racing venue. The atmosphere in the woods is one of a carnival with camp fires, beer and friendly rivalry.

The Grand Prix paddock is a place where a huge range of skills, services and talents are present. The teams' racing transporters, which are used to transport cars and equipment to all of the European venues, are here in abundance, as are the teams' equally impressive hospitality and catering units. In addition, the governing body of motorsport, the FIA, have their full facilities set up alongside units that represent a huge commitment in terms of manpower and technical resource from Formula 1's sole tyre supplier, Pirelli.

The teams' race transporters are specifically designed and manufactured not just as transportation for the racing cars and spares, but also as mobile workshops, data-management suites and a range of meeting rooms and executive suites.

Once positioned within the paddock, they are meticulously cleaned and are perfectly aligned to ensure the paddock exudes an image of total professionalism.

Sprouting tall aerials for their communications and telemetry equipment, it is hard to believe that all of this equipment is set up purely for the few days in each European host nation where races take place. At 'fly away' races, such as the Australian Grand Prix in Melbourne, the trucks are absent, but the equipment levels required by the teams remain constant.

The data produced by the monitoring of the racing cars is seen simultaneously by the on-site team; the engine manufacturers; the rows of senior personnel seated in front of rows of monitors on the pit-wall gantry; the staff back at the respective factories in the UK, USA and Europe; and in the case of the engine manufacturers, at their facilities in the UK (Mercedes), UK/Japan (Honda), France (Renault) and Italy (Ferrari). The data, communications and telemetry are effectively shared globally with all involved elements of the organisations and partnerships to provide the fastest-possible solutions to increase the team's performance on-site.

The scale of the 'show' is simply astonishing. While in Europe, the teams mainly handle their own car and equipment transportation via their purpose-built vehicles and transporters backed up by leading freight organisations. Currently, DHL are the official logistics company for FOM, carrying hundreds of tons of freight to the 'fly away' races via airfreight and seaborne shipping containers, and with global transport costs continually increasing, the team have taken to shipping duplicate sets of equipment to the long-haul overseas races in order to control costs, an example of which is the shipping by sea of a total of fourteen forty-ton containers to Mexico prior to the new Grand Prix there in 2015.

However, large amounts of airfreight are also still sent overseas, with top teams sending as much as thirty-eight tons of equipment each via air transport to the long-haul races and, when taking into account the mobile TV studio that FOM provide, up to seven heavy-aircraft freighters are required to get the materials to their destinations.

When watching a 'fly away' (intercontinental race) on television, just consider for one moment that everything you see in the pit lane, garages and paddock has to be packed, customs-cleared on departure and entry, delivered to the circuit, unpacked, set up and then broken down and shipped back to the teams' base or onto another race, all with very tight time schedules, and you will see just how complex the business of Formula 1 logistics are. The same is true of the entire television production studios and equipment from where FOM distribute the Formula 1 practice, qualifying and race footage for global TV – these again are built and later dismantled for each and every race.

As the sporting and business activities of Formula 1 have increased over recent years, so has the requirement for the teams' garages and on-site combined HQ and hospitality areas to become multi-functional. The mix of engineering challenges and providing VIP hospitality meeting and entertaining facilities has increased exponentially, and therefore the teams' areas and equipment have grown to match these requirements.

The Red Bull energy centre and the McLaren and Mercedes hospitality units are examples of how advanced these all-encompassing centres of weekend excellence have become.

Once based on commercial motorhomes, these latter-day weekend team HQs are superb purpose-built units set within the Formula 1 paddock, and they are carefully controlled in terms of who can access them. Inside, they provide levels of luxury, privilege, services and a quality of food and drink that would shame many full-time international catering venues. Simply put, they are, once again, a reflection of the professional teams that own and operate them. Containing meeting rooms, dining facilities, private offices and areas to relax, they are a haven of comfort within a hectic race weekend.

The actual layout within the paddock of trucks and motorhomes is strictly monitored, with the garages reflecting the seniority of the teams. Again, overseen by an FOM representative, the entire paddock area is laid out with millimetre precision, even within a challenging paddock such as Spa, where two layers of paddock exist due to the geographical position of the garages and with the paddock space effectively 'trapped' within the inner hairpin area of the circuit. Space is at a premium, but again, FOM use every metre to best effect.

The Formula 1 Paddock Club™ is another area that reflects the standards of the sport. This is a designated area for VIP hospitality, the location of which varies at each circuit, where the teams, sponsors and other commercial parties associated with Formula 1 invite their guests for optimum viewing and the highest-quality catering and drinks.

Finally, there are the teams' working garage areas. Once again, these are designed to reflect the identity and personality of the organisation and its sponsors and investors. To step inside a Formula 1 garage is to enter another world. The levels of light, layout and cleanliness have to be seen to be believed, and reflect the teams' factories in their national locations.

The entire interior of the garage area is designed around efficiency and serviceability while offering the corporate world the opportunity to display their corporate logos on the seamless printed panels that feature on the walls; for this is where their own brand, products and services are also on show to the world, and therefore world-class quality is essential.

Large flat-screen monitors display information, timings, logos and other essential race weekend details. The drivers have individual areas for their crash helmets, gloves and seating. Sponsors are given specific areas from which to view the team members working, or to actually view the pit stops in close-up action during the race while being in positions of safety, and all of this is achieved mindful of the fact that the world's media and TV are watching on, ever present.

In among all of this professional imaging, transportation, efficient garage-area design and VIP and media work lies the actual racing weekend and its demanding schedule of sessions and events. In among the deal brokering, VIP and sponsor tours of the garages and the media work lies the need for the drivers, engineers, engine manufacturers, mechanics and technical specialists to concentrate their efforts on practice, qualifying and the actual race on Sunday. Juggling all of these inter-related requirements is again another work of art.

The teams' media, sponsorship, hospitality, on-site race team and factory-based engineers and specialists all require a detailed specific timetable from which to work, an example of which is shown below from the Spa weekend. All is delivered in agreement with the drivers and the team's overall objectives.

As the Grand Prix weekend builds, so does the pressure on every team member. Most are on-site on Thursday (although they get there earlier when the race is at Monaco as it is the only circuit that uses the track on Thursday, Saturday and Sunday, leaving the track to other support races on the Friday), or earlier if it is a long-haul race in order to try and overcome jet lag and travel tiredness. Thursday afternoons are a time to review the layout of the paddock, meet and greet early arrivals and settle into the competitive rhythm of a race weekend.

Friday is a time for circulating the paddock, for searching out specific people and journalists and for catching up on the latest word on the street.

Come Saturday the mechanics, tyre fitters, engineers and drivers can be seen moving between the teams' mobile headquarter and garages, to media briefings, back to headquarters for lunch and private meetings and, if required consultation with the teams' medical specialist or a relaxing massage. Driving a Formula 1 car is a very physical process and requires high levels of mental and physical fitness. In order to keep the drivers in top condition, the teams provide dieticians, masseurs and in some cases coaches to keep their lead men and women perfectly honed throughout the weekend.

Saturday is all about the on-track practice and the all-important qualifying sessions in Q1, Q2 and Q3. Pole position is essential for a competitive start to the race on Sunday and by the end of the day at Spa, it was an all–Mercedes F1 Team 1–2 line-up, with Lewis Hamilton taking pole with a time of 1.47.197, followed by his team mate, Nico

Thursday 20 August 2015		
Formula 1	Press Conference	15.00
Track Activity	Pit Lane Walk (3 day ticket holders)	16.00–18.00
Friday 21 August 2015		
Formula 1	Pit Lane Walk (Paddock Club)	08.45–09.45
Formula 1	Practice #1	10.00–11.30
GP2	Practice	12.00–12.30
Formula 1	Pit Lane Walk (Paddock Club)	12.35–13.45
Formula 1	Practice #2	14.00–15.30
GP2	Qualifying	15.55–16.25
Formula 1	Press Conference	16.00–17.00
Porsche Supercup	Practice	16.45–17.30
GP3	Practice	17.50–18.35
Saturday 22 August 2015		
Formula 1	Pit Stop Practice	08.30–9.15
Formula 1	Pit Lane Walk (Paddock Club)	08.30–09.45
GP3	Qualifying	09.45–10.15
Formula 1	Practice #3	11.00–12.00
Porsche Supercup	Qualifying	12.25–12.55
Formula 1	Pit Lane Walk (Paddock Club)	13.00–13.45
Formula 1	Qualifying	14.00–15.00
GP2	Race #1	15.40–16.45
GP3	Race #1	17.20–17.55
Sunday 23 August 2015		
GP3	Race #2	09.25–10.00
GP2	Race #2	10.35–11.25
Porsche Supercup	Race	11.45–12.20
Formula 1	Pit Lane Walk (Paddock Club)	12.25–13.15
Formula 1	Drivers' parade	12.30
Formula 1	Starting grid presentation	12.45–13.15
Formula 1	National anthem	13.46
Formula 1	Race	14.00

Figure 2 2015 Formula 1[®] Shell Belgian Grand Prix Schedule

Rosberg, with a time of 1.47.655, and yet again the Mercedes drivers appeared to be in control (Figure 1).

Post-qualifying is a time of what appears to be a 'controlled media frenzy'. The drivers and their team's press aides can be seen in the paddock media area surrounded by journalists holding out their recording devices, hanging on the words of the successful and not so successful in order to meet their domestic and international reporting deadlines.

Cameras click, crowds jostle, media coordinators slowly but determinedly move their drivers back to the engineers, who are keen to debrief them on the car's performance and where possible make further on-track improvements for race day.

Saturday evenings can also mean sponsor appearances with senior representatives for the drivers and lead team members. All of this and the track-side activity have to be taken into account, planned for and delivered seamlessly and professionally.

Sunday, race day, 'the longest day', dawns early. Arrive early enough and you will see the first people (usually the team HQ and catering staff) walking to their units and opening up their facilities, meeting rooms and catering areas for the day ahead. Shortly after them come the drivers and their managers, engineers, team mechanics, press officers and of course the all-important team principals.

Within a very short time the paddock is buzzing. The teams are all in, the clock is ticking down to the race start time, the race transporter drivers (truckies) are again cleaning and polishing their cabs and articulated trailers to perfection and the drivers, now totally focused on the day's events, pause briefly for photographs or a final chat with a passing journalist or film crew member. Throughout all of this and over the three days is the ever-present sight of Bernie Ecclestone passing from team HQ to team HQ, garage to garage, ensuring that under his guiding hand the show runs faultlessly and to time.

Amidst all of this action, one cannot but help begin to notice and hear the crowds. When one is within the paddock, it can almost be a trance-like experience, such is the energy created by the comings and goings of the drivers, team members, media and VIPs. But now, with the race start approaching, another noise can be heard . . . that of tens of thousands of people blowing air horns, shouting out their favourite drivers' names. It is the viewing public, the fans, the people who have camped out for days or driven through the night to be here to witness a spectacle unlike any other in the world unfold in dramatic action once the red starting lights on the start line overhead gantry are extinguished.

Here at Spa, looking down the hill after the first hairpin right-hand corner, one can see the grandstands are full; the crowds have congregated at the bottom of the downhill section running into the lightning-fast Eau Rouge left–right flick where the drivers will power onto the uphill straight, taking them up to the highest part of the circuit, where the woods are alive with spectators awaiting the thrill of the Grand Prix.

With final handshakes in the garages, VIPs watch their team's drivers getting strapped into their cars, for the real purpose of the weekend is just minutes away. The pit lane opens just thirty minutes before the start of the race and closes with just fifteen minutes to go before they are off. Failure to be on the grid in your allotted qualifying position within this fifteen-minute window means disaster, as a start from the pit lane exit is your only option if you fail to make your position. The drivers appear calm, team managers focused and the mechanics aware of the challenges facing their drivers, each totally committed to their individual tasks.

One by one the drivers take up their positions on the grid, and in the few minutes before the start of the race they step out with helmets and fire-proof balaclavas off, talking to their engineers and mechanics and, even at this late stage, selected TV reporters such as former Grand Prix driver and now Sky TV Lead Commentator Martin Brundle undertake their frenetic grid 'walkabout', catching key comments from VIPs, Bernie Ecclestone and drivers alike.

With but a short time to go, the grid is cleared of all non-essential people. Standing on the sides of the tracks the engineers and mechanics see their drivers set off on the warm-up lap at the appointed minute and as the last car clears the grid they rush with their equipment, wheels and tyres, car jacks, tools and other essentials to the sanctuary of their team garages.

Meanwhile, completing their warm-up lap, the cars weave frantically to ensure they keep the heat in their tyres which up until the commencement of the warm-up lap have been kept at high temperatures by the electric tyre blankets used to ensure the tyres are at optimum heat for the race start.

The drivers round the last right and left-hand corner and head to their pre-allocated spaces on the starting grid and, once all are in position, with the green flag having been waved at the rear of the gird to indicate everyone is in the right place, the five red lights come on to a crescendo of engine noise, and Race Director Charlie Whiting hits the lights-out button. The 2015 Formula 1® Shell Belgian Grand Prix is underway (see Figure 2 for full schedule).

The paddock area behind the garages is now strangely devoid of people; it is eerily quiet. Everyone is focused on the track, the pit lane and the race order – strategy is unfolding and F1 racing history is being written. One thing, however, never changes in the world of Formula 1 motor racing, and that is the deadline to the next race.

Teams of truck and hospitality HQ staff have already begun to pack away stock and items no longer required. Champagne is of course on ice, but their thoughts are now on the next race venue, the next challenge and the next improvements. Some people, their work done, are already leaving the track to head for the airport, keen to avoid the heavy traffic that a post–Spa GP is also famous for.

The world of Grand Prix racing never stands still, for to do so in reality means going backwards. As the race draws to a close, it is a familiar sight. The two Mercedes of Lewis Hamilton and Nico Rosberg take first and second places, with Romain Grosjean in his Lotus taking a well-deserved third.

By the time the champagne spraying ceremony is over and the media sessions finished, the public roads are becoming clogged with traffic, the helicopters for drivers, team principals and VIPs are leaving and the teams are on the road to next Grand Prix at Monza in just two weeks' time . . . the show goes on.

An introduction to Formula 1 motor racing

The world of Formula 1 motor racing is by all accounts the pinnacle of car racing in terms of technical specifications and global spectacle. In 2015, nineteen races took place in nineteen countries across five continents, and the industry, including its complex supply chain, accounted for an estimated $3 billion in total value. Some 425 million television viewers, 38 per cent of which are women, watched F1 races on television, making it the most watched annual sports series in the world. Viewership is only surpassed by the Olympic Games and the World Cup football tournament, both of which are held only every four years. It is an intense, highly competitive environment where even a hundredth of a second can make a substantial difference to race results.

Formula 1 stands as the longest-established motorsport championship series in the world. Its purpose was initially to provide a racing series which allowed different manufacturers to showcase their cars and technology. A fundamental part of Formula 1 is therefore that each team designs and manufactures their bespoke racing cars each year. There are some automobile manufacturing teams like Mercedes and Ferrari that also design and build their own power units (previously they were called 'engines', but as of the 2014 season they have become very complex, turbo-charged, hybrid V6 power units).

The power unit now encompasses what is known as an Energy Recovery System, or ERS for short. This consists of Motor Generator Units that harness waste heat energy taken from the turbocharger and also waste kinetic energy from the braking system.

This energy is then stored and subsequently used to propel the car. In 2015 an F1 car has two Energy Recovery Systems: MGU-K (which stands for Motor Generator Unit – Kinetic) and MGU-H (which stands for Motor Generator Unit – Heat). These systems are complemented by an Energy Store (ES) and control electronics. ERS is capable of providing 120 kw of power (approximately 160 bhp) for approximately 33 seconds per lap – while complex, this is truly remarkable engineering.

Coming back to the teams, the term 'manufacturer' or 'works team' therefore relates to those who also produce road cars, while the term 'constructor' is used for those who are solely concerned with running a Formula 1 team while relying on a power unit supplier. As stated by Peter Windsor, a well-known commentator on the sport,

The reality of F1 is that it is the only form of motorsport in the world that requires a team to design and build their own car to enter.[1]

To compare the basic differences between Formula 1 and other internationally recognised race series, Table 1 provides a summary of some of the distinctive features of Formula 1.

Formula 1 is an 'open-wheel' formula, which means that the chassis of the car is primarily a cockpit for the driver; the wheels of the car are exposed, and within certain technically specified parameters set out by the Federation Internationale d'Automobile (FIA), the ruling body for motorsport racing, the designers are free to come up with whatever solutions they feel will provide the best race performance.

Table 1 Contrasting F1 with other racing series

Characteristic	Formula 1	NASCAR	Le Mans & American Le Mans (ALMS)	GP2	IndyCar Series	World Rally Championship
International race locations	Yes	No	Yes	Yes	No	Yes
Cars designed & manufactured by teams	Yes	Yes	Yes	No	No	Yes
Open-wheel or full-covered bodies	Open	Covered	Covered	Open	Open	Covered
Based on production cars	No	Yes	No (yes in GT class)	No	No	Yes
Type of track	Tarmac circuit	Tarmac oval	Tarmac circuit	Tarmac circuit	Tarmac oval	Tarmac and rough terrain roads
Weather/light conditions	Dry and wet	Dry only	Dry, wet and night	Dry and wet	Dry only	Dry, wet and night

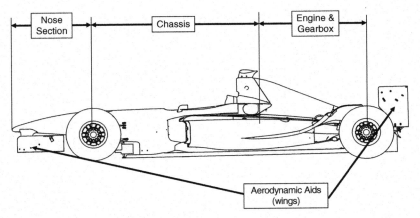

Figure 3 Schematic of F1 car.
Source: Williams F1

Figure 3 offers a simple schematic to represent the typical layout of a Formula 1 car.

Figure 3 identifies a number of important aspects about the car. The first is the chassis, which refers to the main structure of the car. An efficient chassis is critical for the car to achieve the maximum level of *grip*, thereby maximising cornering speeds.

The second is the drive train: a term which comprises the power unit (engine) and transmission, which is located behind the driver at the rear of the car. These components form part of the main structure and are attached directly to the chassis; the drive train provides the *power* and *torque* needed to propel the car around the circuit.

The third group of components are the aerodynamic devices, including the complete bodywork, the most important of which are known as 'wings' at the front and rear of the car. These devices, combined with the overall shape of the car, also provide grip, but do so through using aerodynamic principles to create *downforce*, also known as negative lift. Downforce is created by forward motion in the same way that lift is created in a fixed-wing aircraft, only the wing profiles are in effect reversed, thereby creating negative lift, i.e. suction onto the track surface. A modern-day Formula 1 car creates aerodynamic downforce (in reality, it is negative lift) the equivalent of twice its total weight, meaning that in theory it could run upside down on the ceiling of the famous tunnel seen in the Monaco Grand Prix.

The fourth element introduced into the sport in 2009 was the Energy Recovery System (ERS), as described earlier.

Unlike many other forms of racing, these cars cannot be used on public roads and are not equipped to operate in the dark. However, floodlit circuits have been introduced to the schedule in venues such as Singapore and Abu Dhabi, which enable races to take place at times more suitable for European television audiences, still the main viewing base for Formula 1.

Formula 1 cars are highly specialised, single-seat machines designed to be raced on purpose-built circuits which vary in length from 3 km (Monaco) to 7 km (Spa-Francorchamps, Belgium), with the races covering an overall distance of around 300 km (approximately 180 miles) over ninety minutes. A further important characteristic of Formula 1 is that it is a race championship series rather than an individual race such as the Indy 500 or Le Mans 24-hour sports car event. It therefore takes place over a nine-month season that runs typically from March to November.

Formula 1 motor racing, a brief history

The first ever motoring contest took place in 1894 in France, organised by a Paris newspaper, but it was not until the Automobile Club de France sponsored a race in 1906 that the word Grand Prix was used, which was incidentally a race won by Renault. In terms of what is now considered the Formula 1 World Championship, modern history starts in 1950.

In that year the series comprised seven races that took place in Great Britain (Silverstone), Monaco (Monte Carlo), USA (Indianapolis), Switzerland (Bremgarten), France (Reims), Belgium (Spa-Francorchamps) and Italy (Monza). It was in effect a European Championship with the Indianapolis 500 race included, although only Ferrari actually crossed the Atlantic to compete in the American race in 1952.

According to Autosport.com, there have been a total of 164 constructors involved in Formula 1;[2] we estimate their average tenure as being just under six years (in comparison, the average lifetime of an S&P 500 company is fifteen years). Many great automotive marques have attempted and failed to secure a competitive position in Formula 1; names such as Porsche, Aston Martin and Bugatti were all unable to support their entry into Formula 1 with competitive performances (although Porsche later became a successful engine supplier with the TAG-funded turbo engine, which powered the Championship-winning McLaren cars of 1984 and 1985).

Originally a showcase for manufacturers such as Alfa Romeo and Mercedes to demonstrate the prowess of their cars, Formula 1 soon developed into a more specialised activity, with purpose-built single-seat racing cars manufactured by companies such as Ferrari in Italy (which, in contrast to many of its Italian counterparts, introduced road cars to help fund its race activities rather than vice versa) and Cooper and Lotus in the UK.

Today, Formula 1 is a global phenomenon, as can be seen by the twenty-one venues scheduled for the 2016 season (Figure 4). There exists some concern at the loss of classic Grand Prix races in Europe, and there is a move to protect certain 'heritage' races such as Silverstone and Monza, with many senior figures believing these historic events are crucial to the F1 brand. These twenty-one races encompass five continents.

During the 2015 season, ten teams, each with two cars, competed in the FIA Formula 1 World Championship. These teams were supplied by four engine manufacturers: Mercedes and Ferrari, as mentioned

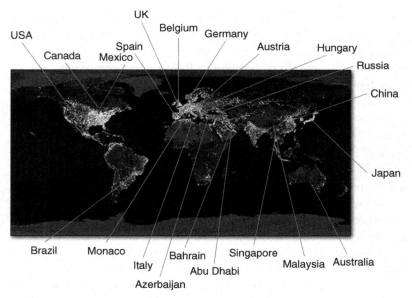

Figure 4 Map of race locations for 2016

earlier, plus Honda and Renault (Table 2). Given the need to continually develop their cars, the constructors will produce around seven chassis a year. However, ongoing development at the detail level to find an extra one-hundredth of a second in speed around the circuit means this is a continual process. According to *F1 Racing*,

McLaren racing produces some form of upgrade to their car every 17 minutes![3]

With budgets often in excess of $300 million and a workforce of up to 800 individuals, these are significant business organisations. They are specialist technology and marketing companies that provide the fundamental elements that underlie the glamour and spectacle of the Formula 1 motor racing series.

The teams have state-of-the-art design and manufacturing facilities which deal with a constant pressure to continually improve and enhance the designs and manufacture of the cars. Most teams also have bespoke wind tunnels that when used in conjunction with Computational Fluid Dynamics (CFD) are where aerodynamic designs are constantly being tested and upgraded.

These facilities have continued to grow in recent years, and a great example of this is the purpose-built MTC McLaren facility in the UK and the CFD centre at Lotus F1 in Enstone, Oxfordshire, where a joint venture between Boeing and the team saw one of the most advanced CFD centres in Europe develop.

The McLaren Technology Centre in Woking, United Kingdom, is large enough to fit nine 747 jumbo jets into its facility.[3]

Teams use complex networks of high-technology suppliers in, for example, areas such as telemetry, computations and measurement in order to respond to the demands for heightened levels of performance from new designs, new materials and new manufacturing processes. About 70 per cent of the car is manufactured in-house by top performing teams. The rest is supplied by partners and a large range of secondary suppliers who are well-integrated into the team's business. The entire system is fed by a sophisticated commercial operation that forges partnerships based on brand synergies and reciprocal marketing arrangements. The teams are led by a range of individuals from corporate managers to entrepreneurs who live, breathe and sleep the sport.

Table 2 *List of competing teams, their power unit suppliers and locations (2015)*

Constructor	Power unit	Location
Mercedes AMG F1	Mercedes HPP	UK/UK
Ferrari	Ferrari	Italy/Italy
Williams F1	Mercedes HPP	UK/France
Red Bull Racing	Renault	UK/France
Force India	Mercedes HPP	UK/UK
Lotus	Mercedes HPP	UK/UK
Toro Rosso	Renault	Italy/France
Sauber	Ferrari	Switzerland/Italy
McLaren	Honda	UK/Japan
Marussia	Ferrari	UK/Italy

What's in it for the teams?

As it is presently constituted, there is little or no incentive for a number of the Formula 1 teams to make money. Commercial organisations such as Williams, however, clearly have to balance their finances as they do not benefit from having a major brand (Red Bull) or a manufacturer (Mercedes) behind them; they are, in fact, stand-alone commercial enterprises.

In fact, the 2014 World Champions, Mercedes F1, lost £77 million ($120 million) during the season. According to the team reports,

operating costs rose by £49.5 m [£190.7 m in 2013 to £240.2 m in 2014] due to significantly higher performance bonuses payable as a consequence of the record-breaking level of sporting performance, and also increased costs arising from regulation change. Another significant impact was a rise in wages from £49.7 m in 2013 to £65.2 m last year, however, the report claims the overall loss was 'within the pre-defined parameters set by the shareholders'. That is despite the fact turnover rose by £21.7 m [£125.2 m in 2013 to £146.9 m in 2014] courtesy of 'higher sponsorship revenue and increased income from the Commercial Rights Holder flowing from improved on-track performance in 2013'.[4]

Nevertheless, the powers that be at Mercedes F1's parent company, Daimler AG, must believe the efforts and financial losses are worth it, as Team Chief Toto Wolff explained:

We are on plan of what Daimler expects from the team. You must just not forget how much the marketing benefit and the branding benefit is of the Formula One exercise. We had $3 billion of marketing value compared to our spending. One thing is clear, we are trying to be very efficient and the pressure from the Daimler mother company is always on and we are on a downward slope in terms of our costs.

Nevertheless, the value we achieve in racing in Formula One makes sense economically to Mercedes and our partners.[5]

The cost of going racing

How does a Formula 1 team fund its business? There are several sources:

1 Prize money allocated to the team based on where it finished in the standings during the previous season.
2 Special funds, called the Constructors Championship Bonus Fund.
3 Sponsors
    a. Cash-paying sponsors for their association with the team.
    b. In-kind contributions from sponsors who provide services and support.
4 Pay drivers.
5 Equity partners.

1. The Formula 1 Commercial Rights Holder Group annual report states operating profit from their activities. Of these earnings, 50% ($1,800 million in 2013) goes to the Formula One Group. The other 50% goes into a Prize Money Fund for the Formula 1 teams ($900 million in 2013). Of this amount, 23.7% of the fund is divided equally among the top ten teams, while an additional 23.7% is divided according to how teams finish in the Constructors' Championship. In addition, 2.5% goes to Ferrari, which has a special contract with Formula 1.[6]
2. The Constructors' Championship Bonus Fund comes from the Formula One Group's 50% share of the Commercial Rights Holder Group, and represents 7.5% of that total. This is a somewhat complicated sharing arrangement but it only involves three teams – Ferrari, Red Bull and McLaren. In addition, there is a special Historical Payment that is made by the Formula One Group to two teams – Mercedes and Williams.[6]

3. Sponsorship is a very important funding source for Formula 1 teams, and we discuss this in further detail in Chapter 8.

4. Most drivers are free agents who are sought after by teams according to their car-driving abilities. Their agents (where applicable) negotiate salary, personal sponsorship deal allowances and race and Championship bonus packages commensurate with their performance and experience. Other drivers might also be fast, but they rely upon their financial backers help them achieve their F1 drives by payment to the team. These are often called pay drivers. While many purists in the sport would prefer this were not the case, their financial backers do enable some teams to go racing when they might not otherwise have been able to do so. One notable driver in this category was Pastor Maldonado, whose backer, the Venezuelan oil producer PDVSA, reportedly paid the Lotus F1 team £30 million ($45 million) per year.

5. There are several business models for Formula 1 teams where equity investment plays a role. This can be in the form of single or shared private ownership, e.g. Sauber; private investment such as that achieved by Brad Hollinger in his shareholding at Williams and limited stock exchange listing, e.g. Williams; or ultimately as the subsidiary of a much larger entity, e.g. Mercedes.

Table 3 shows how this breakdown looked for the teams that lined up in 2014.

Technological change

Like many dynamic industries, Formula 1 has undergone a number of technological shifts over the years which have created new competitors and also destroyed some of the competences of established firms. As with any industry undergoing change, these firms either manage to transform themselves or collapse.

An illustration of the impact of such changes is provided in Appendix B, which details many of the Formula 1 teams who either collapsed or left the sport from 1950 to 2015. Table 4 shows a summary of some of the key stages in the evolution of Formula 1, with technology shifting from the large powerful Italian cars of the 1950s, through to the light agile British cars of the 1960s, through to the focus on aerodynamic grip which began in the 1970s and has made aerodynamics the central

Table 3 *F1 team figures, 2014 season*

Team	Team spending (£ million)*	FOM payments (£ million)**	Number of employees*
Mercedes	335 (incl. engine)	78.6	1300 (incl. engine)
Ferrari	275 (incl. engine)	102.3	750 (incl. engine)
Red Bull	240 (est.)	97.2	690
McLaren	190	61.1	650
Lotus	130	31.8	470 (incl. 40 contractors
Williams	105	51.7	520
Force India	100	37.4	350
Sauber	90	27.4	320
Toro Rosso	90	33.7	320
Marussia	70	29.9	220
Caterham	60	n/a	200

*Autosport.com 30 October 2014.
**The Times 14 May 2015.

competence for creating performance in Formula 1. It is also interesting to note that in the six Formula 1 seasons for each new decade over the fifty-year period featured in Table 4, Ferrari features strongly in every decade with the exception of the 1980s, an issue we will return to later.

In 2009, major changes were introduced to Formula 1 in the form of kinetic energy recovery systems (KERS). Max Mosley, then President of the regulatory body for Formula 1, the FIA, was a key driving force behind this new technology entering the regulation. He explained:

I think it very important that Formula 1 should develop technologies which are demonstrably useful in the real world. With the amount of intellectual talent and money that is now deployed by the top Formula 1 teams, it makes a great deal of sense to arrange the formula so that a performance advantage can be derived from doing something which is socially useful. The KERS technology is a good example because no matter what the means of propulsion of road vehicles in fifty or a hundred years' time, it will still make sense to recycle the energy which would otherwise be lost when the vehicle is slowed.

Table 4 *Key stages in the evolution of the Formula 1 car*

Year	1950	1960	1970	1980	1990	2000	2010
Top 3 cars	• Alfa Romeo • Lago-Talbot • Ferrari	• Cooper • Lotus • Ferrari	• Lotus • Ferrari • March	• Williams • Ligier • Brabham	• McLaren • Ferrari • Benetton	• Ferrari • McLaren • Williams	• Red Bull • McLaren • Ferrari
Key features	• 4.5 litre engine in front of driver • Space frame chassis	• 2.5 litre engine behind driver • Independent suspension	• Aerodynamic wings • 3.0 litre Ford DFV engine • Semi-monocoque construction • Slick tyres	• Ground-effect aerodynamics • Turbocharged engines	• 3.5 litre engines • Carbon composite construction • Semi-automatic gearbox	• 3.0 litre engines • Launch control • Fly-by wire technology • Engine management systems	• 2.4 litre engines • 60 kw kinetic energy recovery systems* • Refuelling abolished
Approx. horsepower & max rpm	• 400 bhp/ 7000 rpm	• 240 bhp/ 8000 rpm	• 420 bhp/ 8000 rpm	• 600 bhp/ 11000 rpm	• 600 bhp/ 14000 rpm	• 820 bhp/ 19000 rpm	• 700 bhp/ 18000 rpm

*KERS systems were not used during 2010, but were available in 2009 and 2011.

This hybrid technology uses mechanical or electrical means to capture energy from the car when it is braking that can be reused to help increase speed or acceleration. Formula 1 has always prided itself on being at the forefront of technology and this provides an important opportunity for the racing imperative to add impetus to the development of these important technologies.

Why do countries and cities want to host a Formula 1 motor race?

The Formula 1 industry has a very unusual business model. If a promotor wishes to host a race, they must expect to pay for the rights to do so and pay for the building of the race circuit in order to meet very exacting specifications for safety and spectator and team facilities; but they cannot expect any sharing of revenue from television broadcasts or the cash flow generated by trackside advertisement and the Paddock Club's corporate hospitality suites. They must effectively cover their costs through ticket sales. With average annual hosting fees of $35 to 40 million over the lifetime of a five to ten year contract, it is clear this is not possible. Added to this is the cost of building a stand-alone circuit, for which we are looking at over another $100 million.

This is why fifteen of the nineteen races during the 2015 season were funded mainly by the governments of the countries that hosted them. For them, the aura of Formula 1 brings a level of prestige to their country which is hard to find elsewhere. During a three-day race weekend, the huge television audience, plus tens if not hundreds of millions of other F1 followers through the press and social media, focus their attention on their city and country. Celebrities and international personalities who appear at the race add to the glamour and image. At the 2015 Russian Grand Prix at Sochi (the second year this was run on the site that previously hosted the Winter Olympics), President Vladimir Putin stood on the podium awarding Lewis Hamilton the first-place trophy.

But there are also some financial rewards for successful hosts. The US Grand Prix returned to the Formula 1 calendar in 2012 after a five-year period when no races were held there. This time it took place at a new, purpose-built circuit called the Circuit of the Americas in Austin, Texas.

At the inaugural race, Smith Travel Research reported that over the five-day period encompassing the full racing event and other attractions, hotels in the Austin area took in $32 million, which is triple the amount made during the same period the previous year. Hotel occupancy in downtown Austin the night before the race averaged at 97.8 per cent, with guests paying an average rate of $300.44. In comparison, on the closest Saturday the previous year, the average rate came to $111.40.

According to Steve Troon at Repucom,[7]

- US audiences have continued to increase for the third consecutive year.
- NBC, which acquired the broadcast rights to Formula 1 in the United States 2013, have since spread the coverage across subscription channels NBC Sports and CNBC, as well as free-to-air channel NBC for selected races.
- Live race audiences have risen by 18.4% compared to 2013. Within this, NBC's free-to-air coverage has risen on average by 6.0% per Grand Prix, whilst its subscription audiences have risen by an average of 65.1%.

Perhaps most importantly, however, Formula 1 is but one part of a government strategy to use sport to boost tourism by increasing Singapore's profile on the global stage. The government has a vested interest in ensuring the race continues to be a success, and so puts an unparalleled amount of effort into turning the race into a city-wide celebration with its affiliated concerts and special events. In the first four years of the Marina Bay round, 100 million people watched the race on television, while between 200,000 and 300,000 people attended each GP. Over the same period, tourism revenues attributed to the race boosted the city's coffers by $410 million.

In contrast, the Indian Grand Prix ran into difficulties when authorities decided to classify Formula 1 as entertainment, not sport. This left the teams liable for large local taxes. When no agreement on the tax issue could be reached, the race fell off the calendar in 2014 after being run there for three years. Also, where location is one of Singapore's strengths, for Korea it was a weakness. The Yeongam International Circuit was five hours from Seoul by express train, and a long drive from any sizeable population centre. Big plans to develop that area did not materialise, funding ran out and the Korean Grand Prix took place there for only four years, from 2010 to 2013.[8]

In 2015, Formula 1 returned to Mexico City after a twenty-three-year absence. Tickets for the event were sold out within days. And in 2016 the first race in Baku, Azerbaijan, will take place on a street circuit laid out across the city. Other countries continue to vie for a slot on the F1 calendar including Qatar.

Why use Formula 1 motor racing to explore management lessons?

Formula 1 motor racing provides many important ingredients to help us explore the nature of organisational performance. The first is a clear, unambiguous performance outcome – consistently winning races and thereby consistently outperforming the competition. The fundamental importance of this measure of performance, and one which is often overlooked by managers striving to improve their organisations, is that it is concerned with **relative advantage**. The notion of competitive advantage is based on the premise that an organisation's performance is superior relative to all available competition.

Formula 1 clearly exhibits this criterion, as a team may make significant performance enhancements to its own car, only to find that it has become inferior to the competition that has made greater advances, and therefore it is the relative rather than absolute pace of improvement that is needed to improve and sustain a competitive position. All too often, managers lose sight of the external relativity of performance and focus too heavily on performance enhancements relative to their own internal benchmarks; in Formula 1 performance benchmarking is always relative to the competition and a team's performance is only as good as the last race.

In the words of the Williams F1's Pat Symonds:

One of the interesting things with Formula 1 is that everything is relative. So, if you ask, 'how fast do I need my car to be?' the answer is 'quicker than anyone else's'; it's not an absolute number. I always say you should win a race as slowly as you can possibly can.

A further aspect that makes Formula 1 a valuable subject for our study is that it integrates all the fundamental resources of organisations: human, financial and technological, and relies on the continual development of knowledge to ensure competitive performance. It is primarily a people-based industry, but also one which requires large sums of cash to fund the technological development and human resources needed to generate superior performance. As we shall explore in later chapters, there are many cases where there is plenty of cash, people and technology and yet these are not integrated in a way that converts such a rich resource base into superior competitive performance.

The longevity of Formula 1 provides us with an important opportunity to consider the long-term implications of performance rather than focusing on those firms which are currently the high performers. This also means that unlike many other performance-based studies we don't have to apply a short-term cross-sectional research approach; we are able to focus on the dynamics of these organisations in terms of their growth characteristics, emergent cultures and the highs and lows of their competitive performance.

The nature of Formula 1 as the pinnacle of motorsport technology allows us to focus on the role of technology in supporting competitive performance. Frequently, technology is seen as an enabler of high performance but also as a huge cost; a potential 'black hole' which can quickly devour an organisation's resources for very little or no increase in performance. Ask most CEOs if they know what kind of return they get on their expenditure on information and communication technologies and the answer will invariably be one of frustration and uncertainty. This is a tension which is particularly evident in Formula 1, where many high-budget teams have been unable to translate their superior technological resources into enhanced performance. Formula 1 provides the ideal context for us to consider this problem.

The Formula 1 industry provides the perfect 'goldfish bowl' for us to examine the components of performance at the critical levels of an organisation:

- The Formula 1 Team itself, along with its partnerships;
- Teams: internal cross-functional and external cross-partnerships and the various groups of individuals who, among other things, create components of the car, coordinate race strategy and change the wheels and tyres during a race; and
- Individuals: how employees are able to sustain motivation and develop the skills and competence needed to perform and keep delivering at the absolute limit of their capabilities.

It is a very unique business and sporting environment, as Toto Wolff from Mercedes told us:

The bizarre thing is that we are meeting each other twenty times a year in that paddock; and within those 2,000 square metres we are confronted with our main competitors, the regulators, the commercial rights holder, our own staff, our sponsors; and all that under the huge magnifying glass of the media, where whatever we say is multiplied by 1,000 and is ending up somewhere in the universe in magazines, TV or the internet. This is why it is so intense and lots is going on around the race weekend – lots of politics, lots of commercial decisions, discussions within your own team, and you're only as good as your last race result. And on Monday the last race result doesn't count anymore – it's void!

While these factors provide a basis for our investigations it is important to be mindful of the limitations of using Formula 1 in this way. Our study is of a very particular and specialised industry. It operates on the basis of a commercial activity to feed a technological system to ultimately create a car to race against the competition. It is therefore less concerned with issues such as customer satisfaction and cost control than other organisations might be, although as we shall see perspectives on the latter are changing.

We are mindful of these limitations, but we do believe that the overall benefits of exploring a performance-rich context such as Formula 1 outweigh some of the concerns around its idiosyncratic nature. It is important for managers to look beyond their own contexts not only in order to help them recognise the distinctiveness of their situation, but also to stimulate new ideas and raise challenging questions about their own performance.

2 | *PATL performance framework*

The research process

The concept for this project first emerged in 2001, when the authors were asked to help design and deliver a management development programme for a leading global law firm, Freshfields Bruckhaus Derringer. Formula 1 was utilised as it provided a stimulating context to consider issues relating to teamwork, project management, client relationships and business dynamics. Our experience in developing this programme led us to focus increasingly on describing, explaining and drawing lessons from the sources of performance advantage in Formula 1 motor racing. The idea that Formula 1 provides not only an exciting context, but also exemplifies how organisations are able to create and sustain the basis for optimised performance, has led us to develop a more rigorous approach to these questions. The objective of this book is therefore to explore these issues in a more holistic and systematic way than we have been able to do so far, and then to develop a structured framework for presenting our findings that represents organisational performance and provides a basis for applying the concepts into other contexts.

Our process has involved three distinct stages. The first was to develop the conceptual framework, which consists of four key elements (organisation, individuals, teams and partnerships) and three core processes (integrating, innovating and transforming). This was done through a review of published sources that have evaluated the performance of Formula 1 teams. One of the benefits (and challenges) of researching the Formula 1 context is that there is an abundance of published information on the Formula 1 organisations and particular individuals such as drivers, founders and CEOs. A review of this material enabled us to draw out some of the key aspects of the performance system in Formula 1, which is summarised in this chapter. A full list of all published sources used is given in the References section.

The second stage of the process was to identify a number of experienced individuals who were to provide the bedrock of our research. In particular, we sought out those who could bring a range of different experiences, either through having worked for differing kinds of Formula 1 organisations or through having worked in other industries. The following outlines some of the organisational characteristics that we endeavoured to represent through our selection of individuals to be interviewed for the book:

1 Exhibited both enhanced and declining performance at different stages in their lifetime;
2 Had undergone a change of leadership and/or ownership;
3 Had created discontinuous innovations which have changed the basis of competition;
4 Illustrated different ownership structures;
5 Illustrated different levels of organisational integration.

In these interviews, we were seeking to gain insights into the process and principles which underlie performance. When researching the original book, this part of the process was perhaps the most challenging as access to these individuals is particularly difficult to obtain; however, through our own efforts and the support of a number of intermediaries and, of course, the individuals themselves, we secured a total of forty-seven interviews. For the second edition we added a further twenty-six interviews, and for this heavily revised third version of our work we completed a further twenty-two interviews, making a total of ninety-five interviews over a fifteen-year period with a total of sixty-five respondents. This provides the basis of our thinking and analysis. Full details of all the respondents are provided in Appendix C.

The selection of respondents was based on the above criteria, but we also wanted to develop in-depth case insights into particular organisations. This meant that to some extent we used the 'snowball' sampling approach, where access to one individual enabled us to identify and contact other relevant individuals.

A further point to our analysis is that, as with Collins and Porras' *Built to Last*,[9] we have also focused on the history and evolution of organisations rather than simply their present-day form. This is because an evolutionary and longitudinal perspective was essential in order to gain a better understanding of the dynamics of performance. We did not therefore simply look at the success stories of those who were at the top of the curve; we considered the way in which such successes were created and formed over time, and also in a number of cases how the success dissolved into failure and the diagnosis of this process.

The final stage of the research involved detailed analysis of the interview transcripts and comparison of this data with the range of published materials that we had collated into a full chronological database. We extrapolated some of the key observations and lessons from the data, which are summarised throughout the chapters and specified in Chapter 10. Our approach to this part of the process was to focus on understanding the details of how these organisations operate, through accounts and anecdotes of specific situations, and also to look for common patterns and themes that emerged. We also sought to pick up on those unexpected, counter-intuitive insights which can add to our understanding of a particular phenomenon or situation.

It is perhaps worth emphasising that this study does not seek to 'prove' that certain factors create success; nor is it our intention to generalise the issues we observe in Formula 1 beyond this specialist context. The purpose of the data collection is therefore not so much to 'validate' but to 'elaborate' the frameworks outlined in this chapter. In particular, we seek to make connections between the processes and elements; for example, in terms of the linkage between innovating and performance. A specific focus for us was to understand the inter-related nature of our four elements (individual–team–partners–organisation). The framework was therefore concerned with rich description and aimed to provide a fine-grained understanding of the processes involved in creating and sustaining high performance in one of the most competitive and dynamic contexts possible.

The performance framework

A Formula 1 team is a highly complex system. It combines many different resources such as human capital, technology, marketing and finance to achieve a performance outcome that is hopefully superior to those of its competitors. It is a critical balance between maximising the potential of individual areas and optimising the overall performance to ensure that the integrated effect exceeds the sum of the parts. For many watching the Formula 1 spectacle, it is all down to the skill of the driver. In our study we conclude that the driver is an important ingredient, both from the point of view of driving skill and also in influencing the motivation and dynamics of the team. But a driver can never succeed without the support of the organisation and its technology behind him.

Appendix A details the Drivers' World Champion for the period 1950–2015. In 1995, 1996 and 1997, three different drivers won the Drivers' World Championship. Each of these drivers moved to a new team shortly following their Championship success and the subsequent fortunes of each were very different. In 1996, Damon Hill won the Drivers' World Championship but left Williams to join Arrows in 1997, and then in 1998 moved to Jordan, eventually retiring at the end of 1999. Also driving for Williams, Jacques Villeneuve won the title in 1997; he stayed with the team during 1998, but then left to help set up the new British American Racing (BAR) team, of which his manager, Craig Pollock, was managing director and a major shareholder. However, he was unable to repeat his earlier success and left BAR, retiring from Formula 1 at the end of 2003.

In contrast, Michael Schumacher was Champion with the Benetton team in 1994 and 1995 and then left to join Ferrari. The technical management team at Benetton followed him to Ferrari a year later and three years after that, in 2000, he became World Champion once again. Schumacher's success at Ferrari continued until his departure at the end of 2006.

In 2005 and 2006, Fernando Alonso won the Drivers' World Championship driving for Renault F1. The following year, full of confidence, he moved to McLaren and found himself embroiled in an intense struggle with his rookie driving partner, Lewis Hamilton. Alonso was able to stay in contention right up to the last race of the season, but both he and Hamilton ended up losing out to Ferrari's Kimi Raikkonen by one point. Alonso subsequently moved back to the Renault F1 team for 2008, where both the team and he found it very difficult to recapture the old magic.

In 2009, Jenson Button won the World Championship by exploiting the double diffuser technology (see Chapter 4) in his Brawn F1 car. Sebastian Vettel then succeeded as World Driver's Champion in the period 2010–2013, benefitting from the advantage of Red Bull Racing's supremacy in aerodynamic development, which came to an end in 2014 when the regulations changed to allow new high-efficiency power units. This put the emphasis back on a more balanced capability between power units and aerodynamics, thereby benefiting teams such as Mercedes and Ferrari, who developed their power units in parallel with their chassis. In 2014 and 2015, Mercedes' driver Lewis Hamilton became World Champion.

The point here is not to explain the demise of some drivers and the success of others, but to illustrate that there are many factors that can influence the lack of performance of a driver, such as the design of the car and effectiveness of the race team. Equally, there are many factors that explain the apparent success of a driver rather than just driving skills. The driver is one part of a team, and in order to sustain success in this highly competitive situation all aspects of the team have to integrate effectively.

It therefore requires **individuals** to be knowledgeable and highly motivated in order to maximise their contribution to the whole system.

To achieve success also requires that these individuals work effectively in **teams**, whether they are the pit crew changing the wheels and tyres of the car in a matter of seconds, the design team creating an aerodynamic component while working with staff in the wind tunnel and the composites department to create the finished article, or the commercial team collaborating to engage a new sponsor, thereby ensuring future funding for technology. Williams F1 Technical Director Pat Symonds describes his ideal engineering recruit:

We want people to be individualistic in their thinking, but they've got to be team players in their actions.

In other words, there's no point in recruiting the most brilliant engineer in the universe if they can't work in a team. As outlined in Chapter 7, teamwork is critical to performance in Formula 1.

Furthermore, these teams and individuals also have to work with their **partners** at the team and individual level. In 2015, this involved tyre supplier Pirelli effectively becoming part of the race team to ensure that the tyre performance is maximised through analysis of wear rates, track temperature and air pressures. It may also involve other commercial and technical relationships, such as data systems, brakes, fuel and lubricants, logistics that allow the team and their partners to benefit. In addition, the system has to work at the **organisation** (or multi-team, cross-functional) level, ensuring that connections are being made between the test team, the race team and the designers to improve the car as effectively as possible, and even where the pit crew are working with the commercial team, to ensure that their most prestigious sponsors get access to the pit garage and team facilities, but without compromising race performance or security.

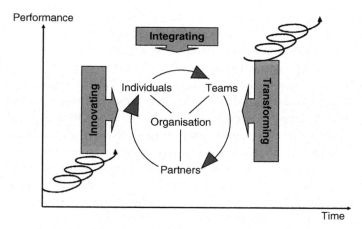

Figure 5 The performance framework

The central framework which we will use as the basis for this study relates to four key elements in the performance system of an organisation: the *organisation* itself, *partner* organisations, *teams* and *individuals*, all working together to produce the outcome of performance.

These four elements are in turn influenced by three dynamic processes which operate continuously across them. These are concerned with: **integrating** – the way in which the organisational system, influenced in large part by leadership and teamwork, brings together all of its diverse but connected activities, providing clarity of purpose and also constantly adjusting the various tensions that need to be balanced to optimise performance; **innovating** – the way in which the system continuously improves and enhances its performance levels; and **transforming** – how the system reconfigures itself in order to create new resources and new performance levels in response to changing conditions and competitive pressures. All of these processes impact on the elements to explain the overall performance outcome, as illustrated in Figure 5. Together they generate the organising framework for the book, which we will now consider in more detail.

Individuals

For the individuals working in Formula 1, this is their dream job. They have always wanted to be in Formula 1 and have now achieved this; their focus is therefore at one level to maintain this situation, but the highly competitive nature of Formula 1 means that they are constantly striving to both establish their worth and also progress in their careers.

There is a vast range of roles encompassed within Formula 1, from working on leading-edge car design to handling the negotiation of multi-million-dollar sponsorship contracts. There is also a huge range of nationalities involved, and not just from those countries which hold Formula 1 races; however, the gender mix is still weighted towards a predominance of male participation. Nevertheless, there are some indications that an already strong female presence will become enhanced, with Claire Williams and Monisha Kaltenborn now in team principal roles and Susie Wolff as the official Williams test driver during 2015. Women are now also heavily involved in marketing and public relations roles, and their skills continue to migrate into the more technical aspects of Formula 1, including aerodynamics and electronics.

Teams

Within Formula 1, the challenges of motivating and coordinating individual talent are central to both creating and sustaining a competitive edge. Employee turnover rates are particularly high in this industry; in this context, turnover often means staff moving to and being recruited by the competition. This means that, on the whole, Formula 1 teams cannot afford to rely on individual knowledge, but on building a wider social capital that underpins the whole organisation and, perhaps most importantly, by melding individual knowledge into the combined capability of a team.

Teamwork is a central element of the Formula 1 organisation. It is recognised that the performance of the organisation is only as good as its weakest link. Therefore, the focus is on ensuring that everyone is up to speed and pulling their weight. In the Formula 1 context we see the team as a small group of individuals who must work together to achieve a clearly defined output.

For example, a team of between twenty-one and twenty-three individuals all have to combine to change all four wheels and tyres on a Formula 1 car in, ideally, less than three seconds; at the time of writing, the current record is held by Red Bull Racing from the 2013 US Grand Prix with a time of 1.92 seconds. At this level of performance, the team has to work together to a degree of precision unimaginable in most other contexts. This kind of teamwork can be described as 'tightly coupled', in that the team works in a clearly defined context where the smallest change in one individual's performance – such as dropping a wheel nut – will have a major effect on the performance of the whole team. There are some valuable parallels in other industries that have transferred some of the concepts of the pit-stop process into their operations, such as hospitals improving the accuracy of patient hand-offs to and from the operating theatre, or short-haul airlines improving the efficiency and speed of their aircraft turnaround times. Learnings from Formula 1 are covered in more detail in Chapter 10.

Teams can also be 'loosely coupled', where individuals may be more dispersed, working on other continents and in other time zones and still be required to achieve a set objective within a timeframe. In Formula 1, this may relate to a team of engineers working on a new suspension component, or producing designs, building models and testing them in the team's wind tunnel. Equally, it can be the fabrication of components with partner organisations in other countries, testing them on the track in a completely different country and then ultimately installing them on the race car at a Grand Prix perhaps on another continent.

In both contexts, teams have to be able to both function effectively within their predefined tasks and to be responsive to changing situations and adapt to them quickly.

Partners

To achieve the highest levels of performance, Formula 1 constructors can never rely entirely on their own activities. They have to work with partners. Even when teams are highly resourced and almost obsessive about secrecy, the teams are still heavily dependent on external organisations for component manufacture and supply, as well as many other products and services.

This is particularly so in the case of tyres. For periods in the history of Formula 1 there has been a single tyre supplier, and so there has been no competitive advantage to be gained. However, there have also been periods when relationships with tyre suppliers became critical in achieving a performance advantage. For Ferrari in 2002, 2003 and 2004 its relationship with Bridgestone was critical to the performance advantage that Michael Schumacher was able to utilise en route to winning the Drivers' World Championships in those years. In 2015, we have a single tyre supplier – Pirelli – and again, the ability of the teams to work with Pirelli and their engineering team to get the most out of tyre performance is a potential source of advantage.

There are of course differing kinds of partners for Formula 1 teams; these range from technical partners who provide key products and technologies, to pure sponsors who have no direct involvement other than the exposure of their brand on the Formula 1 car. More detail on partners and their relationship with the teams is provided in Chapter 8.

Organisation

The purpose of the organisation in Formula 1 is very simple. It is a structure that is designed to generate the revenue streams necessary to design, manufacture and race the fastest and most reliable car. A key part of the flexibility and responsiveness of the Formula 1 organisation is attributed to the importance of the informal organisation. In Formula 1, concepts such as 'grade' and 'structure' are virtually non-existent. What matters is getting the job done to make the car go faster and, while there are clear separations between technical disciplines such as aerodynamics and electronics, to a large extent these are delineated by parts of the car. A team that works on the gearbox is defined by this particular component; moreover, the way it integrates with other areas, such as the engine design, is defined by the component area.

The fact that technical areas are delineated so clearly allows a clarity which is perhaps lacking in other organisational contexts. The hard part is therefore making trade-offs between areas regarding performance, weight and shape, all of which can have major effects on the other parts of the system. While this is a challenging area for today's Formula 1 teams, it is also where potential sources of competitive advantage are to be found.

Another important point about organisation relates to the core processes that are being undertaken. These almost always cut across functional levels, and without them the organisation is unable to achieve its core tasks. In the context of Formula 1, these processes relate to the design and manufacture of the car, with all the resultant issues around supply chains and assembly of components. Additional processes revolve around the continuous development and refinement of the car during the racing season, the mechanisms by which sponsors are engaged and brought into the team and the way in which race strategies are created and executed.

A further aspect of organisation, covered in Chapter 9, relates to culture. While Formula 1 is a particularly close-knit and incestuous industry, with many employees frequently moving between teams, it is also apparent that each team has a distinct set of values and priorities which often mirror the priorities of its founders or corporate parent and imbue all the activities of the team with shared values and corporate culture. For anyone working within Formula 1 the differentiation between these cultures is very clear. For those looking in from the outside the teams all appear very much the same. A winning culture is a critical aspect of these organisations; it directly relates to performance and therefore is a key area of exploration for our study.

Integrating

Integrating is fundamentally about leadership and teamwork. Perhaps an overused term in management, leadership is a descriptor which appears central to both the sustained performance of Formula 1 teams and, perhaps more importantly, to the ability to turn failing teams into Grand Prix winners. The leadership role is fundamentally concerned with integrating; being the 'glue' between the core parts of the operation, which are often in high states of tension. In particular, these relate to the tension between mechanical layout and aerodynamics, between design and manufacturing, between the commercial and technical parts of the business and the tension between the short- and long-term objectives of the organisation. The best leaders in Formula 1 integrate by providing flexibility and clarity for those within the organisation. It is said by many we have interviewed that a Formula 1 team is almost diametrically opposed to the big-business model. Nothing will be achieved through oppressive bureaucracy and burdensome processes. Formula 1 provides some instructive principles for keeping the organisation agile, responsive and fiercely competitive.

Innovating

While cash is certainly the lifeblood of a Formula 1 team, innovation is without doubt the spirit of the team; innovation not for the sake of it, but in search of improved performance in order to improve results on the track. Any team that is unable to sustain a flow of performance-enhancing innovations will quickly find itself at the back of the grid. No team, no matter how small its budget, can afford to stay still when it comes to finding creative ways to improve car performance; and this has engendered some distinctive approaches to innovating within Formula 1.

For example, there are those who have focused on radical new technologies which have disrupted the accepted way in which Formula 1 cars should be built. Such an approach is exemplified by Team Lotus under the leadership of Colin Chapman in the 1960s and 1970s. Others have focused on constantly integrating innovations into their cars, many of which have originated from other teams, but which are combined in highly effective ways to maximise the performance of the car. For example, Patrick Head created the Williams FW14B, one of the most successful Formula 1 cars of all time, through integrating many different ideas from other Formula 1 teams and optimising their performance in one car. Technology is ever changing but innovation is often about reconfiguring and rearranging ideas from both within and outside the industry.

The kind of organisation that is able to perform at the highest levels with total reliability, but which is also constantly innovating and changing the basis for competition, is the ultimate competitive organisation. Every Formula 1 team has to constantly live with this tension, and how they achieve this provides some important insights into managing the uneasy balance between exploiting today's ideas and exploring those of tomorrow.

Transforming

Change is a constant imperative in any dynamic organisation, so much so that management consultants now speak of change fatigue and the importance of stability. Undoubtedly, all organisations are finding ways to deal with the problems of constant change; however, for many this is a necessary evil to be countered, and they seek the restoration of stability as the objective of such initiatives. For Formula 1 teams, change is a constant pressure they cannot ignore. Nevertheless, today this is at the level of continuous improvement based around their current systems and technologies. This has not always been the case, but it is fair to say that really dramatic change only occurs when teams are performing poorly and when new technologies or new entrants require a more radical response.

There is also the issue of change, where organisations have to reinvent themselves. In Formula 1, few teams have the luxury of being able to do this, unless they have the resources necessary to get them through difficult times, such as the case of Ferrari in the 1980s and early 1990s, as described in Chapter 5. Despite many of these firms often being owned by multinational corporations, they are run almost as family businesses. This creates many of the advantages outlined in this chapter but it also creates the kind of inertia which makes radical change especially challenging. This is particularly so when many of the original staff and senior management are still in place – they've seen it all before, and therefore provide a potential barrier to the radical change which may be needed to achieve sustained performance.

Performance

Every Formula 1 team wants to win. Despite perceptions from the outside, no one is going to the race just to make up the numbers. Even the teams at the back of the grid take great pride in the fact that their pit stops can be just as fast as those of the teams at the front. Each team declares that it is its 'will to win' that keeps it going. If they all have an equal desire to win, what then makes the difference? What is important here, as in any organisation, is that there is a clear connection between all the activities which are undertaken and their contribution to performance. However, such connections are difficult to establish in practice. Many managerial initiatives are based on the assumption that there will be a positive impact on performance, but such a relationship is often merely asserted and there is frequently no subsequent effort made to validate this relationship.

In our framework the elements of **individual**, **team** and **partner** are connected to each other to signify the obvious inter-relationships that exist between them. When these components are working in synergy, a virtuous circle of activity can exist that allows the collective efforts of all three to drive organisational growth and improved effectiveness. The processes of **integrating**, **transforming** and **innovating** acting upon the organisation add additional levels of complexity and also create potential conflicts. The spirals in Figure 5 represent the competitive advantages and disadvantages that the interaction between these activities can create for a firm. People or organisations can develop behaviours and momentum that lead to cycles of success or winning streaks. It becomes a virtuous circle involving greater levels of communication and participation. It makes it easier to bond because people respect each other in a group of winners.

This frequently occurs in Formula 1; however, the circle can also become vicious in the sense that this bonding may manifest itself in terms of arrogance and views of invincibility, which allow new competitors to seize the initiative. It is therefore critical that the cycles of winning are tempered with the ability to challenge and adapt as conditions require. Similarly, if performance deteriorates, then organisations fragment into factions which, in the worst case, pass the blame onto each other, making it increasingly difficult to meld the elements back together. It is all too easy for the virtuous circle to quickly become a vicious one!

Performance Pyramid

In addition to the overall performance framework we have found (as discussed in Chapter 10) that a further framework can be very valuable in thinking about how the F1 model can be applied in other organisations. We have termed this the Performance Pyramid, as shown in Figure 6.

The pyramid shows three layers. The real focus of the F1 approach is contained in the middle section, 'constant learning'; it is this process that

Figure 6 Performance Pyramid

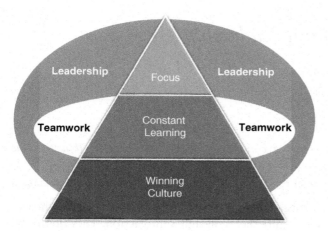

Figure 7 Leadership and teamwork in the Performance Pyramid

can help speed up innovation and performance in general. But for it to work it requires the other two layers – one providing clarity of purpose and the other supporting the values and behaviour that ensure delivery – or, as they are labelled in Figure 6, a clear focus and a winning culture. These three levels are developed further in Chapters 3, 4 and 5. A further aspect of the pyramid is how it is achieved, and as can be seen in a further development of the pyramid in Figure 7, this is driven by the two critical areas of integration – leadership to provide focus and support the winning culture, and teamwork to drive the learning process. The way in which these can be applied in your organisation is discussed in more detail in Chapter 10.

Taking all of the above into account, we believe that Formula 1 provides one of the few organisational contexts where we can get close to the linkage between individual actions, team outputs, organisational characteristics and performance.

3 | *Enabling leadership*

Formula 1 represents a compressed leadership cycle in that there is a performance review every two weeks.

Chris Aylett, Chief Executive Officer, Motorsport Industry Association

As in all successful organisations there is a need for individuals who can spur, motivate and inspire their colleagues into action. They do this by creating harmony within the working environment, which enables the separated but inter-related functions in the business to operate in an integrated manner. In Formula 1 this requires leaders who can coordinate the efforts of many strong-willed individuals so that they can work together cohesively in pursuit of common goals. In short, integrators.

Given the wide range of personalities in Formula 1, it is not surprising to find differing leadership styles. As seen from business experiences across all industries, the most effective managers move seamlessly between different styles and use the appropriate behaviours as situations warrant in order to achieve the organisation's goals. However, it is also true that most leaders demonstrate certain dominant patterns of behaviour in how they deal with their subordinates, peers and bosses. Some managers are more low-key than others, some are more hands-on than others and some are more charismatic than others.

No matter the dominant styles employed, all effective leaders find ways to *galvanise* their followers into achieving high performance. Galvanise is defined as 'to arouse to awareness or action, spur' (the *American Heritage Dictionary*) or 'to shock or excite into action' (*Compact Oxford English Dictionary*). Leaders in Formula 1 are no different. They create a vision of where the team aspires to be. They create the values which govern behaviours that form the team's culture. They set targets and manage expectations. They assess competitor capabilities and build competencies of employees. They spur their teams to ever higher levels of performance in designing, manufacturing, marketing and testing and, ultimately, on the race track.

During the 1970s and early 1980s, an entire Formula 1 team was small enough to fit into a unit the size of a single commercial garage. The team leader oversaw the entire operation by walking through the factory, literally able to touch all the key people and operations of the business. Teams were run like small entrepreneurial businesses. If a new component needed to be purchased, the team principal would immediately work the phones in order to raise the necessary cash. Decisions were made on a day-to-day, even moment-to-moment, basis.

Sponsors were looked upon simply as funding sources. In return for payment, they received an allotted space on the racing car, team uniform or support trucks to advertise their product. Technical suppliers provided their parts and components mainly to place their company logos on the car and in anticipation of the brand association that comes with their relationship to Formula 1. Neither of these types of partnerships was truly integrated into the heart of the Formula 1 team's business activities. These small teams had very limited operating budgets. Much was done through 'seat of the pants' management. Just surviving financially and getting a car ready for the next race was the main goal for most of the teams.

As the Formula 1 industry has grown in size and global reach, so too have the racing teams. Along with size has also come increased complexity. Brand and product sponsors today have a significantly greater call on the whole team in order to leverage their advertising investment. Technical partnerships have become fully integrated into the teams they support. They play important roles in the design, development, delivery and installation of components, as well as the operating functions of the team.

With this complexity and further specialisation, the leader's ability to stay on top of the business simply by walking through the garage has disappeared, although being seen by the staff on a regular basis remains a priority. As with many growing businesses, the tendency for separate departments to develop within the organisation, so-called silos or chimneys, has increased. This, in turn, has required leaders and managers who can cope with the evolving business environment.

We have determined seven key principles of effective leadership that are demonstrated by Formula 1 team leaders. These are familiar to all successful businesses where one sees high-performing leaders:

- Setting appropriate expectations based on a clear purpose
- Integrating the different functional parts of their business
- Focusing on results
- Acting as role models by inspiring others with their own determination and style
- Making rapid and clear decisions
- Protecting their work forces from negative influences from outside
- Understanding that leadership is being exhibited at all levels of the organisation, not just by the top line managers.

Setting expectations and clarity of purpose

Typically, one would expect the leader of a business to create the vision that will inspire the team to achieve superior performance. In Formula 1, this is not as difficult a task as it might be in another industry. The image of what success means is visible to all team members throughout the racing season. It includes their driver, or better yet both of the team's drivers, standing on the winners' podium after a race, receiving their trophies and then spraying a magnum of champagne over their fellow drivers on the podium and anyone watching from the pit lane below.

Maurizio Arrivabene, Managing Director at Scuderia Ferrari, took over an ailing and under-performing team after the 2013 season. He could not have been clearer about communicating his expectations when he announced at that year's Christmas party:

A company is its people and in this case, they are special people. Now we are here to look forward to Christmas, but as from January, I want to see you not on the defensive but on the attack, because the aim is to get the Scuderia back where it should be.[10]

At that same event Sergio Marchionne, the President of FIAT-Chrysler, which owns a majority share of Ferrari, clarified the enabling environment that he intended to provide the team. He stated,

In this room, there are many talented people. I am here to get you working at your best and to give you the necessary resources, which when combined with your ability will put our fantastic pairing in a position to fight for the front row.[10]

He went on to inspire his troops by saying,

Do not fear change, be proactive and have the courage to come up with ideas.
I know you can do it and that is what Ferrari needs.[10]

It took a year of development, but then in 2015, the transformation paid off with Ferrari scoring points once again along with several significant podium finishes.

Another turnaround has taken place at Williams F1. Mike O'Driscoll, Group CEO, talked about the company pressing the reset button a few years ago. It meant management changes at the top positions and clarifying for shareholders, employees and fans that:

The objective in racing terms is to return Williams to the front of the grid and challenge for the Championship. In business terms we need to strengthen the organisation and create a robust and sustainable business so we can continue to race competitively. We are building a strong advanced engineering organisation that can ensure we can withstand the cyclical ups and downs that are part and parcel of any sporting endeavour.

Williams, like Ferrari, have demonstrated that they too can make it back to a very competitive position on the track.

Integrating groups within the company – providing structure

The creation of silos within large and also small organisations has become a key inhibitor for change and development across all industries. Lack of coordination, unproductive processes, unclear sense of purpose and loss of focus on the customer are just a few of the results from functional business groups refusing or unable to collaborate effectively with their colleagues across the organisation. In Formula 1, where teams can reach sizes of up to 800 employees, this attitude and approach would guarantee under-performance on the track.

At the height of their success during a run of six consecutive Constructors' World Championships between 1999 and 2004, the then technical director, Ross Brawn, made it clear to us that in order to succeed as a team it was not just a matter of building the most powerful engine or the most sleek, aerodynamic chassis; rather it was a matter of getting all the parts of the organisation to work together to deliver the final product. Brawn told us,

Ferrari doesn't have an individual feature, perhaps it never has had, but our innovation is an integration of the whole. Our efforts have always been not

to make everything as good as it can be, but to work together as a complete
package.

He went on to add,

It's not an engine, it's not a chassis, it's not an aero-package, it's
a Ferrari.

Many elements go into ensuring that all parts of the business are
functioning in the most productive way. For Toto Wolff at Mercedes
F1, it started with *structure* when he took over the leadership at
Mercedes F1:

What I've found within my work at Williams and then here was to
understand whether the company – and while this is a sports team, it is
fundamentally a company – is structured in the right way. Has it got the
right people in the right places, sharing vision and mission? As a point of
reference you provide the right context and the right environment to make
the best people achieve their targets and therefore achieve the company's
target.

Focus on results

Sir Frank Williams is an extraordinary man. The story of his return
from a crippling road accident has been told many times. It serves
as an outstanding example of a leader inspiring others through his
courage and personal drive. He was in a car crash in the south of
France in March 1986. His car overturned and he sustained verteb-
rae damage to his neck. Remarkably, through intensive care and
rehabilitation, Williams came back to Formula 1 only four months
later to watch his team in the practice sessions at the British Grand
Prix at Brands Hatch. He was able to travel with the team to all
their races the following year and has missed very few since.
Williams is a tetraplegic who is paralysed from the shoulders
down, confined to a wheelchair. Perhaps it is his innate competitiveness, tempered with his personal trials, that fuels Williams' drive
for excellence from himself and his team.

In our workshops and speaking engagements, we have discovered
that one of the most powerful quotes that we included in earlier
editions came from Frank Williams. It distils his *focus* on attaining
results in a simple, very powerful question. When faced with decisions
on any expenditure more than £5,000, he asks,

Will it make the car go faster?

In fact, it is the yardstick against which all key decisions are made at Williams F1.

We have asked countless executive audiences to consider what question they should be asking if, for example, a department requests a budget allocation for something. Can you identify the ultimate purpose of your business? Are your decisions consistently supporting the attainment of the business' key goals?

Even while they are not challenging the front runners as yet, the leadership of the Marussia Manor team, whose journey back into Formula 1 after financial difficulties is described below, believe very much in a structured approach to success. As Graeme Lowdon said,

I quite like a really simple model which says people will be able to do their job if they have three things which are: focus, energy and structure. If we can give focus *so they understand why they are here and what they can best concentrate their efforts on;* structure *– not just boxes and lines, but an understanding of authority, information flow, style, the way we do things here while also recognising the importance of informal structures; and then there is* energy *– it is important to give people energy to help them go and do something that is challenging and difficult.*

Focusing on results might also mean different things for different organisations, especially if you know your collective efforts, notwithstanding a rain-soaked track or some other freak set of circumstances, will enable you to reach the podium. Can you always set objectives that enable your team to strive for improvement? Graeme Lowdon explained:

It's so difficult trying to articulate targets. Every race weekend we look to see what would have been the best result we could achieve with the current package we've got. In other words, we've got to make sure that whenever we get speed into the car we're ready to take advantage of it. How are we doing on pit stops? How are we doing on race strategy? We've got to make sure the team is really on it. If you look at this year we're improving every race in terms of race team performance, but you can't necessarily see it on the result sheet or the time sheet. So a lot of our objectives mean something to us but not necessarily to the outside world.[11]

One aspect of decision-making in Formula 1 which we will address in a later chapter is that the sport tends to be extremely data oriented.

There is a massive amount of information being collected from all components of the car, the racing environment and the drivers. One might expect that all decisions taken are therefore based on somewhat mechanical, analytical principles. And, to be fair, the engineers who govern the design and development of the car do fit that profile. But every once in a while, leaders of F1 teams are reminded that data does not have all the answers.

With fifteen laps to go in the 2015 Monaco Grand Prix, Mercedes' Lewis Hamilton had led from pole position. He built a 25-second lead at one point, and by most accounts was comfortably heading to a race win; however, he ended up finishing third behind his teammate Nico Rosberg and Sebastian Vettel. What happened? His team in the garage and on the pit wall decided to bring him into the pits for a surprising second tyre change when the safety car was deployed. They apparently were concerned by the challenge that Vettel might pose in the final laps and did their calculations, based on the data at hand, that Hamilton would have enough time to make the pit stop and still retain his lead. Instead they got it wrong and Hamilton ended up forfeiting the lead.

According to Toto Wolff,

we got the maths wrong. We got the calculation wrong. We thought we had a gap, which we didn't have, when the safety car came out and Lewis was behind the safety car ... The decision had been made jointly with a lot of information at the same time. Within a fraction of seconds you need to make a call; we've tried to get as much input as possible from the engineers, from the management, from the driver and then take a decision in that case. The algorithm was wrong.[12]

Acting as role models

No matter what leadership styles they exhibit, all Formula 1 leaders exude passion and enthusiasm for the sport that becomes infectious to their employees, sponsors and partners. Great leaders inspire their followers to volunteer their skills, knowledge and energy in order to achieve their shared vision. Clearly they act as role models and embody the performance culture that determines how things are done in their organisation.

As a three-time winner of the Drivers' World Championship, as well as being a successful Team Principal and business advisor, Jackie

Stewart knows the importance of 'walking the talk' for his people. He told us in very matter-of-fact terms:

The man at the top is the example to the others to follow in determining the culture and the manner in which business should be done.

Claire Williams, Deputy Team Principal at Williams F1, obviously carries the name of her father who founded the team and is well aware of that responsibility,

Ours is predominantly a family-owned business. Because I'm a 'Williams' one of my key responsibilities is to make sure that everyone understands Williams, our DNA and our future.

Former three-time Drivers' World Champion, former airline owner and now Non-Executive Chairman Niki Lauda, partner with Toto Wolff in leading Mercedes F1, told us,

For me the most important thing is that the person in charge of a company has to know what the business is for. You have to be clever enough to set the guidelines as to what direction to go. You always have to be the brain. It means you need enough background on all these matters, then take logical right decisions. This is the number one thing. The number two thing is you have to live this life in the company – in your own company. If you tell them things and they do the opposite, that's a bit stupid and this is what a lot of people do. So I make a simple example, when I had my airlines I had the smallest office; they say, 'where do we have the meetings?' 'Here, there's three chairs – what do you want?' If there were big meetings we go to another room. If you want to talk with me, I only need one or two chairs and having the smallest office. They were always surprised; other people have huge offices, employees all want big offices. One guy came to me and said 'my office is small', and I said, 'look at mine! What is the problem?' So you have to live what you try to tell the people ... to be accepted or respected and so the same is here in Formula 1.

So Niki, we asked, how do you instil the appropriate values in your workforce?

Always be straightforward for your employees. Don't tell any bullshit. All this really comes from the top. If the leader does the right thing, the people can follow him, understand what the hell he's doing, it's easier to get them as a team to pull the rope in the right direction.

Rapid and clear decision-making

One absolute difference between Formula 1 and other businesses is the compressed time scales in the delivery cycle. During a race, strategic decisions need to be made in a matter of minutes on the pit wall, not days, weeks or months.

As Mike O'Driscoll, Group CEO of Williams F1, explained:

When I joined Williams I already understood just how quickly a Formula 1 organisation can work. It is an incredibly competitive environment. You get a report card every two weeks and based on that report card you need to take action. You've got a new challenge coming up and the competitors are continuing to evolve, to tackle issues that they have, to improve their competitiveness. This is a business that really never stands still and your reaction time is measured in days and weeks not months and years, and I love that environment. I think everyone within Formula 1 loves that environment and it is something that differentiates Formula 1 from many other businesses.

He added,

The interesting thing about Formula 1 is the speed of reaction that we have to problem fixing. We don't have lead times of once a year – it's two weeks. The Formula 1 team's ability to adapt and make decisions, quick decisions, is absolutely vital for us.

We talked with Peter Digby, Chairman of Xtrac Ltd., which makes the gear boxes for about half of the Formula 1 teams and virtually all other forms of motorsport as well. The discussion moved to how F1 technology has been applied to other industries, and he immediately seized on the difference in time frames that are applied outside motor racing.

It has been a big education where motorsport sometimes has trouble stepping outside of working with people it normally deals with. In motorsport I will get a call on Monday, we have a meeting on a Tuesday, we'll quote on a Wednesday and the order will arrive on a Thursday. In many other industries, each of these stages is six–twelve months and it can be incredible frustrating.

Graeme Lowdon, President and Sporting Director at Marussia Manor, has been a successful investor in start-up technology firms. He thinks,

The start-up mentality suits this sport hugely because the scarcest resource that you have in a start-up environment is time. Of course funding is critical, but there is no market that you can go to to get time – and that's the same in

Formula 1. Tomorrow the race will start whether we're ready or not. In two weeks we'll be at another Grand Prix and the race will start, we can't ring up Bernie and say 'we've got this fabulous new development for the car, but it isn't going to be ready until Monday, so can you please put the start back a bit?'

Lowdon and his colleagues have ridden a rollercoaster of business and emotional experiences over a very short period of time. The team's financial condition in November 2013 required them to seek protection for the business through administration. In his words,

The administrator had to let all the staff go because if the administration runs for more than two weeks, then it has an obligation to retain all the staff and the outlook at the time was too uncertain to do that.

Just before the start of the 2014 season, they found a financial solution to the business. Things had to happen fast and decisions had to be made quickly.

John [Booth, Team Principal] and I sat around a kitchen table and said, 'Right, there's probably ten people that we need now and if we can't get those ten together in the next twenty-four hours we won't be able to be in Melbourne for the start of the race season.' We had to be there as there was no option to join the Championship halfway through the year.

Not only did they have to find the right people, fast, they had to source their cars and equipment.

We had 40 tons of kit that was effectively going to go on eBay. We stopped the auction when we found new investors, but we had to take a static pile of assets and turn it into a Formula 1 team. A huge challenge where decisions had to be made fast.

Protecting their workforce

Formula 1 has always been an active and attractive target for media scrutiny. The level of public awareness and, perhaps from the teams' point of view, invasiveness, has been multiplied exponentially as more social network formats are being employed. Today not only does the large press corps that follows the Formula 1 travelling show has its say, but so does any fan or detractor who wishes to post their views.

This is further exacerbated by the ongoing schedule of Formula 1 – nineteen races within nine months in 2015 and twenty-one races scheduled within that same period in 2016 mean that new issues and stories arise even before the previous headlines have had a chance to die down.

Competition between a team's drivers, problems or even disputes with the tyre manufacturer, leadership issues with the team, financial conditions of the less well funded organisations and technical partnerships that seem to be producing unexpected results are all fodder for the media.

Leaders in Formula 1 teams have an important incentive to shield their employees from the adverse impacts of such attention. Protection is also about ensuring your people have the 'space' within which to innovate and produce without distracting influences from outside. Stefano Domenicali, former Managing Director at Ferrari, took this part of his role very seriously:

A 100 per cent effort is needed from everyone working here, so you need to cover up the pressure that is coming from the outside. You really need to filter that. So this is really what I have to handle, so they do not have to carry it on their shoulders. They really need to be focused on their jobs and try to be as creative as possible and very professional. But with outside pressure it is very, very difficult.

We had heard from people in the paddock that leaders, especially those who are part of much larger organisation such as with the automobile manufacturers, not only have to consider the impact of the media clamour on their employees, but also interference from inside the organisation, from senior leadership at the manufacturer's headquarters. So we asked Niki Lauda about the situation at Mercedes, particularly whether if things do not go so well on the track there is top-down pressure from Stuttgart on them and then on the employees. He replied,

The pressure from the Chairman, from the CEO is on us all the time because we are here to make sure we are going to win. If you win like now, everybody's happy because it's an easy life for us but there have been days or there will be days when it's the other way round, but the main thing is that Stuttgart trusts what management and every employee is doing in England and if the trust is there, then it works. We have established this from day one, and when Toto Wolff came in we have had absolute harmony anyway. Even if times are difficult we ask the question, we give the answer and that's it. They do not interfere.

Leaders at all levels

Leadership in Formula 1 teams is demonstrated not just at the top of the organisation, but at many levels, an important notion espoused by Noel Tichy and other management experts. In the fast-paced, entre-preneurial business of Formula 1, it is crucial that all employees are willing, capable and encouraged to carry the torch when the appropriate moment arises.

As Williams' Deputy Team Principal Claire Williams told us,

I believe that one of the most fundamental qualities of being a good leader is to understand how important people are to your organisation. A good leader is only as good as the team he or she is surrounded by. Bring in lots of clever people and give them the freedom to do their jobs. It's about learning to delegate and give your employees the authority to take action. It's knowing and trusting in others' capabilities.

After struggling at the back of the grid in 2014 and 2015, McLaren are still moving forward as they strive to improve performance. To do so, they have rethought their organisation structure to improve and increase speed in their development processes. According to Matt Morris, Engineering Director,

At every level of the organisation, there is clear leadership. We agree the direction we want to pursue and we bring people with us. The attitude has changed from 'telling' people to 'asking' people; we've integrated people and we share opinions and ideas. The main outcome of that new approach is that people now have a sense of ownership in the car. And they're more motivated and interested as a result.[13]

The Formula 1 driver as leader in the team

Wherever the authors speak at corporate engagements, questions about the drivers and their role are usually at the centre of Q and As. Given this understandably great interest and the drivers' high profiles, it would be remiss of us not to discuss their leadership role within the team. Not all drivers interact with their teams in the same way. Some drivers are actively involved in many aspects of the team's activities. Others restrict their inputs to the on-track performance of the car. In many cases it may be that they are not as integrated into the guts of the engineering equation as one might have imagined.

Nick Chester, Technical Director at Lotus F1, told us:

The drivers have a fairly limited group of people with whom they liaise at the track. They tend to work with their engineers and they talk to mechanics about the car.

We asked Chester if the drivers should have wider contact with the team. He replied,

I think it's surprising how motivating it is when the drivers are in the factory. People like to talk to them and they feel a bit more special if a driver does talk to them. So, I think there are things they can do to help in motivating the team. Everyone wants to feel that what they are doing is important and the more they have this feedback, the more you'll get from them.

David Richards, former Team Principal at BAR Honda F1 and very experienced racing hand, in fact told us that:

The role of a great driver is as much outside the car as it is inside the car. In most companies it is clear where the culture and leadership comes from, the MD or chairman at the top. In a motor racing team you might think that in a conventional structure it comes from the team principal; however, a significant, real influence comes from the driver because it is he who people become passionate and emotional about. As a result, they have a far greater role that they can imagine.

While talking about seven-time Formula 1 Drivers' World Champion Michael Schumacher, Ross Brawn recalled his days working with him at Ferrari while Technical Director there:

Undoubtedly at Ferrari we had the benefit of Michael in that he was a natural leader of people, so he could inspire people, he could motivate people and that does make your life easier. There's no doubt that Michael walking around the factory increased motivation.

We asked Brawn how he did that. He replied:

Within the engineering team he always kept a very level head and always respected everybody and always worked with everybody in being part of a team. That was one of the secrets of his success in that he never tried to pull rank within the team. Everyone was his equal and everyone had a contribution to make. If the team determined it was going to go in a particular direction he would give his opinion and even if he didn't agree he would support the final decision. He might come to you afterwards and say you were right or wrong, but he did that in a proper, quiet, constructive way. Drivers have got to do that.

Other drivers also understand the important role that they can play. Williams Group CEO Mike O'Driscoll recounted what happened after they hired Felipe Massa from Ferrari at the start of the 2014 season:

I remember the first time Felipe walked into the garage, the first test in Barcelona in 2014, he walked around the garage and shook hands with every mechanic and every engineer individually. He didn't just walk straight to the car. He was as interested in meeting the people as he was in what we were going to do that day and that connection he made was really important.

Former Grand Prix driver and 1990 Jaguar Le Mans winner Martin Brundle is a very sage and articulate commentator on Formula 1, which comes from his 158 race starts and other racing activities including driver management. He told us the following when we asked about the role that drivers can play in their teams beyond being fast around the circuit,

Schumacher, Senna, Prost – they realised that they needed to galvanise people around them and have everything pointed at them. Just look at Ferrari and how Vettel's embraced the team, speaking the language, he won in Hungary then changed his flight plans and flew with the team back to Maranello, went to the famous Italian restaurant there and drank and partied with them. The chemistry and the human interaction of that is critical to getting a team behind you.

Staying with Ferrari, Brundle shared his view about the great Michael Schumacher and how he, as a leader, inspired people to offer their very best to enable him to reach greatness:

Michael very quickly found who was married with kids, how their kids were, when their birthdays were and knew their names and what have you.

The team, according to Brundle, sees the driver as

the final link in the chain, to an extent the most important and most visible link; but only a link at the end of the day; and you realise that everybody upstream of you has a direct impact on your achievements.

Former Toyota F1 driver and now BBC commentator Allan McNish shares this view of the driver's role:

The driver provides energy for the team in two ways. One is giving your absolute everything in the cockpit – if you get the most out of it, every single time, every single second you're in the car, it gives a benchmark for everyone in the team to push for as well. And the other is outside of the cockpit – just to remember the things that you say and do can have a very positive impact but also very negative impact, so you need to be sensitive to that.

Like so many sports stars and celebrities, F1 drivers come in different packages. Certainly three-time Drivers' World Champion Lewis Hamilton is living a rock 'n' roll lifestyle. We asked Toto Wolff if he had concerns about that.

A part of my role is like that of a football trainer, you have to understand what kind of environment the driver needs. Some need stable surroundings, some need a creative environment, and others a permanently changing environment – and once you've found out how he ticks, you walk that avenue with him. Both our guys are in a phase of their career where they exactly know what is good for them and what to stay aware of.

In considering the role of leadership in organisations, we can discern a number of management lessons that can be drawn from Formula 1 into other areas. We summarise these as follows:

Lesson 1 Focus, focus, focus

The rigour of a twenty-one-race season puts a heightened premium on getting the right job done at the right time. It seems quite a basic concept, given the industry's often changing regulatory constraints, the budgetary limitations under which many teams operate and very tight deadlines that have to be met. Formula 1 teams must focus on the tasks at hand in order to be on the grid with an improved car, week after week. Even in this context, we have seen examples of where successful teams have lost their focus, lost their edge and ultimately paid a very high price: perhaps most famously through McLaren's departure into high-performance, limited-edition road cars in the early 1990s (the McLaren F1). Likewise, drivers who are facing great demands on their time have to learn to focus on what truly matters, which in the end is performance on the track.

Lesson 2 One team – alignment of goals between individuals, teams and partners

There are two parts to the issue of alignment. One is commonality of goals towards which teams and sub-teams in the organisation are striving. The other is the connection between individuals' actions and the end result. Perhaps this is best illustrated in the way that Frank Williams constantly asks the question when signing cheques: *'How will it make the car go faster?'* against which all can measure the value of their specific contributions on a day-to-day basis. From the Formula 1 team partner's perspective, the question may be different: *'Will it help us sell more products?'* It is the continual alignment of these factors that helps to optimise business processes in Formula 1 teams.

Lesson 3 Build the organisation around informal processes, networks and relationships

Across all of the teams we found a common emphasis on building from the expertise and relationships of the people within the organisation and the partners allied to the business. This approach enables the structure to emerge from these relationships, rather than imposing a 'theoretical' organisation which is populated by rigid, specified roles and job descriptions that do not relate to the pressurised world that Formula 1 teams inhabit.

Perhaps we could criticise those teams who do not have ready-to-hand organisational charts or detailed job descriptions. Clearly these are important aspects of modern organisational life. But in a situation where there is real commitment and passion from employees, the lack of such management tools illustrates how the organisation becomes 'empowered' by removing layers of potentially needless bureaucracy.

In reality, we know that organisation charts rarely reflect how people in the business actually work together or relate to one another in terms of getting tasks completed. The Formula 1 organisation is an emergent structure that is designed to optimise and facilitate the potential of individuals and their relationships, rather than determining and micro-managing such interactions. The conclusion that we reach is that it is only through effectively supporting these interactions and relationships that performance can be truly optimised.

In business management there is a mantra that structure drives strategy, which in turn drives performance. In Formula 1, people and their relationships drive the structure, which in turn drives performance. Perhaps surprisingly given its strong technology orientation, Formula 1 is a very people-driven business.

Lesson 4 Leaders exist at all levels of the organisation

Due to the fast pace of this industry, employees throughout Formula 1 teams are empowered to make decisions, drive processes and take risks. We have witnessed people at all levels within Formula 1 organisations stepping up to be accountable and to lead their colleagues when it is their time to take responsibility.

This means that the more senior roles are concerned with problem-solving and connecting up different parts of the organisation, rather than coaching or directing. At times this can be problematic, particularly where big egos are not in short supply, but the lesson here is to recognise that in the most successful teams people are prepared to put their heads above the parapet and lead their project or initiative. Also, in these contexts, the drivers are not prima donnas but real catalysts for the team, encouraging everyone to play their part to achieve performance at the limit.

Plate 1 Inside the Mercedes garage.
Source: Mercedes AMG F1

Plate 2 Mercedes engineers reviewing data in garage.
Source: Mercedes AMG F1

Plate 3 Team motorhomes upper-level paddock at Spa

Plate 4 Engineers and mechanics arriving on race day at Belgian Grand Prix 2015

Plate 5 Mercedes V6 hybrid power unit displaying engine and battery packs.
Source: Mercedes AMG F1

Plate 6 (L to R) Former driver and now racing commentator Martin Brundle
being interviewed by co-authors Mark Jenkins and Ken Pasternak

Plate 7 Inside the three-storey McLaren motorhome

Plate 8 Offices of the FIA located near race control in the upper paddock area at the Belgian Grand Prix

Plate 9 Fernando Alonso in the McLaren garage.
Source: McLaren

Plate 10 Aerial view of the McLaren Production Centre (L) and McLaren Technology Centre (R).
Source: McLaren

Plate 11 Start of the Austrian Grand Prix 2015.
Source: Williams F1

Plate 12 View along the Spa paddock showing Lotus, Williams and Red Bull motorhomes

Plate 13 Media interviewing drivers after the Saturday afternoon qualifying session at the Belgian Grand Prix while the top three finishers are simultaneously being interviewed on television coverage

Plate 14 Aerial view of Williams headquarters, including factory and conference centre.
Source: Williams F1

Plate 15 Co-author Ken Pasternak with three-time World Drivers' Champion Lewis Hamilton

Plate 16 Co-author Richard West (L) with former driver and now F1 commentator Mark Webber (R) after the 2015 Melbourne Grand Prix

4 | *Constant learning*

Every time you have a negative response to an issue, you're denying yourself the opportunity to improve.

Paddy Lowe, Executive Director (Technical), Mercedes AMG Petronas F1 Team.

The idea that organisations need to learn is not novel, but there are no organisations that have to learn as intensively and as quickly as F1 teams. Speed is the basis of success and time is the currency of performance. Most management students will recognise the concept of the experience curve, often used to map how organisations can reduce costs by learning about the production process. In F1, the focus is on continually improving performance, removing hundredths of seconds from the lap time of their cars in order to stay ahead, or even stay level, with the competition.

At the Formula 1® Shell Belgian Grand Prix in 2015, Paddy Lowe of Mercedes estimated that they were three races ahead of the competition, with each race bringing about one-tenth of a second improvement in the overall performance of an F1 car; in other words, Mercedes estimated that they had around three-tenths of a second advantage at that particular point in time.

Figure 8 shows the learning curve for F1 in the period 1950 to 2015 using the example of the Monaco Grand Prix, which takes place around the confined harbour area of Monte Carlo. The line shows the qualifying lap time in miles per hour, starting with 1950, where Juan Manuel Fangio in an Alfa Romeo managed a qualifying lap in 1'50.2, making an average speed of 64.5 mph, and finishing with 2015, where Lewis Hamilton in a Mercedes Benz managed a qualifying lap in 1'15.1, making an average speed of 100.4 mph. Unlike the theory of the experience curves, this is not a smooth curve, perhaps due in some cases to weather conditions, but in most cases due to changes in regulations.

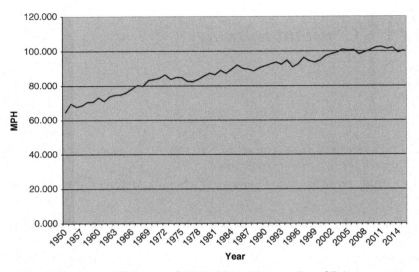

Figure 8 Fastest qualifying speed 1950–2015, Monaco Grand Prix

Regulations and learning

Regulations are one of the most important aspects of the F1 environment, and it can be seen how it impacts on the performance of the cars by the 'saw-tooth' effect in Figure 8, where the speed of the car is increased one year and may then drop down again. This is not due to the teams losing their way, but through the regulatory body, the Fédération Internationale de l'Automobile (FIA), introducing new sporting or technical regulations which then limit the performance of the car.

Appendix D (Figure 19) shows how the regulatory process operated in 2015, with the teams being involved in defining both sporting and technical regulations which are then ratified by the FIA World Motorsports Council.

For example, in 2014 new regulations were introduced which made radical changes to the power units used by the F1 teams. In 2013, they used 2.4 litre V10 internal combustion engines coupled with a 60 kw kinetic energy recovery system (KERS), this enabled them to store energy in batteries and reuse this to provide a performance advantage during the race.

For 2014, the internal combustion engine was reduced to a 1.6 litre V6 coupled with a 120 kw Energy Recovery System (ERS), which harvested both kinetic and heat energy to batteries allowing it to be reused during the race. In addition, the engines had to be raced for 4,000 km – twice the distance in 2013 – and the flow of fuel was limited to 100 kg/hour. These changes resulted in a 35 per cent reduction in fuel usage for F1 cars between 2013 and 2014, due to which the qualifying lap time for Monaco reduced from 1'13.9 (average speed of 102 mph) in 2013 to 1'16.0 (average speed of 99.2 mph) in 2014. It was interesting to note that despite these radical changes to the power units in 2015, the qualifying speed had increased to 100.4 mph; probably by 2016 it will have exceeded the 2013 figure.

The final aspect of regulations relates to how they are enforced. The FIA appoints two distinct groups to enforce regulation – their own administrative team, led by the F1 Director, Charlie Whiting, and the race stewards, which would normally include a local race official and a former F1 driver. The way this works is described by F1 Race Director Charlie Whiting:

We're effectively the police and the stewards are the judiciary.

Although it may not sometimes appear so, there is a great deal of informal dialogue between the F1 teams and the FIA. When teams develop innovations they will usually ask the FIA whether or not they agree that these are consistent with the regulations. Whiting told us:

Ninety-nine per cent of the time the teams accept our opinion. Unless there is a lot of greyness in that particular area they tend to say, 'OK, fair enough, I'm glad we asked otherwise we would have wasted time and money and so on'. Very occasionally we disagree and they will bring the part or system to a race and they will let the stewards decide.

This informal interaction is a key part of the process. Charlie Whiting finds that some teams are better than others in terms of how they find ways to be competitive and yet remain within the regulations:

They [F1 teams] have a lot of very clever people thinking about how to exploit the regulations, that's their job after all. Over the years there have been some very inventive things ... the Brawn Team's double diffuser was an absolutely perfect example of that. So well thought through and of course, my initial reaction was 'no, you can't have that because ...', they said, 'ah,

*but this is an unsprung part of the car and that can therefore shadow this . . .'.
OK, fair enough . . .*

So do regulations limit learning and suppress innovation? Not in the view of Andy Cowell, Managing Director of Mercedes AMG High Performance Powertrains (HPP):

Regulation is an opportunity to show that we can be ingenious, go racing and get a better result than our opponents. When regulations come out everybody reads them and then there's a fixed period of time before you get your exam results at the first Grand Prix – the regulations provide an opportunity to show how good you are.

Pat Symonds, Chief Technical Officer of Williams F1, has a more nuanced view of the impact of innovation:

You know, a lot of people say that Formula 1 technical regulations stifle innovation. They do – the more regulation there is, the more prescriptive things become, the more difficult it becomes to be innovative – but in a way, that can also drive innovation. I think at Williams we are still innovative, there are some aspects of our design that I think are very innovative.

Regulations and safety

One of the key factors in driving regulations has been the imperative of safety in Formula 1, which has steadily emerged since the 1960s, when fatalities were all too frequent and a small number of drivers, such as Sir Jackie Stewart, were outspoken in their criticism of safety standards. In 1978 Professor Sid Watkins was appointed as Grand Prix surgeon, with the remit to develop overall medical standards at Grand Prix circuits. The efforts of Professor Watkins and his colleagues undoubtedly improved the situation, particularly in terms of the care that drivers received when injured on track. However, more urgent pressure for radical change came in 1994, following the serious accident that befell Rubens Barrichello in his Jordan during the Friday practice and the deaths of drivers Roland Ratzenberger and three-time World Champion Ayrton Senna, in separate accidents at the San Marino Grand Prix weekend at Imola, Italy.

Until 1994 there had been a period of eleven years without a single fatality, and many of those working within Formula 1 had never experienced the loss of a driver at a Grand Prix event. There was universal shock within the Formula 1 community, among the Formula 1 fans, but also beyond, among the public at large. Senna's death had been covered by live television broadcasts and there was widespread condemnation of safety levels within the sport from the press, governments, sponsors and even the Vatican.

Max Mosley, then FIA President, stated at that time that the only acceptable safety objective was zero fatalities and zero serious injuries. Mosley established the FIA Safety Committee, chaired by Sid Watkins, to explore how this objective could be achieved. Since then, safety regulations have covered many areas from the construction and testing of the cars, to the equipment worn by the drivers and the design of the circuits to protect both drivers and spectators. As the racing car designers constantly strive for enhanced performance, so must the regulators respond to meet increased speeds with appropriate measures to ensure the safety of all those involved.

Regulations and disruption

From the perspective of competitive racing, the regulations seek to minimise any areas of competitive advantage a team may develop in order to maximise the competition on the track. There have been various regulations passed over the years in order to try to reduce the technological advantage of particular cars. However, it is interesting to note that invariably these regulations lag behind the innovations. This is perhaps not surprising, in that a regulation can only be drafted once the source of advantage is more widely understood or 'codified', thus enabling the regulation to effectively remove it. For example, it took a number of years before the principles of ground-effect aerodynamics were fully disseminated around the Formula 1 paddock. It was only when these concepts were fully understood that regulations were changed banning ground effects, in order to prevent continually increasing cornering speeds, which were considered too fast and potentially dangerous at that time.

There have also been situations where cars have been banned on their first race, or even beforehand. In 1978, Brabham designer Gordon Murray developed the Brabham 'fan-car', which used a mechanical fan to enhance the ground effect which other cars were achieving aerodynamically. However, the fan created a dust cloud behind the car as it raced around the track and it was banned on safety grounds after winning its first Grand Prix at Anderstorp in Sweden.

Another example was the Continuously Variable Transmission (CVT) system developed by Williams in the early 1990s. This system removed the need to change gear, with a belt and pulley system ensuring that the wheel speed was matched to the track conditions, the engine running constantly at maximum power. The system was based on technology used on the DAF road car, which had been developed by Van Doorne Transmission. The car appeared at a test session at Silverstone in 1993, driven by then Williams test driver David Coulthard. It was rumoured that a number of competitors had identified the huge potential of the system during the test, and somehow regulations were drawn up banning the use of CVT by the end of the year. Therefore, despite all the time and cash Williams had invested, it was never able to race the system in a Grand Prix.

Regulation for reducing costs

Within the regulatory body a new imperative has developed, albeit one that has, to date, not found a sustainable basis on which it could be implemented – an imperative whereby Formula 1 stays in touch with changes in the broader global environment and also addresses the increasing problem of cost inflation relative to the entertainment value of the sport.

Regulation has also been used to reduce costs by stipulating certain standardised components to be used and reducing the usage of certain items. For example, in 2004 a regulation was passed which stipulated that each driver could only use one engine during a race weekend (this was extended in 2008, from which point an engine had to last two races or the team faced penalties should replacement of an engine be required), the intention being to prevent cost escalation by reducing the number of engines used over the course of a season. The impact of this change was significant to the engine builders. They now had to change their specifications regarding the lifetime of engines, resulting in many components having to be redesigned in order to cope with this change. As observed by Cosworth Racing's former Commercial Director Bernard Ferguson, while the objective of the regulation was to cut costs, that was not necessarily the outcome:

The biggest cost for an engine manufacturer is obsolescence, so for us, the less change the better.

In addition to the changes created by the competition on the track, many changes were also created by the commercial demands of Formula 1.

Until the 1970s Formula 1 teams were funded either by car manufacturers or by private individuals such as Rob Walker, who funded his racing activities from the wealth created by his family's Johnnie Walker whisky business. Walker successfully ran his own team with cars purchased from Lotus and Cooper using top-class drivers such as Stirling Moss and Jack Brabham. When car sponsorship was introduced, the teams needed to develop marketing and sales operations in order to both recruit and manage sponsors. During the 1970s, 1980s and early 1990s, much of this sponsorship came from the tobacco companies who, due to increased legislation on tobacco advertising, had fewer and fewer alternatives to promote their products. In the 1990s, Formula 1 enjoyed huge growth, both in terms of the television exposure and viewing figures, which ultimately attracted the car manufacturers back on a far larger scale than had been the case for many years.

The learning loop

So, how is it possible that F1 teams are able to learn so fast while many other organisations seem unable to learn at all or, at best, very slowly? Like most answers in life and business there is no one single factor, but a combination of aspects which, when combined with the hyper-competitive context of F1, create learning at a speed which is unparalleled elsewhere.

First, we refer to the Performance Pyramid, which we outlined in Chapter 2; constant learning requires two other critical elements which are discussed elsewhere in this book – a clear focus and a winning culture. A clear focus is concerned with clarity around what the organisation is trying to do (see Chapter 3 – Enabling leadership); this gives the learning process a clear purpose and a clear basis for understanding whether or not the changes made are impacting on performance, as without a clear focus it is virtually impossible to progress learning to the levels achieved in F1.

But similarly, even with a clear focus learning will not be effective unless it is underpinned by a winning culture (Chapter 9). Two key aspects of the winning culture are the no-blame philosophy, which is critical if you want individuals and teams to take risks and innovate, and the one-team mindset, where everyone is clear that ultimately they are all part of one team and that learning is about improving the performance of that one team, not the many silos that can grow in

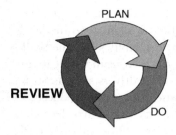

Figure 9 Plan–Do–Review cycle

organisations. There is no point in having the best F1 gearbox in the world if the rest of the car does not perform to this level; similarly, there is no point in having the best sales force in the world if your product is poorly made and your aftersales non-existent. 'One-team' recognises the interdependency and openness that need to exist across the entire organisation and its partners.

So if we assume that we have a clear focus and we have the winning culture to support learning, how does the learning process itself work? One of the aspects of F1 that really surprised us when we started our research in 2004 was the teams' obsession with reviewing performance. Figure 9 illustrates the simple 'Plan–Do–Review' model often used to represent the learning cycle in organisations and to emphasise the importance of planning.

In this context the aspect of the model that is the real focus of activity is the review stage (hence the large font), and also how the review feeds into the next planning cycle. In our work with companies we often find emphasis on planning and execution, with little effort made at harvesting the learnings from what has been delivered. For F1 teams, the critical event is the race, and since at times during the season races take place with only single-week intervals between them, extracting every last element of learning from them is absolutely critical. Back in the days when he was Team Principal of Ferrari, Jean Todt provided us with an interesting perspective on this process:

After we win a race and the champagne has been drunk, we stay one-and-a-half hours together making the debriefing or talking about what did not work.

At one level this sounds quite negative – why beat yourselves up when you've just won the race? At the time Todt gave us this quote, they

(Ferrari) were winning all the time. In F1, reviewing to address potential problems is not seen as negative, it is seen as what you have to do to stand any chance of winning the next race. Reviewing through a debrief process is as natural as racing in F1, and in fact for many it is the most important part, as Mark Webber's comment on Red Bull Racing Technical Director Adrian Newey reveals:

What I loved about Adrian was his attitude. The race result was generally invisible to him; even if we had dominated with a 1–2 finish, fastest lap, pole position and fastest pit stop, he was still pushing the team to improve and that's why we were as good as we were.[14]

So how does this review process work? What goes on? In his autobiography, Mark Webber describes the process at Red Bull Racing:

At the height of Red Bull Racing's success our post-race debrief would involve up to 25 people plus another 10 or so back at the Milton Keynes factory linked up by video stream and radio. Everyone would listen as we gave individual breakdowns on how our race had gone before the race engineers and other departments contributed. The meeting could take between 90 minutes and two hours – often longer than the actual race![14]

A more detailed insight into this process is provided by Paddy Lowe Executive Director (Technical) from Mercedes. He has a very clear view on how this process works by working through a series of development loops that operate at all levels:

I think what generally drives the great pace of development in Formula 1 is the process of constant innovation and feedback. This goes on at all levels and involves all sorts of different processes. It may be one guy at his computer innovating on a design to find an optimisation or it may be a larger loop around the whole department developing a new wing or it may be the whole organisation. Probably the biggest loop we have when you're talking about car performance is about actually putting parts on the car, driving it around with the real driver and seeing how it works either from data or from his comments. Everything we do is about development loops and the key point is cycle time: the quicker you can rotate the process, the quicker you can try the next experiment.

Figure 10 shows how Paddy Lowe's concept of development loops looks at different levels within the organisation.

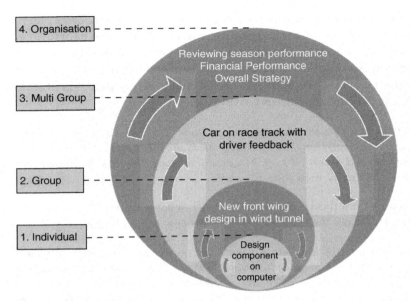

Figure 10 Formula 1 development loops

- Level 1 refers to individuals doing specific tasks, such as an individual working on a design on a computer. As the design progresses, the designer may submit this to various analyses or even a simulation to assess how good the ideas are. This provides feedback that allows the design to be refined further.
- At level 2, there are designers and engineers developing a more elaborate design, such as a front wing, which requires them to work as a team, perhaps with different expertise and responsibilities relating to the materials used or particular component elements of the final assembly. In this case they have to come together as a team to formulate a design and then try it out – perhaps this time by building a model which can be used in the wind tunnel. Again, a lot of data is captured and analysed, changes are made and further tests are carried out.
- At level 3, we have multiple teams coming together to assess the overall performance of the car – aerodynamicists, simulation experts, race engineers, powertrain engineers, tyre engineers, systems engineers and the drivers all taking part in a debrief to review performance, based on data, and then decide what changes need to be made to improve performance further.

- The final level, level 4, refers to inputs from the entire organisation maybe over an entire year or the first six months. How have we done? Is the strategy right? Is the structure right? Do we have the right business model? Do we have the right funding in place?

The key with F1 development loops is the speed at which they occur. Over a F1 Grand Prix weekend there will be up to fifty meetings, with the explicit focus on learning and improving performance. In 2015, the team's two cars were both involved in three free-practice sessions, a qualifying session and a race, with each of these five learning opportunities involving a full debrief process.

In the case of the free-practice sessions, the debrief will involve both the drivers and around thirty engineers based at the circuit, as well as a further thirty back in the factory. In Mercedes' case, this would be at the team's base at Brackley, Northamptonshire, UK.

These sixty-two individuals will all be connected via intercom (a necessity at most tracks due to the noise from supporting races). They will be chaired by the chief engineer and follow a preset agenda, an example of which has been kindly provided by Mercedes and is shown in Figure 11.

The purpose of the debrief is to glean as much information as possible concerning the performance of each driver and their cars in order to learn how to improve further for both the qualifying session and the most important part, the race. Although the teams are swimming in a sea of data (see later in this chapter), they are concerned at this point with how everything translates into the drivers' experience and how the entire system is likely to operate – a key part of the one-team culture.

Whereas everyone has clearly defined responsibilities, they are all focused on ensuring that the overall race performance is maximised. These are not long, protracted meetings – there isn't the time. They will last around fifteen minutes and then everyone will focus on how they can improve things in time for the next experiment. Clarity and speed of delivery are vital here.

Learning and data

A Formula 1 car is bristling with technology and a key part of this relates to providing the team with real-time data in order for them to learn and develop the car as quickly as possible. Pat Symonds

DRIVER DEBRIEF SHEET

	HAM	ROS
Balance and performance issues		
Priority 1		
Priority 2		
Priority 3		
Priority 4		
Tyres		
Stint 1		
Warm-up		
Graining / degradation		
Balance		
Stint 2		
Warm-up		
Graining / degradation		
Balance		
Stint 3		
Warm-up		
Graining / degradation		
Balance		
Stint 4		
Warm-up		
Graining / degradation		
Balance		
Race Start		
Performance (Laps to Grid & Race Start)		
Power Unit		
Contact with other cars?		
Powertrain		
Overall Power		
Consistency		
Driveability		
MGUK Turn Off Points		
Engine Braking		
Refind		
Systems		
Steering Wheel Layout		
Dash Display		
DRS		
Shift Lights		
Upshifts		
Downshifts		
Pit Limiter		
Diff Control		
Radio Operation		
Comfort		
Seat / Pedals / Belts / Mirrors		
Buffeting, Helmet Sealing and Ventilation		
Drinks Bottle		
Driver Cooling		
Brakes		
Brake Bias		
Locking		
Stopping Power		
Warm-up		
Brake Pedal Consistency		
General		
Ride / Kerbs		
Steering		
Bottoming		
Vibrations		
Pit Board Visibility		
Any other comments		

Figure 11 Debrief agenda.
Source: Mercedes AMG F1

of Williams F1 described how the use of data has evolved in F1, noting that a key aspect was developing sensor technology that worked in a race situation:

We had to spend a lot of time working on the transducers themselves because even something like a pressure sensor would be made for a ground-based plant and we had to work on miniaturising pressure sensors, accelerometers, gyros – all these sort of things. And that was a very, very long process; many years were spent developing these in the last decade. Now we've achieved the ability to measure pretty well anything we want to measure on the car.

This has led to 'big data' being a key issue in F1, with the teams now totally overwhelmed with data, as Pat Symonds describes:

I think there are, in terms of actual transducers, there are probably about 150 or so on the car, but what's more significant is the fact that we recall a lot of states of things, and we produce other virtual channels; so, in actual fact, our current systems have a limit of 1,000 channels of information if you like and that's full, we use all 1,000 of them.

All of this requires a different perspective to learning and means that the teams are using both judgmental approaches – reading graphs and interpreting trends, but also developing algorithms to create measures that were beforehand well beyond their reach. Pat Symonds again:

So, a lot of work is now going into smart ways of looking at data and interpreting and aggregating it to produce virtual things that you couldn't see, otherwise it's very difficult to measure understeer on a car, an understeer meter if you like, but now we have the potential to aggregate steer and lateral acceleration and vehicle velocity to produce an understeer channel. The real secret now is to use that data in a smart way, and that's still an area I feel that we've got a long way to go.

Coupled with these developments is the need to use the data to improve performance. This underpins the learning cycles shown in Figure 10 – the whole basis of development is the use and application of data. Part of the reason that F1 teams are able to review in such an 'objective' way is that they have a huge volume of data charting not only their progress through the race, but the progress of their key competitors. But the debrief process is not one of pouring over lots of graphs and spread-sheets; they don't have the time. Individuals have to be able to interpret the key issues and bring these into the discussion.

Learning and innovation

There's a cliché about motor racing being like war and it's absolutely true. You know, war accelerates technical development astonishingly.

Joe Saward, Formula 1 journalist.

Innovation in Formula 1 is usually thought of strictly in terms of technology, but the sport has in recent years witnessed remarkably creative ideas in the marketing arena. The impact of Red Bull's involvement in Formula 1, for example, has not just been related to an injection of cash, it has introduced a number of marketing innovations to Formula 1, as described by Team Principal Christian Horner:

Red Bull has brought a very refreshing appeal back to Formula 1 with the introduction of concepts such as the 'energy station', an open-house facility that is open to any F1 pass holder, which was unheard of previously. We also have some fun initiatives that we have partnered with film promotions, Formula Una [a Formula 1-based beauty contest] or the Red Bulletin [a daily newsletter printed during a Grand Prix weekend], so there's so many initiatives that Red Bull has brought to Formula 1 which I think without which Formula 1 would be a much duller place.

So what are some of the pressures and demands of innovating in the context of Formula 1? Two factors emerged from our research: *speed to market* and the *challenge of innovating in organisations which are growing larger and larger.*

Speed to market (or the track)

Whereas there are many similarities between Formula 1 and other businesses, there are real differences in terms of the *pace and intensity of innovating.* The pace of innovation is significantly faster in Formula 1 than other technology industries. Here, innovating is a continuous process, with a constant array of design changes and new components being incorporated into the car. This is shown in Figure 12, which was kindly provided by Ferrari. The top part of the figure shows how Ferrari develops its production engines, which are used in its high-performance road-going cars. We can see that the total development period for a production engine is forty-two months, if we exclude the time for the concept study up to the start of production (SOP). In contrast, during the same period within Formula 1, there have

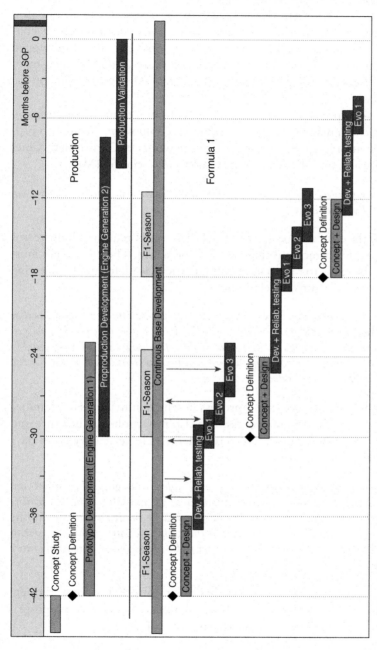

Figure 12 Ferrari engine development, F1 vs production cars.
Source: Ferrari SpA

been three new engines designed, built and raced each with three iterations or evolutions (EVO 1, 2, 3) of the design. It can also be seen from Figure 12 that within Formula 1 the development process is continuous, meaning that the engine is being both raced and developed simultaneously. For Formula 1, we therefore see a total of nine stages of development compared to the single stage of development for the production engine.

Such compressed cycles of development put a tremendous stress on supply chain management, requiring that components blend into production at precisely the right time. In the words of Chris Aylett, Chief Executive of the UK Motorsport Industry Association (MIA):

In motorsport we do not know how to deliver late – no race has ever been delayed by a late delivery from a supplier.

One of the critical aspects of Formula 1 is that it requires all the teams to attend fixed race meetings around the world. Therefore, cars must always be ready to race at each event. Patrick Head, former Engineering Director at Williams F1, elaborates:

We are driven very much by specific dates and programmes. That means that with a new component the chief designer will know when the design needs to be issued, how long it's going to take to do the design, he'll know roughly how long it will take to manufacture and he can then target a test for the component to be evaluated.

All of these factors require a process in which individuals are familiar not just with the design process, but also the whole manufacture and development cycle; a fact which is underlined by legendary Formula 1 designer John Barnard:

The key to speed in innovation is being able to integrate the design and manufacture processes. A good designer will go and talk to the fabricators or machinist to find out how the part would be made; it may be that by making some small design changes at this point the part could be easier to manufacture and therefore both quicker to be released and potentially more reliable.

However, Barnard also believes that this means that more traditional management methods such as those used in aerospace are inappropriate for the flexible and responsive context of Formula 1:

The problem is that in a context like aerospace, people can almost determine their own production times, their own lead times. If you sit down and do the project timescale properly you just keep adding on and, 'That'll take this long and then I have to do that and once I've got that done I do this', and so on. You'll end up out here and that's your project lead time. It doesn't happen like that in racing because there's your lead time, there's your project time, that's the race; now you make it fit, and you do whatever that takes.

The ethos of 'doing whatever it takes' means that teams have to go beyond the bounds of their highly pressurised development programmes to stay competitive, as illustrated by Williams F1's former COO Alex Burns:

In 2008, we were developing a new front wing aimed at Monaco, so it was planned to go to the Ricard test [the Paul Ricard circuit in the South of France] and then go on to Monaco; in testing we found a significant performance gain, so we actually rushed one through two weeks earlier to the Turkish Grand Prix, so Nico was racing with that at Istanbul. That call was made on the Sunday of the Spanish Grand Prix [two weeks before the Turkish Grand Prix], and we hadn't quite finished designing it at that point, so there's an opportunity to say, 'That's going to give us an advantage at Istanbul therefore can we push it through in nine days in order to get it out to Istanbul in time for the race.'

A complicating factor is the variability of the different tracks used in Formula 1, which means that innovations are often track-specific. Monza and Monaco are very good examples of this. With the Monza circuit being the fastest circuit in the Championship year, a major redesign of bodywork, wings and end plates is required to ensure the minimum of drag on the car while on Monza's super-long straights. Likewise, the brakes and their cooling require attention, with the manufacture and fitting of different-sized cooling ducts. The exact opposite of this requirement is Monaco, where due to the confines of this street-based circuit different ratio steering racks have to be fitted to cope with the very tight corners, and aerodynamics are almost the exact opposite of Monza to gain the maximum amount of downforce and therefore grip on the slow corners. Alex Burns bears this out in more detail:

A lot of the aero [aerodynamic] design work is track-specific. There is an underlying thread of upgrade that goes through the year; you are in a constant state of development but, we'll have a specific package for

Monaco, a specific package for Montreal and for Monza. Then you'll have general upgrades that go through for the bulk of the races, so the high downforce races of Barcelona, Magny Cours, Silverstone, Hockenheim; all of these will be relatively similar.

Another key part of speed to track is the various simulation approaches that are used to predict performance prior to reaching the circuit, and therefore it is in simulation technologies that Formula 1 has also made significant progress, as Alex Burns observes:

It is important that our simulation for brake cooling is accurate, so if we go to a circuit and we project the brakes will be at this temperature, we'll be using the same simulation package to predict it for the next races, even though the cooling will be a different package. But if our simulation package isn't correct, we need to correct it, otherwise we are going to have a problem. The brakes might run substantially cooler than we were expecting, that should flag that there's an issue with the simulation and we'd want to fix that before the next event, because you're losing performance by running them too cold and if you're running too hot, you're going to ruin the brakes during the race; you're not going to survive the race. So, you need to get these things right, you need to be accurate with simulations.

Who benefits from innovation?

The history of Formula 1 is littered with innovations where teams have created a step forward in performance, but the innovating team has not always been the one who has enjoyed the most race success as a result of its innovation.

In business strategy, there is often talk of 'first mover advantage' – the idea that being first with a new innovation is the basis of success. However, there is growing evidence that often the more profitable and successful strategy is to be the second mover – to watch, learn and copy, as outlined in Shenkar's analysis of 'copycats'.[15] Such a phenomenon is also evident in F1. In Table 5, we can see that often the innovator is not always the prime beneficiary of the innovation. While Cooper undoubtedly enjoyed success from its mid-engine layout, it was Colin Chapman of Lotus who took the design to a more refined stage and was able to overtake the Cooper concept when it came to performance. Similarly, while it was Lotus who pioneered the development of the Ford Cosworth DFV engine, which required a different concept in chassis design (the engine formed a structural part of the car), it was

Table 5 *Who benefits from innovations in F1?*

Innovation	Innovator	Beneficiaries
Mid-engine	Cooper	Cooper/Lotus
Cosworth DFV	Lotus	All British constructors
Ground effect	Lotus	Lotus/Williams
Flat 12 engine	Ferrari	Ferrari
Turbo engine	Renault	Honda
Active Suspension	Lotus/Williams	Williams
Six-wheel car	Tyrrell	Tyrrell
Composite monocoque	McLaren	McLaren
Semi-automatic gearbox	Ferrari	Ferrari
Tuned mass damper	Renault	Renault
Double Diffuser	Brawn, Williams, Toyota	Brawn

Ford's decision to make the engine available to other teams. This meant the performance potential was dispersed across a range of constructors, effectively creating Grand Prix winners out of teams such as Matra, Tyrrell, McLaren and Brabham.

Renault entered Formula 1 in 1978 with a car using a lightweight turbo-charged engine. The regulations at the time stipulated that engines were either 3.0 litre normally aspirated or 1.5 litre turbo-charged. It was generally believed that no one would be able to build a 1.5 litre turbo which would be competitive against the 3.0 litre engines. Renault did so, but in the nine years it raced the turbo engine it failed to win a World Championship. In contrast, Honda, which entered with its own turbo-charged engine in 1983, was able to win three World Championships between its entry point and the end of the turbo era at the close of the 1988 season with the Williams and McLaren teams.

But there have also been instances where the innovating team was able to capture much of the value of its ground-breaking work. Ferrari's 'Flat 12' engine was developed originally to be fitted into an aircraft wing, but found its true potential in the Ferrari 312T racing car. The powerful twelve-cylinder format with a low centre of gravity meant that it posed a significant threat to the well-established Ford Cosworth DFV. While there were attempts to copy the Ferrari format, most notably with Alfa Romeo supplying the Brabham team with a Flat 12 engine, these were uncompetitive and Ferrari enjoyed a prolonged period of success before the engine was rendered obsolete by new ground-effect aerodynamics.

More recently in 2009, the development of the double diffuser concept was initially created by three teams, all of whom were using Toyota engines and therefore had similar issues in the design of the rear of the car. The rear diffuser is a device that manages the airflow as it reaches the rear of the car and is critical in terms of maximising the aerodynamic grip that can be created underneath the car. Toyota, Williams and Brawn (who have now become Mercedes F1) all came up with designs which exploited a loophole in the regulations (see Charlie Whiting's comment earlier in this chapter) to create a more powerful aerodynamic effect by using twin diffuser structures to manage the airflow more effectively. However, it was the Brawn interpretation of the concept that proved the most effective and best integrated this innovation into the design. This advantage over the other teams was critical to Brawn's World Championship success in 2009.

These examples raise some important questions about how Formula 1 teams are able to protect their ideas. In 2007, one of the most notorious episodes of espionage – Spygate – illustrated the lengths some individuals would go to in order to acquire information on their competitors, as former President of the FIA Max Mosley summarises:

It [Spygate] involved the entire IP of the current Ferrari Formula One car, 780 pages of drawings and technical data, plus full information about how the car was operated. It revealed all the technical secrets, everything necessary to build and run the latest Ferrari, and was an absolute gold mine for any other team.[16]

It did not take the significance of 'Spygate' in 2007 to highlight that secrecy is a big issue in Formula 1, but it is something that Patrick Head believes can be taken too far:

Some Formula 1 teams are so concerned about secrecy and the loss of IP that they literally build physical walls around departments to ensure that if someone leaves from the transmission department, they won't have an idea of what's going on in the suspension department; in contrast, we have the view that providing we're progressing and developing it's more positive to have an open internal exchange of information than the risk of losing IP when somebody goes.

From Ferrari's point of view, its location outside of the UK's Motorsport Valley could be a benefit here. Ross Brawn, former Technical Director of Ferrari, said:

If you've got an innovation you're lucky to keep it for three or four months, particularly once it goes out on the circuit. I guess we gain and lose from that because we don't have the grapevine feeding us, but generally I'm happier with the degree of isolation we have.

Another potential concern is the frequent movement of drivers around the teams, but in Patrick Head's view this is not a problem:

Most drivers are only aware of what we're doing on the surface, they know that if they press this button it does that, but they've got no idea of what goes on inside.

Of course, another possibility is that the potency of the innovation is masked by the fact that other aspects of the car perform poorly. Gordon Murray, former Technical Director at Brabham and McLaren, said:

Where we've had a massive innovation and we think we're going to walk it and the driver makes a mistake, the engine fails, you choose the wrong tyres or whatever and you have a series of races where other things go wrong. That happened to us a lot. It can be a bad thing if you cream the first race as everybody panics.

Balancing innovation with growth

Formula 1 teams enjoyed particularly high levels of growth in the period between 1993 and 2003. During this time, the typical number of employees in a Formula 1 team grew from around 100 to 500. This, however, created new problems for how they were going to maintain their flexibility and responsiveness, the essential ingredients of competitiveness.

The nature of technological growth in Formula 1 meant that there was a need for increased specialisation, particularly around the areas of aerodynamics and electronics.

This need for increased specialist expertise meant that the process by which a car was designed had changed from essentially a step-by-step linear process to one which now involves many activities occurring in parallel, as summarised by former Williams F1 Engineering Director Patrick Head:

Probably fifteen years ago the design team would be working on the gearbox for one week and then the next week they'd be designing the rear suspension and then the next week they'd be in the wind tunnel sorting out the aerodynamics; you tended to be involved in every aspect of the car. Today we have specialist areas working in parallel, so we have to deal with the problem of how the transmission, for example, integrates with the rest of the car, how it satisfies the aerodynamic requirements of the diffuser [a structure which manages the airflow under the rear of the car], how it deals with the loadings coming from the rear suspension, etc.

Williams F1 dealt with this problem by the senior management focusing on the integration of these groups:

Fundamentally my job is to ensure that we are producing the quickest car, as opposed to the best transmission or the best rear wing mounting. It's a different way of working and it means that you have to have frequent contact between these groups. We have an open-plan design office and encourage people to liaise with the other departments who have an interest in their work.

The teams had to create structures which were able to bring together these specialists and the necessary equipment, but at the same time they had to ensure that these groupings did not become ghettos of specialists, detached from other parts of the team. Alex Burns relates some of the steps which have been taken to address this at Williams F1:

We're trying to deal with this by creating smaller units and ensuring that we get the interaction between design and manufacturing and align this to the testing and racing operations. I think that once you get above 200 there's a real shift in the culture in a company. You ideally need 50 to 60 people to make things happen quickly. Within these groups you ideally need teams of no more than a dozen, and then ensure that they understand how they fit into the other groups.

In addition to creating appropriate structures, Burns notes:

It's also important that each group has something which is clearly related to the car, rather just, say, your delivery performance against your works order due dates must be high. For it to work in Formula 1, everyone has to be able to relate their activities to the performance of the car.

While individuals such as Patrick Head have experience in all the component areas of the car, which they bring to bear when making trade-offs between different aspects of the car, many of those coming up have tended to have been specialists in one particular area, most notably aerodynamics. He said:

One of the problems created by this growth is that you see some people who were very capable in one particular area, such as aerodynamics, being headhunted to be a chief designer or technical director in another team, [a combination that is] completely wrong for the individual and the company.

Current Williams F1 Chief Technical Officer Pat Symonds also reflects on the challenge of developing all-round technical expertise to support the innovation process:

As a young engineer I was working track-side, I was working on the drawing board, I was running a wind-tunnel programme. I was looking at R&D, I was learning electronics and computing and how we could apply it to everything. Now, someone who is doing CFD is doing CFD, he's not even doing broad aerodynamics; he can be a CFD specialist. As a designer, I was designing – and certainly capable of working on any part of the car. Now, if you look out there, there are an awful lot of people designing, they tend to be very specialised; I mean, we have someone whose speciality is designing front wings. We have someone who is on cooling systems and things like that. So, that's a huge difference that's occurred in the last two decades.

Examples of innovation in F1

In Formula 1, there have certainly been a number of notable innovations over the last fifty or so years. Here we pick a number of particular examples to consider some of the general principles of innovating within Formula 1. The Ford DFV engine in 1968; the six-wheel Tyrrell of 1976; the 'pit stop' Brabham of 1982; Ferrari's paddle gear change; the active suspension Williams of 1992; the all-conquering Ferrari F2004 of 2004 and most recently the tuned mass damper of the Renault R25.

Changing the face of Formula 1: Ford DFV engine

The Ford DFV engine was a disruptive innovation in Formula 1. It changed the way Formula 1 cars were designed and effectively further shifted the basis of competitive advantage away from the engine to the chassis and aerodynamic aspects of the car. In many ways it was this engine that created the regional cluster of expertise in the UK, known as Motorsport Valley; now the core competence needed was focused on chassis and aerodynamics rather than engine design. Its contribution to Formula 1 and the motorsport industry more generally is highly significant.

The basic concept of the Ford DFV was that it replaced the need to construct a full chassis along the entire length of the car. The DFV was part of the car and was attached to the chassis behind the driver with the rear suspension and gearbox attached to the back of the engine. This created a significant increase in the power-to-weight ratio of the racing car.

As an innovation, the Ford DFV was a joint development between Cosworth Engineering, which developed the engine, and Formula 1 constructor Lotus, which designed its type 49 car around the engine, allowing it to be attached to the rear of the chassis. The Ford Motor Company sponsored the project with a capital investment of £100,000, and after this the engine was also known as the Ford Cosworth, with the famous Ford oval logo carried on its cam covers. With a total of 138 wins to its credit, the Ford DFV engine sponsorship was probably one of the most successful in motorsport history.

One of the main catalysts for the innovation was a change in regulation. In November 1963, the FIA announced that from 1 January 1966, Formula 1 engines would be either normally aspirated 3.0 litres or 1.5 litre turbo-charged. Prior to this point, the normally aspirated 1.5 litre engine had dominated, most notably with that produced by Coventry Climax and used by successful teams such as Cooper and Lotus. However, Coventry Climax decided that the development costs of a new 3.0 litre engine would be too high for it to bear; it announced its withdrawal from Formula 1 at the end of the 1965 season.

Colin Chapman of Lotus approached Keith Duckworth of Cosworth to see if he could design and build a new 3.0 litre engine. Chapman then sought support from Ford, from which he received the aforementioned £100,000 from Walter Hayes, who was responsible for Ford's motorsport activities.

Duckworth developed a novel layout for the combustion chamber using four valves per cylinder. At the same time, Ford had also commissioned a smaller four-cylinder Formula 2 engine using the same layout. The Formula 1 engine effectively doubled up two four-cylinder blocks into a V8 formation. It was therefore given the name 'DFV' for Double Four Valve. The car and engine were developed during 1966 and made their first appearance at the Dutch Grand Prix at Zandvoort on 4 June 1967. It won the first race and went on to dominate the rest of the season. While Lotus and Cosworth were delighted with the situation, Ford's Walter Hayes was not so sure:

Almost at once I began to think that we might destroy the sport. I realised that we had to widen the market for the DFV engine, so that other teams could have access to it.[17]

In 1968 the Ford DFV, which had been instigated by Colin Chapman of Lotus, became available to other teams for the sum of around £7,500 per unit. This started a tradition in Cosworth in building customer engines. In 2004, Cosworth was still supplying 'customer' engines to Minardi and Jordan, although the supply contract by then ran into many millions of dollars per annum.

However, as has frequently been the case, while Chapman was the innovator he was not fully able to capture all the benefits of the innovation. Hayes' decision to make the innovative engine available to other teams ensured that while Ford dominated Formula 1 through the late 1960s and early 1970s, Lotus, although it enjoyed some success, did not.

Four isn't enough: the six-wheeled Tyrrell P34

Tyrrell Racing was one of the most successful Formula 1 constructors of the early 1970s (in the late '90s it was sold to British American Tobacco as the formation 'base' for the BAR Honda F1 team). However, its success, which had been based partly on the Ford DFV engine, had waned and Technical Director Derek Gardner was looking for a new way forward:

In about 1974, it was becoming apparent that the Ford engine had lost its edge, it was still producing the same horsepower that it always had, or a little more even, but with the success of the Ferrari, the possible success of engines like Matra or anybody else who came along with a Flat 12, V12 or 12

cylinder whatever, you're going to be hopelessly out-classed ... I wanted to
make a big breakthrough.

Gardner's idea was a radical one that had started in the late 1960s, when he had worked with Lotus on a series of cars for the Indianapolis 500:

So I thought about the six-wheel car and looked at it in a totally different light to the way I had as a potential Indianapolis car. I thought if I could reduce the front track and keep it behind this 150 cm [maximum body height stipulated by the Formula 1 regulations] then I'm going to take out all those wheels and their resistance, but above all I would take out the lift generated by a wheel revolving on a track.

Although Ken Tyrrell had his reservations, he decided to give Gardner the opportunity to develop his ideas:

It was Derek's idea [the six-wheel car]; Derek had wanted to do it the year before [1974] but I didn't think that we were long enough established as manufacturers to go to something so radical. But he finally convinced me that we ought to try it, so we grafted four front wheels onto our existing car and created the six wheeler. We decided to show that car [to the press], we explained this was an experimental car which we were going to test, and if it was any good we would race it.

A key aspect of the development of the six-wheel concept was the input of tyre manufacturer Goodyear, which at that time supplied all the Formula 1 teams with tyres. Gardner shared his ideas with Goodyear, which responded to the challenge by creating a tyre with a 10-inch width and a 16-inch diameter. The introduction of the six-wheel P34 temporarily restored the fortunes of Tyrrell Racing, as shown in Figure 13, which charts their progress from 1970 to 1980.

However, despite a promising performance in 1976, when Tyrrell finished in third place in the Constructors' Championship, 1977 proved to be a different story, with the P34 becoming uncompetitive relative to conventional cars. The reasons for this appear to have been due not to any fundamental aspect of the concept, but to the speed of development of specific components that were supplied by external suppliers to Tyrrell. Ken Tyrrell said:

It became difficult to get big enough brakes to fit inside small front wheels. Because everyone else was using a standard front tyre, it became politically difficult for Goodyear to develop the small tyre for us. The car became too

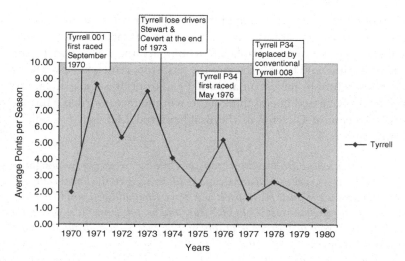

Figure 13 Performance of Tyrrell Racing Organisation, 1970–1980

heavy with our attempts to put bigger brakes in it and at the end of the second year we had to abandon it.

Derek Gardner commented:

Where I think we went wrong was that Goodyear were supplying most of the teams with rubber, they were only supplying one team with very small front wheels. Therefore, the development of the tyres which are continually going on, it meant that almost with its first race the development of the front tyres went back – they just didn't develop as fast as everyone else. Whereas the rear tyres were being developed with the existing front tyres, so in effect you're having to de-tune the back of the car to stay with the front which was, really, not what it was all about.

As a result, Tyrrell returned to using a conventional chassis with the Ford DFV engine. Derek Gardner left Tyrrell to return to industry and it wasn't until he had retired and became involved with the Formula 1 Thoroughbred Racing Series, in which historic Formula 1 cars race, that he was able to work with the six-wheel car once more.

Innovating the whole system: the Brabham pit-stop car
Pit stops have been a feature of Formula 1 for many years. But contrary to popular belief, they were not introduced by regulation to liven up the racing. Contemporary pit stops were created by the innovative Brabham

BT50 or pit-stop car. The point of the pit-stop car was that this was not just a technical innovation, but an innovative race strategy which enabled a lighter, more nimble car to outpace the opposition to the extent that it would be able to enter the pits, stop, refuel, fit new wheels and tyres, return to the circuit and still be in front. It is a classic case of problem-solving and lateral thinking to win the race. Gordon Murray, former Technical Director of the Brabham and McLaren Formula 1 teams, said:

I was the one who introduced pit stops in Grand Prix racing by designing a half-tank car – to get the advantage of the lower weight, the lower centre of gravity. But it wasn't just pit stops; it was a plan that allowed you to achieve advantage through a faster, lighter car and a pit stop. It's just pure mathematics; you just draw a graph of the race – you draw the car's weight, the centre of gravity and the benefit per lap as a curve and then you take a chunk, a negative curve out of the middle bit where you lose say 26 seconds slowing down and coming into the pits and refuelling and if the total equation's better, then you do it.

But Gordon Murray's idea created other problems, such as tyre temperature. The performance of a Formula 1 car is very susceptible to changes in the condition of the tyres. When a race starts, the tyres are relatively cool and performance is only optimised as they warm up to operating temperature. The challenge with the pit-stop car was that this problem was multiplied two, three or even four times in a race. So its success was also dependent on the tyres being able to get to their optimum temperature as soon as possible. Gordon Murray said:

We developed these wooden ovens with gas heaters in them to heat the tyres up so the driver didn't lose the time and smacked those on at the last minute with the fuel.

One surprise for Murray was that the other teams were relatively slow to respond to Brabham's innovative approach:

In the first four or five races the turbo chargers kept failing, I said to Bernie [Ecclestone – then Brabham Team Principal], well that's it, we started in Austria, we only had four races left to end the year, everybody's going to turn up at Brazil with a pit-stop car. But no! Williams had it – but it was a kit that could be put on the car, it wasn't integrated into the design of the car.

Politics and innovating: the Ferrari paddle-shift

Perhaps of all the innovations in Formula 1, the paddle-shift gear change is the most recognisable that found its way into road-going, high-performance cars. The paddle shift utilises a semi-automatic gearbox where the driver does not operate the clutch but selects gears by a pair of 'paddles' located left and right on the steering wheel; pulling one side towards the driver changes up a gear and pulling the other towards the driver changes down.

It was developed by John Barnard, who was trying to find a way to improve the performance of the turbo-charged Ferrari Formula 1 car. However, the problem with this innovative idea was that it meant that the car had to be either designed as a paddle-shift car or a conventional gear-shift car; there was no possibility of producing a competitive car which combined these two features. Barnard said:

There was a massive amount of politics around the whole paddle-shift concept. It actually happened at the time when Enzo Ferrari died. Vittorio Ghidella, who was running Fiat Auto at the time, came into Ferrari to take over Enzo Ferrari's mantle. Towards the end of 1988 I was designing the 1989 car, which was a more developed version of the 1988 test car, but I was designing it such that it would not take a manual gear shift; you could only have a paddle-shift gearbox in it, which was a pretty big commitment to make. Ghidella was so nervous of the fact that it wouldn't work, that he insisted that they built a manual version alongside it. I resisted heavily, because I knew that we didn't have the capacity to do that properly, but they did it and modified the car to put the manual version in and Mansell [driver Nigel Mansell] ran it for a few laps at Fiorano [Ferrari's dedicated test track] and said 'Forget it, give me the paddle shift again'. So that was a diversion caused literally by politics by the head guy at Fiat. I had to literally lay my contract on the line to be able to do it. My contract said that I had overall technical authority on all the cars and the race team and I used that. I put my contract on the line such that if it didn't work or there were unseen problems with it, then effectively I go and commit hari-kari. So that was how it was done, which puts a lot of pressure on that you really don't need when you've got enough technical pressure as well.

Barnard went ahead with the paddle change on the elegant Ferrari 640, which won its maiden Grand Prix on 26 March 1989 at the Brazilian Grand Prix in Rio de Janeiro.

However, the 640 suffered from reliability problems and despite also winning Grand Prix in Hungary and Portugal that year, Ferrari finished third in the Constructors' World Championship. The paddle-shift gear-box was quickly imitated by many other designers and is now a standard feature of a Formula 1 car. It is also used on some of the higher-performance Ferrari, Alfa Romeo and Subaru cars, as well being a common feature on many videogame steering wheels!

The gizmo car: Williams FW14B

The Williams FW14B won the first five races of 1992, with Nigel Mansell at the wheel; a record which even survived the dominance of Ferrari and Michael Schumacher in 2002 and 2004.

The FW14B was a highly innovative car in that it incorporated many of the leading-edge ideas of the day. Its designer, Patrick Head, had incorporated semi-automatic gearboxes, drive-by-wire technology and Williams' own active suspension system. The significance of these ideas was that many of them had been initially developed by other teams such as the carbon-composite monocoque (McLaren and Lotus), semi-automatic gearbox (Ferrari) and active suspension (Lotus). The source of advantage was therefore not one particular innovation, but the way in which they were all brought together, as summarised by David Williams, who was General Manager at Williams F1 at the time:

I think we actually were better able to exploit the technology that was available and that led to a technology revolution. We were better able to exploit it to the full, before the others caught up. It wasn't just one thing but a combination of ten things, each one giving you another 200/300th of a second; if you add them up you a get a couple of seconds of advantage.

The Williams car was so successful that many questioned whether this was a case of technology taking over Formula 1 and whether the skills of the driver were becoming replaced by the technology in the car. This led to further regulations to remove many of these so-called driver aids from the cars.

The total package: Ferrari F2004

Ferrari dominated the Formula 1 Championships for a period of time with cars such as the Championship-winning F2004. So, what innovations were applied to make these cars so competitively outstanding? Ross Brawn, former Technical Director at Ferrari, explained:

Ferrari doesn't have an individual feature, perhaps it never has had, but our innovation is an integration of the whole. Our efforts have always been to make everything as good as it can be, but to work together as a complete package.

Ferrari's innovation is in process and mindset rather than in the technology itself. Since the Ford DFV engine was first raced in 1967 it shifted the dominant design of a Formula 1 car to the chassis, with the engine simply being bolted into the rear of the car (instead of its conventional position in the front). This approach enabled many teams to be Grand Prix winners and developed into a situation where engines were invariably 'outsourced' from engine partners; and, even where the engines are 'in-house', these can easily be made at a different site, perhaps in a different country, as is the case with Renault F1.

However, when he joined Ferrari as Technical Director, Ross Brawn wanted to maximise the unique characteristics of Ferrari – having their chassis and engine design in one location, in the small town of Maranello near Modena, in northern Italy. He said:

When I left Benetton we were using a Renault engine but so were Williams and there was always a conflict about what sort of engine they wanted and what sort of engine we wanted. I really felt that if we could get into a situation where the engine was completely integrated into the car then that must be the best situation. So one of the things that was very important to myself and Rory [Chief Designer Rory Byrne] was to have someone here who understood that and luckily Paolo Martinelli [former Ferrari Engine Director] very quickly appreciated our ideas and was completely receptive to the idea of a fully integrated engine as part of the car package.

One of the key ways in which they achieved this was by maximising the integration between the engine and the other systems of the car, as outlined by their former Engine Director Paolo Martinelli:

I think the integration of the work [between chassis and engine] has been a continuous process and is ongoing, so I think year by year, we are continuing in this direction. I think it was very important that there was trust from the top management and the direction given from the top, from Mr Montezemolo [President] and from Jean Todt.

We do have some cross-functional areas; for example, electronics. We do not have electronics for the chassis and a separate group for the engine and gearbox; they cover the whole car and they help us to integrate the designs between chassis and engine. It is the same for metallurgy; they cover the whole car. Within each area we have experts who also work together, for example, in the area of CFD [Computational Fluid Dynamics] where someone in the chassis group may be working on design of the airbox and someone in the engine group is working on the flow of gases in the engine, they may often share ideas and calculations.

The tuned mass damper: Renault R25

In 2005 Renault introduced the concept of the 'tuned mass damper' (TMD) to Formula 1. Interestingly, applications of the concept of the mass damper have been around for some time and can be found in objects such as the domestic washing machine and the Citroen 2CV. As with most great innovations, the concept of the mass damper is ingeniously simple. Dampers absorb vibration and by locating a tunable damper – the damper is adjustable to absorb particular frequencies – in the body of the car, Renault was able to both create a performance advantage and develop an innovation which was difficult for the competition to imitate quickly. The value of the tuned mass damper is that it cancels out the natural vibration of the tyres, which is transmitted through the chassis of the car, thereby increasing the adhesion of the tyres and reducing wear.

Renault had exclusive use of the TMD during 2005, as the other teams had not been able to quickly recognise the system or develop a response. However, in 2006 it was believed that a number of other teams had developed their own interpretations of the Renault system. Controversially, the FIA made the decision to ban mass dampers half-way through 2006, at a time when Renault was leading the World Championship. Despite the ban, Renault was able to secure both the Drivers' and Constructors' titles in that year. Interestingly, following the ban both McLaren and Ferrari developed damping systems which were smaller and integrated with the suspension systems, and, therefore, less likely to fall into the category of a moveable aerodynamic device – which was the basis for the ban by the FIA.

The 'J' damper (apparently a random letter used by McLaren) uses a spinning mass inside the device to absorb the vibrations from the tyres, thereby producing a similar beneficial effect as the tuned mass damper.

The drive for innovation

So what makes successful innovation in Formula 1 possible? One of the most gifted and influential designers over the last thirty years is John Barnard. Many of his ideas form the basis of the conventional Formula 1 car today. He summarised some of his ideas around being innovative in design:

If it's a really innovative project then that means that I can't be 100 per cent sure that it's going to work. So the one thing I always try to do when I'm either sitting down to design something, or I've got an idea in my head, is to have a back-up solution. I would generally try and think as I'm doing it, 'OK, if it doesn't work what do I do?' so that I'm ready for that catastrophic event that there is something that we haven't foreseen that is so bad there is no other way to go but dump it. I tend to approach things like that, because you're not going to get too many chances to be very innovative in any business and you have to recognise that everything is going to have some sort of problem. That problem is either fixable in a fairly short space of time, hopefully, or it's so big that you've got to think of another direction. Effectively, don't get caught, be ready for the unimaginable, that your brainwave idea doesn't work.

Underlining Barnard's approach is the fact that truly innovative thinking has to be methodical, structured and above all have the total commitment of those behind it. He continued,

Give it a bit of time. Get to understand more about what you're trying to bring this innovative idea into, what sort of field you're coming into and understand more of the problems, and strength of character really. Most times I would say eight out of ten people will rubbish an innovative idea. Carbon monocoques and all the rest of it all got rubbished by people in the business, paddle shift, all the rest of it, all got rubbished. 'Why, what's the point? It'll hit something, be a cloud of black dust!' Be ready for that and don't let it put you off, because it's very easy to be steered away from it by someone you think should know what they're talking about.

In considering the role of learning in organisations we can discern a further number of management lessons that can be drawn from Formula 1 into other areas. We summarise these as follows:

Lesson 5 Make quick decisions and learn from the results

Seeing the opportunity, being decisive and then learning from the result of one's actions is central to continual improvement of performance in this fast-paced environment. These ideas fit closely with the concept of the learning organisation, where continual experimentation and learning provide the basis from which firms move forward. Formula 1 teams have to continually learn from their mistakes otherwise they soon fall off the pace and lose the interest of their sponsors.

But for it to work, it also requires a culture where individuals are not constrained from trying something, and where failure does not undermine their position or credibility in the organisation.

Lesson 6 *The real gains come at the boundaries*

The real performance gains occur at the margins, at the boundaries between the various interfaces, whether these are component areas of the car, between partner organisations or between different teams and sub-teams. These are the gains that are particularly difficult to achieve and sustain, but they are the ones that will make the difference in performance if all other areas are working effectively. When teams are operating at the top of their game, their focus moves from building up particular specialist competences to integrating the whole system and ensuring that it operates to the maximum. In order to deliver the best racing package, barriers between functional departments must be eliminated so that communication between and across them can be clear, constant and directed towards achieving their common goals.

Lesson 7 *Measure everything*

Formula 1 is first and foremost an engineering-based industry. In that context, the delivery of the key product, a fast Formula 1 car, is entirely contingent on design, manufacture and refinement, using the latest in software, telemetry and computer capacity to measure everything. Measurement comes into play at the factory, in the pit lane, on the track and also, as we have seen, in the physiological readings of the drivers.

Like all people in business, Formula 1 teams have to determine what useful information can be drawn out of the massive amount of data that is captured. They must apply reasonable thinking to utilise that information, to make strategic and tactical decisions. In turn, those decisions need to evolve, usually very quickly, into actionable tasks. Once delivered, the impacts of those tasks are measured, and the process starts over again. Recording of input and measurement of output goes beyond the teams themselves, and is the primary process by which sponsors determine whether their investment in the sport provides the returns they are seeking.

When a business is using scorecards of some sort or re-engineering techniques, it is embracing a model of measurement, evaluation and action in the organisation, just as Formula 1 teams do.

5 | The power to change

I think we've learned a huge amount in the last two years about what it takes to manage through this kind of constant chicanery of industry change. This industry, at a detailed level, has changed enormously in the last five years and each time they change it you've got to assess your business and say, 'is the structure right?' 'Is the capital base right?' 'Are the people right?' It's required constant change, it's been hard work, when you look back you think, 'I'm not surprised we're all worn out'.

Graeme Lowdon, President and Sporting Director, Marussia/Manor F1 Team

Change is all-pervasive in Formula 1, whether it is the hundreds of small design changes made to a car during the course of a year – McLaren have estimated that a new component for their car is created every seventeen minutes during an F1 season – or the fact that the individuals employed within Formula 1 are likely to work for eight different teams during the course of their careers.[18] The teams themselves have an average lifetime of less than six years – Appendix B lists sixty-one teams who are now in the Grand Prix graveyard – and are frequently either dissolved or acquired by other teams, creating a constant state of flux.

There are many explanations for the constant pace of change that pervades Formula 1. Not least is the incessant search for technological advantage. As a consequence, many radical ideas have disrupted the evolution of the Formula 1 car. These have included such developments as gas turbines, four-wheel drive and six-wheel cars.

In addition to the changes created by the competition on the track, many changes were also created by the commercial demands of Formula 1. As discussed in Chapter 1, until the 1970s Formula 1 teams were funded either by car manufacturers or by private individuals such as Rob Walker, who funded his racing activities from the wealth created by his family's Johnnie Walker whisky business. Walker successfully ran his own team with cars purchased from Lotus and

Cooper using top-class drivers such as Stirling Moss and Jack Brabham. When sponsorship was introduced the teams needed to develop marketing and sales operations in order to both recruit and manage sponsors. As was noted earlier, during the 1970s, 1980s and early 1990s much of this sponsorship came from the tobacco companies who, due to increased legislation on tobacco advertising, had fewer and fewer alternatives to promote their products. In the 1990s, Formula 1 enjoyed huge growth, both in terms of television exposure and viewing figures, which ultimately attracted the car manufacturers back on a far larger scale than had been the case for many years. In 2015, we see a different situation where teams are struggling to find the levels of sponsorship they need to be viable. This is discussed in further detail in Chapter 8 on Partnerships.

Formula 1 teams have transformed from micro-businesses – in 1971, the Brabham team employed seven full-time people,[19] whereas the Championship-winning Tyrrell team had nineteen[20] – into medium-sized enterprises. In 2015, the Mercedes team employed around 820 people at its facility at Brackley and 400 at their facility in Brixworth, which is the home of Mercedes Benz High Performance Powertrain (HPP). These factors have combined to create an organisational landscape which is continually changing and placing new challenges on those teams who seek to compete in Formula 1. While at one level it looks a particularly challenging environment, Sir Frank Williams has no illusions as to how well-protected the Formula 1 world can be:

Many people say if you went into the real world you'd be a billionaire. I think it's quite the reverse. Formula 1 is a protected environment, outside it's a lot more cut throat. Look at the retail world, I don't think we'd last ten minutes outside.

For sure, the priorities of a small team struggling to stay alive against better-funded competitors are very clear. Several years ago we asked Paul Stoddart, who owned and ran the Minardi team that was eventually sold to Red Bull and renamed Scuderia Toro Rosso, what made his situation different from that of the larger teams:

It sounds a simple answer but it's one word, survival. That is our biggest challenge, and simply put we're competing on less than 10 per cent of the budget yet expected to consistently produce 96–98 per cent of the performance.

This kind of situation still remains in F1, with Manor Grand Prix now struggling at the back of the grid in a similar situation to that which faced Minardi in 2004. Manor's President and Sporting Director, Graeme Lowdon, is clear as to what the focus of the team is about:

We're quite a small team, we don't make anything else; we don't have a parent company that makes medium-sized people cars or energy drinks or whatever; all we do is race. It's a really straight forward kind of DNA.

But like Paul Stoddart before him, he has no illusions as to where they sit relative to the other teams as they are running a year-old power unit:

Engine development between 2014 and 2015 was massive and so in straightforward performance, without any questions, it doesn't matter how well we set the car up or whatever, we don't have the performance to compete with any other team.

So how do the different teams deal with the constant pressure for change and what are some of the factors that explain how some are able to adapt whereas others do not? One perspective on organisational change is that organisations find it relatively easy to change incrementally – or in small steps – because such change fits with their dominant paradigm or mindset. In the context of Formula 1, the pace of incremental change is probably far higher than in the average organisation, because of the flexible, problem-solving and informal basis on which they operate.

However, even though change is pervasive and impressive in Formula 1, it is nonetheless incremental change; it occurs in discrete steps within a dominant mindset, and therefore produces relatively predictable outcomes. Incremental change in the context of Formula 1 would cover aspects such as changing sponsors and technology partners, adapting to new regulations, bringing in new people, systems and so forth. The rate of change will also vary by team. For the smaller teams, issues such as partnerships can change even race by race, presenting them with a very different problem when compared to Ferrari or McLaren, as examples, whose major partners would be retained on three to five-year contracts, as in the case of the new Shell five-year contract signed in November 2015.

As an organisational type, we suggest that the flexible and responsive Formula 1 teams are able to deal with higher levels of incremental change than their counterparts in other kinds of industries. However, the challenge comes when they have to achieve more radical steps in performance improvement, which require fundamental changes in mindset, rather than continuous improvement within the existing organisational framework.

These radical changes are required when the competitive landscape is changing faster than the organisation's ability to change with it. If an organisation fails to respond to these changes it is unlikely to survive in the longer term. Perhaps one of the most disastrous attempts was Lola cars in 1997. Established by former quantity surveyor Eric Broadley in 1957, Lola became a highly successful manufacturer of racing cars, at one time dominating the CART/Champ Cars series in the United States and winning the Indianapolis 500 in 1978 with Al Unser. It had a number of forays into Formula 1, first with a Broadley-designed car in 1962, and then in 1974 designing and building cars for Graham Hill's Embassy-Hill team. After several projects during the late 1980s, it attempted to re-enter under its own name in 1997. The outcome was that the major sponsor it had anticipated failed to materialise and while the cars arrived for the opening race at Melbourne in Australia, it was unable to take part. Lola Racing folded with debts of $9 million in 1997, also forcing the parent company into administration.[21] While Lola was subsequently turned around by new Chairman Martin Birrane, its 1997 entry into Formula 1 remains a dark period in the company's history.

Case studies in change

We consider a series of cases where F1 teams have responded in differing ways to the pressure for change.

Tyrrell Racing

Figure 14 shows the success of Tyrrell Racing during the period from 1970 to 1998. Tyrrell enjoyed a particularly successful period as a Formula 1 team, but eventually succumbed to an environment which was changing faster than its ability to adapt.

Interestingly, it was never Ken Tyrrell's intention to become a Formula 1 constructor. Ken was a naturally gifted Race Team Manager and talent spotter in the early 1960s, who ran his own team

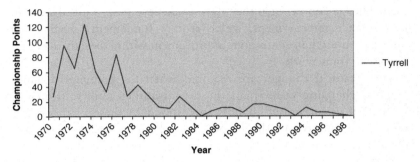

Figure 14 Tyrrell Racing 1970–1998

in the smaller Formula 3 category, with cars provided by Cooper. In 1964, he had signed the up-and-coming young driver Jackie Stewart to drive for his team. In order to improve their performance, he negotiated with French aerospace and performance engineering conglomerate Matra to build a specialist chassis for the car. This it did, and the relationship eventually moved into Formula 1, with Tyrrell running a Matra chassis and a Cosworth engine to win the 1969 World Drivers' Championship title for Jackie Stewart and also the Constructors' title for Matra. However, Matra's desire to develop its own engine led to a parting of the ways, as Ken Tyrrell outlined:

Matra came to us and said if you want to use our car in 1970 then you have to use our engine. So we tried the engine. We put it in the car and took it to Albi in the South of France [north-east of Toulouse], it made a very nice noise, but it actually didn't go very fast, so we made the decision to stay with the Ford DFV. We tried to buy a car from the established people – Lotus Brabham, McLaren, etc, but nobody would sell us a car. Fortunately, March Engineering [FIA President Max Mosley was one of the founders] had just formed and they were prepared to build cars for anyone. So we had a car to go racing in 1970, but it was a bit of a lump, and the writing was on the wall. If we wanted to stay in Formula 1 [and be competitive] we were going to have to build a car ourselves. I'd met Derek Gardner at Matra and I asked him whether or not he'd like to design a Formula 1 car. He said, yes he would, and that's how it all started. If Matra had stayed with the DFV we would have been with Matra now, we didn't want to become a constructor, but we had no choice.

In the early 1970s, the Tyrrell team had dominated Formula 1. With World Champion driver Jackie Stewart, Designer Derek Gardner and with funding from the Elf petroleum company, Ken Tyrrell had put together a winning team, until Stewart's retirement in 1973 and the untimely death of the talented Frenchman François Cevert, who was being groomed as Stewart's successor. During the mid-1970s Tyrrell was a strong midfield team, which was still winning Grand Prix and was also technologically quite innovative. In 1976, it surprised the Formula 1 community with its radical P34 six-wheel car. In 1991, it produced the first 'high nose' Formula 1 car, a design feature that was adopted by the other teams and became the dominant nose feature in the sport. But the real problem for Tyrrell was the changing business of Formula 1.

During the late 1980s and into the 1990s, all the teams were developing highly professional marketing departments in order to secure the funds needed to operate in the long term, allowing them to build up the technological infrastructure in areas such as dedicated wind tunnels, which cost tens of millions of pounds in capital cost. Many had also secured strong relationships with manufacturers to supply them with engines. Most of the teams were run as profitable businesses with state-of-the-art factories. Tyrrell, on the other hand, still operated from the original wood yard site at Ockham in Surrey, where he had started his motorsport activities in the 1960s. It was this site that had hosted the Championship-winning cars of the early 1970s and so held a great deal of the history of the team, but it was nonetheless a fairly basic facility, as former employee Jo Ramirez commented:

Ken ran the tightest and most efficient team in the business but, as I arrived in Long Reach near Ockham, I couldn't believe that the World Championship-winning car had been built and run from this place. There were three sheds, three Portakabins, and a muddy yard for a parking place; the whole ensemble was enough to put off a travelling salesman.[22]

Some of the key problems the team faced in the 1990s were summarised by Mark Gallagher, who became Head of Marketing at Tyrrell, and who had gained his initial experience with the team in 1994. (Latterly he also worked for Jordan F1 and Cosworth.)

We got the job at Tyrrell by being blunt about their situation. That entailed telling Ken and Bob [Ken's son, who was Managing Director] that a media survey viewed their team as being like a family shop, one that hadn't moved on ... The sport had moved on in many respects and the fact was that we had to find a way of raising the team's profile and finding the money to do the job.[23]

In 1995, Nokia had become a major sponsor of the team after supporting Finnish driver Mika Salo, but this still didn't resolve the situation. He continued:

Nokia had been sold the deal that Tyrrell could go from a low ranking towards the top and that all they needed was money. Nokia gave them quite a big cheque, believing this would be the answer. The difficulty was that the selling of Tyrrell was always being done on rediscovering past glories. We've won three Championships with Jackie Stewart, okay, twenty years have gone by, but we still know the magic ingredient. But that was wrong, because they didn't have the infrastructure, the development facilities or the manufacturer behind them.[23]

The Tyrrell team won its last Grand Prix at Detroit in 1983, which was also the 132nd and last win for the Ford Cosworth DFV engine. The years that followed became a constant struggle for cash and resources and the team was purchased by BAR at the end of 1997. The original plan had been for Ken to run the team as Tyrrell Racing in 1998, with it being renamed BAR in 1999. However, due to differences over the choice of drivers, Ken resigned from the team at the end of February 1998. The final race of a Tyrrell car took place at Suzuka, Japan, in November 1998 without the presence of the founder of the team. Ken Tyrrell passed away on 25 August 2001. He left a legacy of the values of the team owner of the 1960s and 1970s who undoubtedly played a major role in the history and development of Formula 1, but was ultimately unable to adjust to change.

Brabham

Founded by Jack Brabham along with fellow Australian designer Rob Tauranac in 1962, Brabham was one of a number of teams founded by drivers to support their racing activities but which eventually became a successful constructor in its own right. Figure 15 shows the performance of the team from the period 1962 to 1992.

In contrast to Tyrrell, which enjoyed success almost immediately as a constructor, it took Brabham a few seasons to establish and build up the performance of the team. However, once this had been achieved it became a successful operator, using a series of different engine suppliers

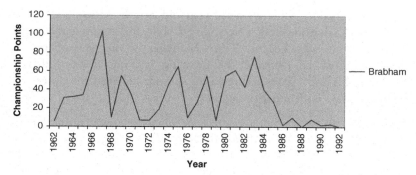

Figure 15 Performance of Brabham 1962–1992

such as Coventry Climax, Repco and Ford Cosworth. In 1966, at the age of forty, Brabham became the only driver to win the Drivers' World Championship in a car bearing his own name – the Brabham BT3 (the model number using the first letter of the two partners' surnames). This was followed by a further World Championship for both the Constructors' Cup and the Drivers' award, but this time with New Zealander Denny Hulme at the wheel. At the end of 1970, Brabham retired from driving, having sold his share of the team to Tauranac a year earlier, and departed for Australia to take up farming and a number of other business ventures. Interestingly, following Brabham's departure, Chief Mechanic Ron Dennis and his number two Neil Trundell also left, to set up Rondel Racing. Dennis went on to create a series of racing organisations including Project Four Racing, which eventually metamorphosed into McLaren International in 1982, hence the designation of MP4/ on each year's race car (McLaren/Project4).

Tauranac found the commercial pressures of running the team, as well as designing and overseeing the construction of the cars, an unsustainable burden to bear. In the autumn of 1970, he sold the company to Bernie Ecclestone, while he became joint Managing Director with responsibility for car design and engineering. This situation remained until early in 1972, when Tauranac left the company and Ecclestone assumed full control.

Ecclestone set about restructuring the Brabham operation. He sacked four of the five-man design team and promoted the remaining

designer, Gordon Murray, a 24-year-old South African, to Chief
Designer. Ecclestone had a very direct style for running the team.
Keith Greene, who became Team Manager of the new operation,
described how he resolved the growing friction between drivers
Graham Hill and Carlos Reutemann, as both believed the other was
being supplied with superior engines:

*Bernie said, 'Right, I'm not going to have any more arguments with these
drivers. What we are going to do now is decide their engines for the year,
OK?' So he got the drivers to alternately call out heads or tails while he
flipped a coin and that decided who would have which engines for
the year. Once the draw was finished he said: 'I don't want to hear any
more about engines.' And he was gone and there were no further
complaints.*[19]

Ecclestone set about making some other changes to the operation. He
had both the workshops and cars painted white, and redesigned the
layout of the factory. Former Brabham employee Nick Goozée commented on the changes:

*We found the changes, which were introduced quickly, a little over the top,
but, in fact, we were not an efficient company. We were very basic in some of
our methods, which had been fine in the '60s but once Bernie bought
Brabham, change was both inevitable and necessary.*[19]

In the early 1970s, the Brabham budget was around £100,000 per
annum and the company employed seven full-time people. It was
a very demanding time for all those involved, but the new team at
Brabham had the sense that this was a new beginning with new opportunities, as outlined by Chief Designer Gordon Murray:

*Bernie gave me the opportunity to be first of all Chief Designer and then
Technical Director. And that was good and bad. The good thing was, and the
reason the performance started to climb, that he had the trust in me to do
a brand new car. He said to me: 'I'm tired of all these bits and pieces, I want
a completely new Formula 1 car; we need a clear head, a clean sheet of paper.'
And that's why we started climbing and we led the first race in fact with the
new car, and won in 1974 for the first time.*

But things were very stretched and while Brabham's operation could be
described in today's terms as an agile organisation, in that it was both
lean and flexible, it also placed a great deal of strain on the individuals
working within it:

The bad part was that he fired everybody and made me Chief Designer and, at the time, I was pretty hard headed about doing everything myself. I couldn't delegate, I wanted to draw the whole car, draw the gearbox, the body and the aerodynamics, everything. And I went far too long without any help. In fact, I was on my own, running Brabham, designing and doing the truck spares and organising everything until 1978; that was far too long, by then people had an engineer on each car as well as a technical director; I was Technical Director and I was also engineering both cars, in the same race.

In addition to the organisational strains that Brabham was enduring, the competitive situation was also changing. Brabham, like most of the British-based Formula 1 constructors, was using a Ford DFV V8 engine. In 1975 Ferrari, which designed and built its own engines, was beginning a renaissance that was seeing a new kind of engine dominate the circuits – the Ferrari 'Flat 12'. The engine used four more cylinders than the DFV, and while it was heavier, the extra power it provided made it dominant on many circuits in the Grand Prix series. Ecclestone and Murray were very quick to respond to this new development and began to look around for an alternative engine to the Ford, which could provide the performance levels being enjoyed by Ferrari. Midway through 1975, they reached agreement with one of Ferrari's historic rivals, Alfa Romeo, to build them a twelve-cylinder engine similar to that currently being used by Ferrari. However, this meant that Murray had to begin work on designing a radically new car and engine combination, the Brabham BT45, midway through the 1975 season:

The BT45 was a completely new car. Well obviously it was a Flat 12 engine, it was a non-structural engine, so you couldn't use the current structure, so it was a total rethink. I had six months to design and build a Flat 12 Alfa car for the beginning of the 1976 season. And I was still halfway through the 1975 season, travelling to every race, every test, engineering both cars and running the company, and I was just about dead, basically.

In Murray's view, Brabham's desire to change radically at this point cost it the 1975 World Championship:

If we'd stuck with the [Ford] DFV, in retrospect, and developed the BT44 theme [the 1975 car], we would probably have matched Ferrari. The new team had only been together for three years and we were very understaffed, underfunded and we were learning to work together. I was running it like a really tight, small family.

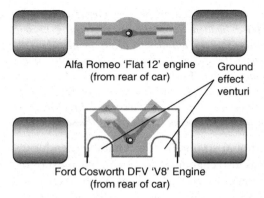

Alfa Romeo 'Flat 12' engine
(from rear of car)

Ground
effect
venturi

Ford Cosworth DFV 'V8' Engine
(from rear of car)

Figure 16 Car profile for ground-effect aerodynamics

Brabham had some success with the Alfa Romeo engine, but it took far longer to develop into a competitive package than had been anticipated:

We had no way of judging what sort of engine Alfa would make – we just assumed that it would be a reasonably good engine. The engine was very big, very heavy and incredibly thirsty. It didn't work, basically, it took most of the practice sessions to get the thing to run, let alone race, at the first Grand Prix.

While the technical team at Brabham was struggling to develop the Alfa Romeo engine, a new innovation was being developed by Lotus, which was to revolutionise the basis of Formula 1 car design, this time by making use of the airflow under the car to create a low-pressure area. The car was effectively sucked onto the track. This innovation, which became known as ground-effect aerodynamics, provided the cars with hugely increased downforce. The problem for Brabham was that this development was impractical when using a Flat 12 engine layout, because it meant that there wasn't the same capacity for airflow under the car as with the Ford DFV 'V' formation engines. This is shown in Figure 16.

Murray therefore had to face the problem of again radically redesigning the Brabham car:

I'd said to Bernie, 'we're just about getting up there again, we've shot ourselves in the foot by going with Alfa, we're just starting to climb up again and now this ground effect,' and he said 'What's ground effect?'

Bernie's essentially non-technical and I got up and drew this thing, and I said I can't get past the engine – right where the venturi diffuser [the shaped underside of the car that creates the area of additional performance] wants to start expanding, we've got a twelve-cylinder engine sticking out there and exhaust pipes. So he said 'Well, what are we going to do?' We sat there racking our brains, thinking how else can we do this – you know, we've got to have a ground-effect car. How can you have ground effect or downforce with a Flat 12 engine? The fan-car [another radical design where the mechanically operated fan assisted ground-effect performance] bought us time to go back to Alfa and say, 'we need a V12 engine'.

In fact, Alfa Romeo was able to respond more quickly than Ferrari to this new development, and provided a new V12 engine for Brabham to start to race in 1979. By this time everyone was returning to the Ford DFV as the ideal engine to use with ground-effect aerodynamics. Brabham bowed to the inevitable and switched to the Ford DFV at the Canadian Grand Prix in September 1979.

The fortunes of the Brabham team took a marked upturn in 1981, when driver Nelson Piquet secured the Drivers' World Championship title by a margin of one point, in the ground-effect car with the Ford DFV engine. In 1982, it switched from the normally aspirated Ford DFV to a turbo-charged four-cylinder BMW engine. Renault had entered Formula 1 with a turbo engine in 1978, and won its first Grand Prix in 1979. With the banning of ground-effect skirts in 1982, Brabham was able to emulate Renault and Ferrari and switch to a turbo-charged engine supplied by BMW partway through 1982. However, the BMW engine, while hugely powerful, suffered from reliability problems.

In 1983, these problems were resolved and, when combined with Gordon Murray's revolutionary 'pit-stop' car (as discussed in Chapter 9 on Innovating), Brabham was able to win its fourth and final World Drivers' Championship. Brazilian Nelson Piquet took the Drivers' Championship for Brabham BMW in 1983, with Brabham also coming third in the Constructors' Championship.

This was the last positive highlight in the history of Brabham. With Ecclestone increasingly involved with the Formula One Constructors' Association (FOCA), and also becoming central to the negotiation of television and advertising rights for the Formula 1 series as a whole, Brabham was left more and more to its own devices. Nelson Piquet, who had given the team many victories, quit at the end of 1985, being unable to agree terms with Ecclestone for the 1986 season. In 1987, a dispirited Gordon Murray left to join the McLaren team, with whom he enjoyed a successful period as Technical Director, as well as going on to develop a series of high-performance McLaren road cars alongside another McLaren Director, Creighton Brown.

During 1987, Brabham only managed eighth place in the Constructors' Championship. In 1988, it did not submit an entry to compete in the World Championship and Bernie Ecclestone sold Brabham and its holding company, Motor Racing Developments, to Alfa Romeo.

Alfa intended to use the team as a basis for a production car racing project. Later in 1988, Brabham was again sold, this time to Swiss financier Joachim Lüthi.[19] However, the team was kept afloat with support from Japanese sponsor Nippon Shinpan, and in March 1990 was purchased by the Middlebridge Group of Japan. Brabham did manage to keep going up to 1992, with the Italian female driver Giovanna Amati. It also introduced driver Damon Hill to Formula 1. Hill finished eleventh at the Hungarian Grand Prix of 1992, Brabham's final race. Hill went on to become World Champion in 1996, driving for Williams.

In 1993, the FIA declared that Brabham would not be allowed to enter the World Championship in 1994 unless all its debts were settled, a demand it was unable to meet. This brought to an end the journey of a team that had been the first Championship winner for an owner-driver, had produced many highly innovative and striking cars and also provided the basis by which Bernie Ecclestone became President of FOCA and subsequently a Vice-President of the FIA. While the company disappeared, many loyal Brabham employees such as Herbie Blash, Alan Woolard and Charlie Whiting took on key roles with the Formula One Administration. In fact, so much in evidence were the former employees of Brabham that they became known in Formula 1 circles as 'BOBs', or Brabham Old Boys.

Ferrari

Founded by Enzo Ferrari in 1929, Ferrari is the oldest Formula 1 team by some margin. It is the only team that has been in Formula 1 since its inception and at the end of 2008 was the most successful team in the history of Formula 1. Figure 17 shows the performance of the team

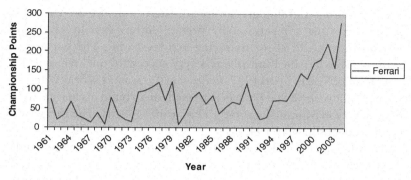

Figure 17 Ferrari performance 1961–2004

from the period 1961 to 2004, which is examined in this section of the chapter.

In 2004 Ferrari won its sixth successive World Constructors' Championship title, the first time this had happened since the award began in 1958. Furthermore, driver Michael Schumacher won his fifth successive Drivers' World Championship, the first time a driver had achieved such a concentrated dominance. His previous World Championships for the Benetton team in 1994 and 1995 also meant that he surpassed Juan Manuel Fangio's record of five World Championships with a total of seven, making him the most successful World Champion since Formula 1 began in 1950. However, this success had not come without controversy. At the Austrian Grand Prix of 2002, Ferrari was accused of unsporting behaviour, when its second driver, Rubens Barrichello, who had dominated the race, moved over on the last corner to allow Michael Schumacher to win, thereby maximising Schumacher's World Championship points. While there was a furore in the press, the Ferrari management remained stoical about its approach. After all, this success had been a long time coming – its 1999 Constructors' Championship title had been their first for sixteen years, during which the honours had been dominated by the British-based Williams, McLaren and Benetton teams. Ferrari's focus had always been to secure the Drivers' Championship, and Schumacher's title in 2000 had been Ferrari's first since Jody Scheckter in 1979; a gap of twenty-one years.

In 1929 Enzo Ferrari, a former driver with the 'works' Alfa Romeo Grand Prix team, created Scuderia Ferrari (SF) based in Modena,

between Parma and Bologna in north-eastern Italy. SF prepared Alfa
Romeo cars for competition by private enthusiasts; in 1932 Alfa
Romeo outsourced all of its racing activity to SF. The partnership
between SF and Alfa Romeo was a very successful one, winning 144
out of the 225 races up to 1937. Following the Second World War, Alfa
Romeo split with SF and Enzo Ferrari went on to build his first car at his
new factory in Maranello, some 10 km from Modena. The Ferrari 125
made its debut in May 1947.

A key feature of the 125 was the Ferrari supercharged twelve-cylinder
engine, the first in a long line of *dodici cilindri* to feature in Ferrari
cars. The 125 was entered into the first season of Formula 1 in 1950,
which was won by Alfa Romeo. In 1952, Ferrari secured its first
World Drivers' Championship (the Constructors' Championship did
not start until 1958) for Alberto Ascari. Ascari went on to win a further
Championship in 1953 and this was followed up by Mike Hawthorn in
1958. Around this time the red Italian cars of Ferrari, Alfa Romeo and
Maserati were beginning to be outpaced by the smaller, lightweight
Coopers and Lotuses whose designs focused on maximising mechanical
grip through better weight distribution and improved suspensions. This
was in contrast to the philosophy at Ferrari, where the engine was always
the starting point of car design and the search for enhanced performance.

Enzo Ferrari had a rather enigmatic approach to running his company. After the death of his son Dino he very rarely left the Modena
area, and hardly ever attended a race, preferring instead to spend his
time either in the factory or at the Ferrari test facilities. He relied on the
Italian media – which had always reflected Italy's strong interest in
Ferrari – and his closest advisors for information. This often created
a highly political atmosphere in the team.

Ferrari initially resisted the trend being pioneered by the British
constructors, whom he referred to as '*assemblatori*' or '*garagistes*'.
He defended the engine layout of the Ferrari with the analogy that
the 'horse' had always pulled, not pushed, the cart (although he later
denied having made this statement). Not an engineer himself, the
designers who Ferrari employed up to 1980 (Alberto Massimino,
Gioachino Colombo, Carlo Chiti and Mauro Forghieri) had first learnt
their trade as engine designers, and so the design of a new car would
always start with the engine. Ferrari himself often referred to '*the song
of the twelve*', underlining the distinctive high-pitched note of the
Ferrari power unit.

However, by 1960 the dominance of the British cars was clear, and Ferrari had to build a lighter rear-engined car, which it did using a highly effective V6 engine. The Dino 156 (1.5 litre, V6) or 'shark nose' dominated 1961 and gave Ferrari a further Drivers' title (for American Phil Hill) and Constructors' World Championship title. However, the advances made in chassis construction by other teams had meant that it was increasingly uncompetitive and, in 1964, the Ferrari 158 was launched with a similar monocoque-type chassis to the Lotus 25 of 1962.

Also in 1964, Ferrari first tried out the Flat 12 engine developed by Mauro Forghieri. Originally commissioned for an aircraft application, the Flat 12 was designed to fit into the wing of an aircraft. However, it was powerful, relatively light and its flat profile gave it a low centre of gravity, which would help in improving mechanical grip. It was this twelve-cylinder unit that was seen to be the future for Ferrari.

Merging with Fiat
In the late 1960s, Ferrari merged with Italian automotive manufacturer Fiat. This was, in effect, a benign acquisition, with Fiat acquiring 40 per cent of the equity in Ferrari, thereby providing a huge injection of cash to support research and development. This allowed the construction of a private Grand Prix circuit at Fiorano adjacent to the SF factory in Maranello. The technical team used this facility to engage in a period of intensive development focusing on the Flat 12 engine.

The new ownership and influence from Fiat meant increased resources, but also increased pressure for results. In the early 1970s, Formula 1 was dominated by the Ford DFV engine (see Chapter 9). Built by Cosworth Engineering near Northampton and funded by the Ford Motor Company, the DFV was Formula 1's first widely available purpose-built engine; it was light, powerful and relatively inexpensive. In 1968, the engines were available for £7,500 per unit and were fully capable of winning a Grand Prix. This enabled the British constructors, who specialised in chassis design, to become increasingly competitive. In 1971 and 1973 every Grand Prix was won by a car using a DFV engine. Its impact was that it made the cars both very light and very powerful; at a time when tyre technology was relatively primitive, this left the designers searching for other ways to increase grip. The answer came from aerodynamics with aircraft-type 'wings' being used to create downforce (a term used to describe what is actually negative lift), described technically as aerodynamic grip, allowing the cars to both enter and exit corners at vastly increased speeds.

1970s renaissance

During this time, Enzo Ferrari had been suffering from ill health. Now in his seventies, he made the decision to appoint a Team Manager to run the day-to-day activities of the Formula 1 team: Luca di Montezemolo, a 25-year-old lawyer who was also connected to Fiat's Agnelli dynasty, was chosen. In addition, Mauro Forghieri had been recalled to Ferrari in 1973, as Technical Director. In 1975, the fruits of Montezemolo's team building, Forghieri's creative ideas and the intensive testing at Fiorano were exemplified in the new 312T, which featured a wide low body with a powerful Flat 12 twelve-cylinder engine and a revolutionary transverse (sideways mounted) gearbox which improved the balance of the car, making it handle extremely well. While the new car was not ready until the season had already started, driver Niki Lauda, with the support of teammate Clay Regazzoni, was able to easily secure both the Drivers' and Constructors' World Championships.

The Ferraris dominated the 1975 season. With their elegant styling, handling and the power advantage of the engine, they were in a class of their own. Ferrari success continued, winning in 1976 (Constructors' Championship), 1977 (Drivers' and Constructors' Championships) and 1979 (Drivers' and Constructors' Championships). But perhaps its greatest moment was in the 1979 season, when Ferrari finished first and second at the Italian Grand Prix at Monza. This sent the fanatical Italian fans, or *tifosi*, and the Italian press into a complete frenzy.

By 1980, however, the 312T5 car was outclassed by the competition. New innovations in aerodynamic design brought about the 'ground-effect' revolution, pioneered by Lotus and quickly adopted by Williams (see Chapter 9). While the Ferrari's engine was one of the most powerful, it was a 'flat 12', meaning that the cylinders were horizontal to the ground, creating a low and wide barrier, which gave little opportunity to create the ground effect achieved with the slimmer V8 DFV engines (see Figure 16).

In 1979, as engine supplier to Brabham, Alfa Romeo had launched a V12 engine to replace its Flat 12 for this very reason. No such initiative had been taken at Ferrari, which had concentrated on a longer-term project to develop a V6 turbo-charged engine. *Autosport* correspondent Nigel Roebuck commented on this change of fortune:

Maranello's flat 12, still a magnificent racing engine, is incompatible with modern chassis. Villeneuve and Scheckter were competing in yesterday's cars.[24]

The lowest point came in the Canadian Grand Prix, when the reigning World Champion, Jody Scheckter, failed to qualify his Ferrari for the race, the equivalent of Italy failing to qualify for the soccer World Cup. Once again the full wrath of the Italian press descended on the team.

The Ferrari GTO

In the mid-1980s, more and more investment was poured into the Italian facilities, but with no effect on performance. A key problem was that new developments in aerodynamics and the use of composite materials had all emerged from the UK's Motorsport Valley.

In 1984, British designer Harvey Postlethwaite became the first non-Italian Technical Director of Ferrari and in 1986 British designer John Barnard was recruited to the top technical role. Barnard was responsible for the introduction of the carbon-composite chassis into Formula 1 in 1981 with McLaren; this material created a lighter and stronger chassis than the aluminium monocoques which had previously been used. It is now accepted as an essential and central part of Formula 1 design.

Barnard was not, however, prepared to move to Italy as he felt that his technical team and network of contacts in the UK would be essential to his success in the role of Technical Director. Surprisingly Enzo Ferrari, now eighty-eight years of age, allowed him to establish a design and manufacturing facility near Guildford in Surrey. Barnard said:

Through intermediaries, Enzo Ferrari contacted me and the outcome was that I didn't want to go to Italy, but he wanted me so he said, 'Okay, do you want to set something up in England?' and given that opportunity I said 'Yes'. So we started what was called 'GTO' which stood for Guildford Technical Office. Ferrari was at that time [1986] fundamentally an engine company and the chassis was always second place. Enzo saw what was going on in the British side of Formula 1 with the introduction of composites and so on, so he wanted to give the chassis side a boost.

The fact that Barnard was defining the technical direction of Ferrari meant that he became increasingly involved in activities at both sites. The geographical separation between the car and engine departments led to the development of various 'factions' within Ferrari, making Barnard's job increasingly difficult. In 1987, on arrival at Maranello, he became famous for ordering a ban on the consumption of wine at the midday canteen:

When I went racing and testing with them in '87, in the middle of the day out come the tables, out come the white tablecloths, and a bottle of Lambrusco or something on the table, and they all sit down and tuck in. You know, pasta, a glass of wine, that's what they tended to do for their lunch. Marco Piccinini, Enzo's right-hand man, said 'What did you do at McLaren?' I said, 'Well we'd have a few sandwiches and a cup of tea and get on with it', you don't stop, you just have a quick snack and then you were eating at 6 o'clock in the evening or something like that because it's all going on and you've got to get ready for qualifying and so on. 'Yes,' he said, 'I thought so.' He said, 'Do you want to change the way they do this? Because it's up to you if you want to change this . . . we can . . .', and I said 'Well yes, I think we should Marco, you can't sit down in the middle of the day, it's completely unrealistic, if you've got work to do on the car, you've got to be keen.' 'Right', he said, 'Well leave it to me.' And of course the next thing you know – 'John Barnard bans wine', it was a classic, and Marco climbs in there and said 'Mr Barnard, he doesn't want the glass of wine . . . sorry but what can I do, he's the boss' and I thought, 'Right, I'll watch you mister!' but at the end of the day it's what needed to happen. It was probably things like that, that Enzo saw were fundamentally wrong with the team, but he didn't know how to change them.

Enzo Ferrari's death in 1988 created a vacuum which for a number of years was filled by a series of executives from the Fiat organisation. It was written into the contract between Fiat and Ferrari that on Enzo's death, Fiat's original stake would be increased to 90 per cent. This greater investment led to attempts to run Ferrari as a formal subsidiary of the Fiat group.

Barnard became frustrated with the interference and politics of the situation and left to join Benetton in 1989. Ferrari had recruited World Champion Alain Prost to drive for it in 1990, but while the GTO-designed 1990 car was highly competitive (an example of that year's Ferrari 641 was displayed in New York's Museum of Modern Art), the organisation was falling apart, and in 1991 Prost was actually fired by the Ferrari management for criticising the car and, thereby, the sacred name of Ferrari. Former driver Patrick Tambay commented on the situation:

No one's in charge anymore. When the Old Man was alive the buck stopped with him. Maybe he took some curious decisions – but at least he took them. I'm not saying that Ferrari will never win again, but the fabric of what the name meant has gone. There are so many layers of management, so many bosses reporting to bosses, until ultimately it gets to Gianni Agnelli [Chairman of Fiat].[23]

Transforming the Prancing Horse

At the end of 1991, Agnelli appointed Luca di Montezemolo as CEO, with a mandate to do whatever was needed to take Ferrari back to the top. Since leaving Ferrari in 1976, Montezemolo had taken on a range of high-profile management roles, including running Italy's hosting of the Soccer World Cup in 1990. Di Montezemolo accepted the role on the basis that Ferrari, and, in particular, the racing operation, was independent of Fiat. Montezemolo understood he was about to embark on something different:

I have not been in the Fiat management stream for ten years. Maranello is another world and has to be treated as such.[25]

In an article in *Autosport*, he described the situation as follows:

After I arrived last December [1991] I spent five months working to understand the situation. To understand the manpower, to understand the potential of the car. Once I had absorbed all this I decided to approach the whole situation in a completely different manner. Ferrari had become an inflexible monolith of a company, which was no good for racing. As a result I decided to divide it into three small departments: future developments and special projects in the UK under John Barnard; the engine department in Maranello under Paolo Massai; and finally the Scuderia Ferrari under Harvey Postlethwaite, which is the place where we build the cars and manage the team.

I also wanted to build up a strong relationship between our UK facility and Italy in order to take full advantage of the Formula 1 'Silicon Valley' in England for chassis development and specialist sub-contractors while still harnessing the huge potential of Maranello.[26]

When asked why he was repeating the 'GTO' initiative that Enzo Ferrari had set up with Barnard and which had ultimately ended with Barnard leaving and taking the facility with him, Montezemolo had a very clear response:

I think that the GTO concept of Enzo Ferrari was a super idea. Unfortunately, at the time Ferrari was very old and the situation was managed in a bad way. But the fundamental idea was very good. For me the approach is slightly different. First of all, I am in charge of the company with full powers, so I can take a decision without anyone else taking a parallel initiative. I take my responsibilities and I want the people in the company to follow my ideas. If they follow, I am very happy. If they don't then there are many other doors, many possibilities available to them outside Ferrari.

My objective is to create a smaller racing department which contains less bureaucracy. Of course there will be a lot of discussion between the engine and chassis departments. In Maranello we have a huge organisation geared to building cars, but I want to take advantage of the UK facilities, and for a worldwide company like Ferrari it is certainly not a scandal to have an affiliate in the UK. If you want to make pasta, then you have to be in Parma; I want to make a sophisticated Formula 1 project, so I want to be involved in England. Then it is up to me to put everything together.[26]

In August 1992, John Barnard signed a five-year contract with Ferrari to design and develop its new cars. In an effort to avoid a 'them and us' situation between the UK and Italy, a number of Italian technical people were recruited to work for Barnard in the UK. The re-established UK operation was called Ferrari Design and Development (FDD) and was a Ferrari-owned subsidiary.

At the launch of the 1992 car, Luca di Montezemolo broke with tradition and introduced a new numbering system based on the year a car would be racing, an approach which has been followed from 1992 up to the Championship-winning F2004. Prior to this, the numbering of many Ferrari cars had been based on the characteristics of the engine – the 312 of 1971 representing <u>3</u>.0 litre and <u>12</u> cylinders; the 126C4 of 1984 representing a <u>120</u>° 'V' angle with <u>6</u> cylinders, and C standing for '<u>C</u>ompression' or turbo-charging. Montezemolo said:

At Ferrari we have always devoted and will continue to devote, great attention to racing; racing is part of the history, the culture and the traditions of this company. We live in a country in which, especially in recent times, people have yelled and complained a bit too much. We hope that the only noise around here will be our engine as it sets new lap records at Fiorano. We are looking for a revival here, and with an eye to the future we have tried to put together a group which combines young engineers, many of them with the highest qualifications, and people whose enthusiasm and abilities will make a notable contribution. We have a lot of work to do; we have a lot of ground to make up on the opposition. We have code-named the new car F92A to demonstrate that we are turning a new page in our history.[25]

When asked about drivers in 1992, he also gave some further indication of his thinking:

The main priority is the new organisation. We are lucky because it is a big challenge to offer a driver the chance to help re-establish Ferrari to a competitive level. I want a driver who is motivated and prepared to work with us. Motivation is everything in a driver, as Niki Lauda reminds us![26]

In addition to the structural changes, di Montezemolo had also brought in some familiar faces from Ferrari's successful period in the mid-1970s: former driver Niki Lauda acted as a consultant to the team and Sante Ghedini took on the role of Team Manager. With an Englishman heading up design, di Montezemolo followed this up with the appointment of a Frenchman, Jean Todt, to handle the overall management of the team. Todt had no experience in Formula 1 but had been in motorsport management for many years and had recently led a successful rally and Group C Sportscar programme at Peugeot with 1982 World Champion Keke Rosberg at the wheel. Driver Gerhard Berger commented on Todt's team-building skills:

I was able to bring some links in the chain to Ferrari, but it took Todt to join them together. Ferrari is now working as a team for the first time. He has made a huge difference.[26]

Chief Mechanic Nigel Stepney joined Ferrari in 1993, but his first impressions were not positive:

When I joined Ferrari at the beginning of 1993, it was like being thrown into the lion's den. I was in a non-position, regarded as John Barnard's spy and not allowed to take any responsibility.

However, he recalled the arrival of Jean Todt as a turning point in the team:

It was like Julius Caesar every day. People getting sacked and leaving every five minutes. You never knew who was boss – not until Jean Todt arrived, took control of the situation and instilled organisation, stability and loyalty into the team.[20]

The physical separation between design and development in Guildford and the racing operation in Maranello led to increased problems and, in early 1997, Barnard and Ferrari parted company for the second time. This opened the way for Ferrari to recruit not only driver Michael Schumacher but also a number of the key individuals in the Benetton technical team which had helped him to his world titles in 1994 and 1995. The arrival of Schumacher provided new impetus for the team, as Nigel Stepney recounted:

Once Schumacher arrived, everyone started putting us under incredible pressure. We weren't quite ready as we still needed key people, but at some point you just have to go for it and get the best driver around. He was the icing on the cake and it sent out signals that we were serious again.[20]

Todt and di Montezemolo also chose not to make a direct replacement for the role of technical supremo who would both lead the design of the car and the management of the technical activity. They split the role between a Chief Designer, Rory Byrne, who had overall responsibility for designing the car, and Ross Brawn, who managed the entire technical operation. These were roles which both had had when working with Schumacher at Benetton. However, on leaving Ferrari, Barnard had purchased the entire FDD operation from them. As most of the existing staff remained working for Barnard, this meant that Byrne and Brawn faced the task of building up a new design department from scratch – around fifty people, this time based in Italy. The engine department continued to develop Ferrari's engines, but in line with new technologies and regulatory requirements, these were now lighter V10s to compete with the Renault and Mercedes engines, rather than the beloved, but now dated Ferrari *dodici cilindri*.

As part of its recruitment in 1996 of Michael Schumacher, Ferrari entered into a commercial partnership with tobacco giant Phillip Morris to expose its Marlboro brand on the Ferrari cars. In a special arrangement Philip Morris, rather than Ferrari, paid Schumacher's salary, and also made a significant contribution to Ferrari's annual operating budget. However, there was one price to pay which was too high for many long-term Ferrari *aficionados*, the blood-red Ferrari of old was now replaced by a bright orange red, because it was more closely matched to the Marlboro colour scheme. Most importantly, it was more effective on television than the original Ferrari red.

In addition to Marlboro, Ferrari also entered into a long-term partnership with Shell, to provide both financial and technical support to the team. This was a departure for Ferrari, which had previously always worked with Italian petroleum giant Agip. With these kinds of arrangements, Ferrari led a trend from just selling space on cars to long-term commercial arrangements, with coordinated marketing strategies enabling commercial partners to maximise the benefits of their investments.

To many, the team now revolved around Schumacher, in contrast to past decades when drivers were honoured just to work for Ferrari. Jean Alesi, a former Ferrari driver, commented on this change in attitude at Ferrari:

Schumacher does whatever he wants, and they do whatever he says.[27]

Enzo Ferrari had famously rejected a number of top-class drivers because they wanted too much money, such as Jackie Stewart in 1970 and Ayrton Senna in 1986, whose wage demands Enzo described as *'imaginativo!'*[27]

This rejuvenated team provided the basis for Michael Schumacher's dominance of Formula 1. In 1997, Ferrari's fiftieth anniversary, there was great anticipation that would be its year, but the team fell just short, finishing second in the Constructors' Championship with the Barnard-developed Ferrari. As Nigel Stepney recounts:

1997 was a great disappointment for the team as we so nearly won the Championship, we felt we had the right way of working; we just had to keep at it and not panic.[20]

Ferrari's competitiveness continued to improve and in 1999 it won the Constructors' World Championship – although the Drivers' World Championship went to Mika Hakkinen in a McLaren-Mercedes. Stepney recalls:

It was a very stressful year; we lost Michael Schumacher after he broke his leg at Silverstone. Then we made mistakes such as the pit stop at the Nurburgring. But although we paid the price in one respect, we gained from the experiences. We realised that as a team, we had to pace ourselves, to switch off and recharge our batteries sometimes.[20]

In 2000, Ferrari secured both World Championship titles, a feat it repeated for the following four years. It was at this point that it felt it had truly returned to the glory of the mid-1970s.

Red Bull Racing

Changing the way Formula 1 teams operate to deliver enhanced performance is a key imperative for senior management. No one knows this better than Christian Horner, Team Principal of Red Bull Racing. He took over the organisation shortly after Red Bull's acquisition of Jaguar Racing from the Ford Motor Company and had the job of moving the team up the grid:

The initial observation that I made upon joining Red Bull Racing was that previously there had been a large corporate entity trying to run a corner shop. Formula 1 and mainstream automotive industry are two very different things. You have to be very reactive within Formula 1, moving to the demands of the business and at the end of the day you have got eighteen weekends [the number of races at the time of this interview] that you are judged upon. Many of the fundamental areas were quite sound but the team lacked technical direction, technical leadership and so basically we focused from a very early point on addressing the technical structure.

Horner's recognition of the need for technical direction meant that a top-line Technical Director needed to be recruited to the team; one who not only had the breadth of technical skills necessary, but one whose very presence would motivate and inspire existing staff and encourage new talent to move to the team. Perhaps surprisingly, in Formula 1, this was not the work of a moment:

Through the first twenty-four months we went through a process of identifying the key individuals and recruiting them into the company, obviously Adrian Newey being the most significant as Chief Technical Officer. Recruiting Adrian was a key appointment for us. One of the later key appointments was Geoff Willis, who had recently been at Honda and BAR as Technical Manager. This allowed Adrian to continue to focus on the strategic direction of performance technologies, with Geoff being very much the facilitator to make it happen within the team.

Recruiting Adrian Newey from McLaren was only the start of the process for Red Bull Racing. What then had to follow was putting the right infrastructure in place, to allow the technical team to deliver the performance needed:

We've really invested heavily in the technical infrastructure, and then the operational structure as well in manufacturing and the trackside operation. So in many ways we kept what was working efficiently from the old Jaguar regime, and had a bit of a clear-out across the technical and operational groups, to put in a focused and disciplined structure with clear technical direction. We've also spent a lot of time investing in the tools you need to get the job done, in the wind tunnel, in CFD, in various other dynameters and simulation tools, so we really have started to move the team into the twenty-first century.

The rest, as they say, is history. The success of Red Bull Racing (RBR) is up there with Ferrari as one of the great stories of transformational change in F1 – from Jaguar Racing, without a single win to their name over 85 races, their best results being two third places, to RBR achieving four consecutive Drivers' and Constructors' World Championships in the period 2010–2013. At the US Grand Prix of 2015, RBR had achieved 50 race victories from 200 races. However, the dynamics of F1 can be merciless and the change in regulations for 2014 meant that the power unit of an F1 car once again became a potential source of competitive advantage, having previously been 'frozen' by the regulations, which had had the effect of focusing competitive prowess on aerodynamics. This change led to an acrimonious breakdown in the relationship between RBR and their power-unit partner, Renault. At the time of writing it remains unclear as to who will provide power units for RBR in 2016; indeed, it is also unclear as to whether they will continue in F1 in their present form, such are the dynamics of this ruthless industry. However, Christian Horner remains upbeat and sees no real difference in the kind of challenge the team now face:

It's just the same challenge, just different mapping because, you know, when you're winning, the pressure of retaining that performance is there and when you losing, it's about going back into being in a winning position. So, it's no harder or no easier.

Williams F1

Williams F1 are rightfully regarded as one of the heritage teams of Formula 1. Since Frank Williams became an entrant in 1969, and then a full blown constructor as Williams Grand Prix Engineering in 1978, the team has always borne his name. Although they have enjoyed race wins as recently as 2012, their last World Championship success was in 1997 (see Appendix A). By their high standards the last ten years have been a less than successful period, as Group CEO Mike O'Driscoll admits:

Williams between 2004–2013 went through what can only be described as a fairly lean patch. With a deterioration in track performance comes a reduction in the following year's revenue and also lower sponsorship because you're attracting fewer sponsors, you're retaining fewer sponsors and you find yourselves in a vicious circle where poorer performance reduces revenue – lower revenue gives you less to spend on motor racing which reduces performance and that's essentially a recipe for extinction. We needed to put a stop to that, we needed to press the reset button here at Williams in order to create a sustainable future.

A central part of the Williams F1 approach was to have a very clear rationale as to what they were trying to achieve going forward. A key challenge was culture change – to remove a blame culture and move back to a winning culture (see Chapter 9):

We focused very much on people and on putting in place the technical leadership that could unite the disparate functions within the Formula 1 technical organisation. A culture of blame had permeated the organisation over two or three difficult years and we needed to bring people together; we needed to find a way of capturing the talent that was there, the latent talent in the organisation and we needed a strong technical leader who would be able to do that, and of course we turned to Pat Symonds.

The appointment of Symonds as Technical Director in 2014 was a critical point in the change process:

He's done it all, he's won the World Championship and had a great career in the sport and we knew he had the knowledge, the skills, the experience but, probably most importantly, the personality to be able to bring people together.

Symonds himself saw his contribution in terms of helping not only the people, but also the process:

Process is one of the things that delivers performance quickly. When I came to Williams, I think people got fed-up of me saying the two 'P words' all the time – it's all about performance and process, get your process right and focus on performance.

The recruitment of Symonds was important, not just in terms of the individual leadership he brought, but also in terms of further recruitment generated by his appointment, a similar effect that Red Bull had enjoyed when they had recruited Adrian Newey from McLaren. According to O'Driscoll:

And of course in bringing Pat in, he then acted as a magnet to attract other technical leaders that we needed to bring in to supplement the great talent pool that we already had here at Williams. We brought in about a dozen people over a period of about six months under Pat and really strengthened the technical organisation.

In addition to rebuilding the technical side of the F1 operation, another key element was the development of Williams Advanced Engineering (WAE), a separate business unit which focused on generating revenue through technology transfer from F1, a similar approach to McLaren with their McLaren Applied Technologies operation, both of which are discussed in more detail in Chapter 10. As O'Driscoll explains:

At Williams it's still majority owned by founder Frank Williams, whose passion and drive and energy is all about motor racing. We compete against teams with much larger budgets than we have available and in the absence of cost controls within Formula 1 and the competitive environment we're operating within, we needed to put in place a structure that was sustainable and the Formula 1 team depends on its sources of income from two principal areas; the first is Formula 1, where we receive money on an annual basis based on our participation and on our performance. We generate revenue from sponsorship through major partners, but we needed a third leg to the stool and advanced engineering provides us with that stability.

In addition to the focus on WAE, the transition at Williams involved finding a new engine partner, which resulted in the team ending its relationship with Renault to work with Mercedes Benz:

We also made the decision to go with Mercedes Benz HPP for our power unit. We did a lot of due diligence on power unit source of supply and believed that Mercedes HPP had a very well developed thought process on the new power unit. We were very comfortable that they knew where they were going, that they knew what they needed to do to be successful. Now of course, in retrospect, it looks like a really smart decision but certainly that was important.

Interestingly, when organisations run change programmes they are framed as internal initiatives focusing on internal process, structures and people; but paradoxically here the most externally obvious sign of change was the fact that Williams managed to secure a new title sponsor, a company which had had a long history and association with motorsport, Martini:

The combination of Williams and Martini blew the dust off both brands. The creation of Williams Martini Racing was a way of demonstrating publicly the changes that we were making internally, and became both an internal and an external rallying cry moving forward. We were able to demonstrate that we were back in the game and it was different. We were fighting again!

In referring to the change process, Mike O'Driscoll underlined that it was not about one or two factors but a number of elements in addition to the recruitment of Symonds and the focus on growing WAE. Importantly, these had both internal and external impacts: the decision to go with a new engine partner – Mercedes HPP; the decision to find a new driver – Felipe Massa; and working with a new commercial partner – Martini. All of these together signalled a new era, or as he describes it – '*pressing the reset button*'.

Marussia/Manor F1 team

In Appendix B you will see the Grand Prix graveyard, which features sixty-one teams who are no longer part of F1, even though many of the people and facilities morphed into other teams. In this list there have been very few who returned after falling into administration. Even Team Lotus, who had often dominated F1 in the sixties and seventies, only returned recently in name with no direct connection to the original team.

An exception to this occurred during 2015, when the Marussia F1 team, which had gone into administration in 2014, managed to resurrect themselves and return to the F1 grid. But tragically this was not just a story of fiscal recovery, but one of deep emotional trauma caused by the loss of one of their drivers, Jules Bianchi. Following an accident on 5 October 2014 at the Japanese Grand Prix, Jules sustained catastrophic head injuries, causing him to lapse into a coma from which he never recovered. Jules died on 17 July 2015, the first F1 driver to receive fatal injuries during a race since Ayrton Senna at Imola in 1994.

When we talk about organisational change there can be few situations that carry the depth of trauma experienced by the Marussia/Manor F1 team.

The financial problem which the team faced was that their business model had been based on a proposal from Max Mosely, who was then FIA president, that new teams could enter in 2010 with a budget cap of £40 million per annum operating costs and enjoy beneficial technical support to help them be competitive. Unfortunately, neither the budget cap nor the technical support came to fruition; and of the three teams that entered under this arrangement (Caterham, Marussia/Manor and HRT) only Marussia/Manor are still in F1 in 2015. Manor's case is remarkable because financial problems meant they went into administration in 2014. According to Graeme Lowdon,

We worked very, very hard and got to a position where we were able to bring the company back out of administration. It's the ideal solution and it's what an administrator always hopes for, but it's not always what happens.

But the biggest challenge was picking themselves up after Bianchi's accident in Japan. Graeme Lowdon summarises the approach he and Team Principal John Booth took to work through this situation:

I subscribe to that kind of fairly simple view of management which is we don't get paid to let the inevitable happen, we're here to do something, but equally we're not here to micro-manage other people, I quite like that really quite simple model which says, people will be able to do their job if they have three things which is focus, energy and structure. So if there's some kind of focus that we can set so that they understand why they're here, what to concentrate on and some kind of structure – and when we say structure not just boxes and lines, but an understanding of authority, information flow, style, the way we do things, and we had to make sure that everybody still had the energy to go and do something that I'm sure they really didn't want to do [to race again, straight after the accident in Japan] and that was partly the reason why we prepared Jules' car.

At the Russian Grand Prix in 2014, which was only one week after the Japanese Grand Prix, the team had prepared two cars, even though Jules was in a coma in a Japanese hospital.

We knew, medically, he was in a difficult way, but it was really important to prepare the car for Jules, because it's a message. We thought it was quite important, as a race driver, to know we are preparing a car for him; and

secondly for the guys, to give them the focus to be doing something that they've put a lot of energy into.

Sadly, Bianchi would not race his car again and the team had to endure the news of his death halfway through the 2015 season:

And then earlier this year, sadly, Jules lost his fight and even though we were very aware of the situation, it was still a shock and it had a big effect on the team, there's no question about it.

As we sit in the small Marussia/Manor F1 Team hospitality unit across the Paddock from the towering McLaren facility, Graeme Lowdon reflects on the even more imposing challenge they face for 2015:

I always think of the company travelling along a timeline and on that timeline you get all sorts of different scenarios and in the last twelve months we've had all sorts. The way we've prepared for this season is not the optimum way to prepare a Formula 1 racing team because if it was then everyone would do it this way and quite clearly they don't, and they don't for a reason; it's a massive, massive challenge, we're here and we're certainly playing catch-up at the minute.

Haas F1

In September 2015, while announcing their first driver, Romain Grosjean, who was moving to Haas F1 from Lotus F1, owner Gene Haas was asked why Haas F1 will succeed when the last three teams that entered Formula 1 had failed (although one did revive). In his reply, Haas explained two key components of his team's approach to entering the sport,

I think they were under a real time constraint. They had probably almost six months to put together a whole team, and I think when people think about entering Formula One ... you really have to build everything from scratch. I think that's what really tripped up the previous teams was ... they just didn't allow enough time to actually build their cars so, when they got on the grid, they were really, really behind. Not only are you trying to develop and design your car, but you're also trying to race, and trying to do those things simultaneously is probably impossible. That's probably the biggest difference with us.[28]

Haas, a successful businessman in the United States and a motor racing enthusiast who is also a partner in a NASCAR team, has made it clear that his main motivation to enter was in order to internationalise his Haas Automation organisation and build a global brand. He told CNN's The Circuit programme,

Just the association of being with F1 basically takes a brand from nobody to the stratosphere. If I can achieve an extra billion in sales, we will pay for whatever F1 costs.

Haas and his key advisor from the start, Guenther Steiner, had not only observed the demise of recent new entries, but he had also seen the failed efforts of another American entry in 2010, USF1, that never even made it onto the starting grid. So he took on board these two key lessons – take your time and find a way to not necessarily build your own car. So firstly, he took his time by postponing Haas F1's start in Formula 1 by one year to the 2016 season. Haas once again:

The more time you have, the more time you have to develop the relationships that you need and secure the people, equipment and other parts of the puzzle that just takes time, and time is what we need, and when we get to the grid, we won't be developing a car, we'll be ready to go ...

We're taking quite a bit more time, actually, to get our car prepared and, at the same time, we're also able to put together some very important relationships with obviously Ferrari and then Dallara, plus our UK operation. We were very fortunate to be able to obtain a race shop that had a lot of facilities that we really needed. If we had to do that in a short of timeframe, I don't think any of that would have happened.[28]

And there is the other difference in the Haas F1 model: working closely with partners to complete the whole package. According to Haas,

Our business model in Formula One is based on our NASCAR race team where we use other people's engines and chassis.[29]

Haas F1 is taking full advantage of F1 industry rules that allow significant support and components to be supplied by another team. So in addition to getting their power unit from Ferrari, they will maximise any other support that is permissible from this iconic, experienced partner in Maranello, Italy.

In addition, the Italian single-seater specialist, Dallara, is designing and building the Haas F1 chassis.

In the words of Guenther Steiner, Haas F1's Team Principal, who is also credited with bringing and selling the F1 entry idea to Gene Haas,

We came up with a different plan that has a strong focus on collaboration with somebody established, and therefore we don't start from zero ... The crucial thing is that we work together with somebody and buy all the stuff that is allowed by the FIA regulations. That is the big difference.[29]

Realising that it would be difficult to run a Formula 1 team only from their Kannapolis, North Carolina headquarters, Haas purchased the former Marussia team's headquarters in Banbury, England. So along with Ferrari's and Dallara's experience, this puts them in the middle of the UK's Motorsport Valley. Immediately taking advantage of the expertise available there, Haas hired ex-Marussia staff Dave O'Neill and Rob Taylor as Team Manager and Chief Designer, respectively.

So this three-location approach breaks down as follows, according to Greiner:

The headquarters is in North Carolina – the administration, CFD and machining; in the UK we will have the race team; and in Italy the design and aero department. We are running out of three countries. Sure, not the easiest thing, but doable – and technology helps a lot. For sure it would not make sense to run the race team out of the US, so we needed a European base.[30]

6 | *Right people in right places*

The battle on the race track is happening alongside the continuing struggle – as seen in all businesses – to find, nurture and retain top talent. In this chapter we will take a look at the people who populate this sport and several of the dynamics associated with working in such a highly competitive industry.

In terms of attracting talent, Formula 1 has a special allure. It is perceived as the pinnacle of international motorsport and people working in it, at all levels, believe they are involved in the ultimate racing endeavour. They enjoy a unique opportunity to participate in a global sport and business arena associated with glamour, international travel and the excitement that comes from advanced technologies, powerful engines and high speeds. As one writer put it:

Formula 1 is the archetypal glamorous sport: a heady mix of brilliant and brave drivers, electrifying speed, billionaire backers, debonair celebrities and pioneering design and technology.[31]

Engineers, technicians, mechanics, designers and other specialists find their way into Formula 1 typically from related industries like aeronautics and automobile manufacturing. Some are now even recruited directly out of higher education institutions that cater to motorsports talent development. Suppliers are also tapped for skilled people, as we were told by Peter Digby, Chairman of Xtrac, a UK-based company that is a leading supplier of high-performance products such as transmissions and gearboxes to all forms of motorsport teams:

Each year I am losing three or four engineers to Formula 1 because we have become the Rolls Royce of training regarding motorsport engineers. If you want a really good engineer, someone who understands assemblies, fits and tolerances and everything else, and how to produce parts at a reasonable cost, we do all of that.

Being a major supplier to ten Formula 1 teams is a double-edged sword, as Digby notes:

Because we supply a lot of teams, if we lost ten guys that would be a problem. Most teams respect this, but not all. I often feel like an employment agency and sometimes feel we should start to charge a finder's fee!

Formula 1 is a relatively closed community of experts, where one sees revolving doors of staff moving from one to team to another. This is what might be expected in a situation where the United Kingdom, quite proudly, has created a Motorsport Valley industry cluster. Seven of the ten teams competing during the 2015 season have factories based in a reasonably small region in the UK. This can be a challenge for team such as Sauber, which is located in Hinwil, Switzerland. Team Principal Monisha Kaltenborn explains:

First you have to look at Sauber as a medium-sized enterprise and start with our location. We have to determine our strategical role, where we want to invest, the situation of the Swiss Franc, and also how do attract people to come in this industry to Switzerland because Switzerland is not known for motorsport.

In business life it is usual to work with people who demonstrate a wide spectrum of personality types and behaviours. This is also true in Formula 1. But a closer examination of the mechanics, technicians, engineers, managers and drivers in the sport reveals certain common characteristics. We have identified several that consistently cut across all Formula 1 teams. Formula 1 people demonstrate:

- Passion and drive;
- Focus and competitiveness;
- An entrepreneurial mindset; and
- Attention to detail.

However, before taking a closer look at these, we start with a few comments about the people who lead Formula 1 teams.

Team principals sitting at the top of every Formula 1 organisation are lightning rods for praise, dissent and media gossip. Egos among this group of individuals often run high. This is not a position for someone without a high degree of self-confidence. All team principals are passionate about the sport and work the same long hours as everyone else in their team.

Many Formula 1 leaders have been self-made men and may have been associated with the motor industry in some way before moving up to Formula 1. Until recent years, the majority had learned through experience, and therefore their leadership methodologies tended to be rather ad hoc. But given new organisational and commercial realities, this has had to change. The teams have grown to the size of major companies. The amount of money at stake has increased significantly over time. Team principals have needed to learn about operating in a different, more professional environment, and in some cases they have had to bring in management talent or outside advisors to help provide guidance for their businesses.

While listening to Christian Horner, Team Principal at Red Bull Racing, for example, one can hear the more measured approach of someone who considers himself, first and foremost, a professional manager. He shared his approach to building a successful Formula 1 team:

Invest in people, give them support and the tools to do their job. Don't tell them how to do their job, but give them the right guidance and the right backing and they will deliver for you.

He has also clearly given great thought to creating the right kind of atmosphere that will encourage people to perform at their best:

Within the team there is a steely determination to achieve its objectives. We have a very non-political environment here, a very good team spirit and a group of people pulling together. We've never struggled to recruit people. This is a dynamic team that looks after its employees and rewards success.

For most senior leaders it is about getting the right talent in the right positions. As Mike O'Driscoll at Williams explains:

In the end, organisations are made up of people. This business like any other business is about finding great people. Over the last couple of years, we've been very focused on ensuring we had the right mix of people to be successful and reignite our Formula 1 organisation that had such a legacy of success in the past; and alongside that, create an advanced engineering organisation.

As with most successful executives, Toto Wolff of the Mercedes team takes his role of finding the right people, especially at senior leadership levels, very seriously:

If you are leading an organisation like ours, you need to have a feeling for the people you work with, empathy, which is necessary to see how an individual fits into the organisation and whether an individual is able to understand your vision. If it doesn't click with the person, it's not going to go well.

All the senior people we've recruited since I arrived, I interviewed every single one of them. I need to feel whether the person fits. If somebody doesn't fit and I don't have the feeling that they share the same values around integrity, loyalty, working hard – we are not going to pursue looking at the best CV ever.

He went on to add:

You need to put the guys in the right places, because sometimes people have developed into the wrong positions, as with 'The Peter Principle'. This is a common problem in Formula 1. You develop somebody who is really good in his current role and he moves on to something where he is not good at all.

Managing people in this industry is not easy. As Pat Symonds pointed out when he was at Renault:

The interesting thing about Formula 1 is they're all rather difficult people to manage because they are a self-opinionated, arrogant sort of people, in the nicest possible way. To be honest, that's what we look for at Renault. We look for people who think laterally, who never accept that something is impossible and who are prepared to work hard. They've got to be team players, while they've got to be individuals. They should be individualistic in their thinking, but team players in their actions.

Passion and drive

The one word that would encompass the mindset of all the Formula 1 people the authors have interviewed is *passion*; an all-encompassing passion for just about everything that revolves around their participation in this sport. This goes from the people at the top of the organisation, to the mechanics, to the commercial directors dealing with sponsors. Given that, it's not surprising to learn that what Frank Williams looked for in new employees:

People who have intellect, strength of character, humanity and a sense of humour, but above all, passion.

His daughter, Claire, now Deputy Team Principal at Williams, not surprisingly is carrying on this approach, especially where passion comes into play:

A great team is all about the people you have, how they behave and the attitudes that they have. One of the secrets of our success is passion and everyone at Williams being passionate about what we do. I think in any business you have to be passionate about your product. If you don't believe in your product, then how are you going to look after it, help it grow, nurture it, encourage it to be the best it can be? So for me, one of the most important things is demonstrating that we believe in what we're doing as a leadership group and making sure that that permeates throughout the business. Show that passion; and the best way you can do that is to be strong in communications.

This passion is evident not only in the long hours that are put in, but in the energy with which every task is approached. It overflows into the non-stop discussions about the sport, business and personalities within Formula 1, whether they are on the job or away from the track and factory.

Of all the Formula 1 teams, Ferrari holds a special position when one talks about passion. In our first edition, we spoke with Raoul Pinnell, who was at the time in charge of global marketing at Shell, a major sponsor of Ferrari. He told us about the passion associated with Ferrari:

It is just extraordinary and it extends beyond even Formula 1. There are countries in the world in which Shell operates where there has never been a Formula 1 Grand Prix, it's hardly ever on the television, nobody in those countries has ever owned a Ferrari, never seen one in person – but people know Ferrari.

Ross Brawn, former Technical Director at Ferrari during its amazing run of success from 1999 to 2004, told us:

Where Ferrari is different is the sheer passion of the people who work here. If you work at Ferrari and you go home your family ask you about the job, your nephews, nieces, neighbours, everyone asks you what's going on at Ferrari because there's so many people interested in what we do and in supporting what we do.

Ferrari stands out in that it not only garners millions of loyal fans, but also represents the hopes and aspirations of the Italian nation. Seven-time World Champion driver Michael Schumacher put it this way:

Driving for Ferrari is more than special; Ferrari is more than a team. In Italy it is kind of a religion. If you win or if you lose, there is a whole country behind you. It took me a while to understand that, and maybe I have learned it the hard way, but now I feel part of that feeling and part of that family.[32]

And more recently, Sergio Marchionne, President of FIAT-Chrysler, stated in November 2014,

We all know how important a healthy team spirit is, particularly at this time ... The kind of spirit that can come only from a group of people who believe strongly in a project and are prepared to share the commitment, sacrifices and results.[33]

This all-encompassing passion extends beyond Ferrari, in fact from all the Formula 1 teams, to the millions of fans and supporters who follow the sport on television, through the printed media, online communities and at the track. And it is this passion, translated into brand loyalty, that Formula 1 team sponsors and owners (particularly in the case of the car manufacturers) hope to tap into in order to spur additional product sales.

Matched with their passion, individuals working at all levels in Formula 1 do nothing by half measures. They are, in a word, ***driven*** (and the authors apologise for the obvious pun that cannot be avoided). Some are propelled by the heady excitement of powerful engines and high speeds, some by the leading-edge technology employed, some by the racing competition, and still others by the wealth that has accrued to quite a number of successful participants in the sport. No matter the reason for their involvement, anyone working on a Formula 1 team knows only one credo; that is, working flat out in order to push oneself, one's teammates and ultimately their cars to the limit.

According to Jackie Stewart:

The level of driven people in Formula 1 is probably more clear than any other business segment. They work to closed-loop procedures because there's a race every two weeks from March until November and there are deadlines to meet. The ability to duck under the fences and make things happen is more clearly obvious than any other business that I know.

Formula 1 people are always being pushed by deadlines, competitive pressures and budget concerns. In Stewart's words:

When you're designing a racing car, the design is always running to the limit, the manufacturing is always running to the limit, the number of spares you're going to take to the first race is running to the limit. The people you've got

working for you would work, in Melbourne for example, for three nights, non-stop, and work all day. Those people do that, and they would not do that in any other business, so this fever or this allergy that they all have is the same one. It's 'do it yesterday', not ever tomorrow.

Focus and competitiveness

Successful Formula 1 teams *focus* on maintaining steady improvement and obtaining results. To succeed in Formula 1, according to Jackie Stewart,

it takes a special individual with total commitment and total focus ... nothing like it exists in the corporate world.

From Frank Williams' point of view:

Focus is pretty common among all the top teams. It's partly borne of passion, partly borne of a strong competitive spirit.

Focus is generally thought to be a positive force in business, but when applied to the wrong strategy or at the expense of the business that can need development, it can be detrimental. Such was the case with Enzo Ferrari's obsession with engines. He believed that motor racing teams lived and died on horse power. It has taken a great deal of effort to change internal mindsets at Ferrari, but that focus had to be re-channelled. While still at Ferrari, Ross Brawn explained:

A few years ago it used to be an engine and a chassis. Ferrari was renowned for having very powerful engines, but the chassis was not very good. Today, we would never take that view. It's the car that matters. It's the result of the car on the track that matters and the junction between engine and chassis is seamless. We apply that principle to all areas of the car: electronics, engine, chassis, aerodynamics, structure – it has to be a whole. There is no point in having one area very strong and the other areas weak.

Formula 1 people are very *competitive*. They work in highly pressured situations and always under tight deadlines. The very nature of the business is about going faster; improving performance while maintaining consistent quality and reliability. They are constantly measuring themselves against the clock. This pertains not only to performance on the track or changing wheels and tyres in the pit lane, it also relates to making minute but important changes in the chassis, gearbox, engine or electronics so they can reduce lap speeds by a fraction of a second at the next race. Formula 1 people are strongly motivated to improve on each previous performance. Their successes and failures in this sport are on display for everyone to see within the industry and, thanks to the enormous media coverage, on view for hundreds of millions of fans and enthusiasts.

Ron Dennis, Team Principal at McLaren-Mercedes, has said:

If you are in Formula 1 and you are not a competitive individual, and I mean anywhere in Formula 1, you are going to struggle and have a tough time. It is a cut-and-thrust business where the rewards for success are massive and the penalties for failure are punitive. When you go into the Grand Prix environment you are constantly trying to out-manoeuvre and out-think your opposition, and I don't mean only in how you are going to run the car in such a way that you win, I am talking about every single aspect of Grand Prix racing: the politics, the sponsorships, the way you portray yourself, how you race, how you look, how you attract investment and how you optimise or shape your performance.[21]

Entrepreneurial mindset

While the Formula 1 industry has seen its share of large car manufacturers take positions on the starting grid, the guts of the business are still grounded in individuals who, in fact, act like entrepreneurs. When comparing Formula 1 to other industries, Jackie Stewart said:

Formula 1 operates at a faster pace, requires more decisive decision-making, is less well structured, and has little or no bureaucracy. It is very entrepreneurial, very leadership driven and extremely teamwork related.

Or, in Christian Horner's words,

The interesting thing about Formula 1 is the speed of reaction that we have to have with problem fixing. We don't have lead times of once a year – it's two weeks and we're judged every two weeks. The Formula 1 team's ability to adapt and make decisions, quick decisions, is absolutely vital.

But as teams have grown to sizes of up to 800 employees, maintaining the entrepreneurial spirit has become much harder to do. As a former Team Principal and then advisor to Jaguar Racing, Jackie Stewart has had to caution his colleagues that, even though they are owned by the Ford Motor Company, they must *keep in mind you're a small company where your attention to detail is better and your urgencies are faster. You have to think like you are running a corner business.*

Formula 1 teams have recruited from other industries to fill expertise gaps, but as Pat Symonds points out:

We have always recruited from other industries, particularly aircraft industries. We don't think people need necessarily motorsport experience, but they do need the attitude and mindset that you find in our industry.

While trying to bring in more managerial techniques from large companies, such as formal performance reviews and performance appraisals, Formula 1 teams have attempted to maintain the small-firm feel about them.

Eddie Jordan was one of the more colourful team principals in the days of Jordan F1. He originally entered motor racing as a driver before getting into team management and ownership:

Some people might classify me as a form of entrepreneur, but that is only because I'd probably be unemployable in a regular business.

He recalled discussions with Honda in the late 1980s, when they were interested in purchasing his team and suggested putting him under a contract to them:

This gave me a big shock. It meant that I could be hired and fired. Therefore, the only way to guarantee the project is to do it myself and continue myself.

His entrepreneurial nature set the tone for the entire Jordan racing team.

Attention to detail

Formula 1 is a sport where winning and losing is measured in fractions of a second, so it is not surprising that team members pay a great deal of attention to detail. While the vision of a podium finish is crucial for individual and team motivation, day-to-day performance depends on thousands of precise measurements in the wind tunnel, sophisticated aerodynamic and stress simulations on computers and parts manufactured and assembled to tolerances within thousandths of a millimetre. Every element of design, development, manufacture, assembly and car set-up impacts the fractions of a second that the teams are striving to shave from their lap times. Therefore, focus on detail is paramount.

McLaren-Mercedes' Ron Dennis is renowned for his attention to detail:

I have a view that every single thing in a company is important; the entire spectrum, from how a toilet roll dispenser functions, to who drives our racing cars ... The great companies are those that have the intentions of being the best at everything. And this envelops the whole environment.[34]

But attention to detail must be seen in context of what a team's priorities are and how big their budget is, as explained by Pat Symonds, Chief Technical Officer, at Williams:

Because of the tight regulations in Formula 1, once you've got the fundamentals right, an awful lot of the incremental performance comes from real attention to detail. Attention to detail is bloody expensive because you need a lot of people working in a lot of different areas and that's where the budget gets increased massively. The return on investment of that higher budget is low in absolute terms but it is that important bit that moves you forward. So, a team like Williams operating on a relatively limited F1 budget can get the basics done very well indeed, but we have to be very careful about choosing our added-value areas. We can't just blanket everything and say right, we're going to have five people working on tyres, we're going to have twenty people working on suspension, etc. We have to choose our project carefully.

An important aspect of attention to detail is to have appropriate performance management and performance measurement systems in place. As Toto Wolff of Mercedes told us:

We have a very structured management performance system, where we measure people all throughout the organisation. Management performance is crucial here and we never forget that this is still a mid-sized company; in a global context, this is a tiny little thing so we don't want to make it too corporate and too multi-national.

Before completing this section on the people in Formula 1, we would be remiss if we did not ask the question, 'Where are the women?' After all, women make up 38 per cent of the viewing audience of Formula 1 races, but how are they represented on F1 teams?

According to the CNN programme 'The Circuit' broadcast in August 2015, which focused on women drivers in Formula 1, since the World Championships started sixty-five years ago, there have been 835 male drivers, but only 5 women. Physical differences have been used by many to explain the disparity; but Susie Wolff, test driver for Williams, has stated that a woman's 30 per cent less muscle mass is not a barrier. She says the key is strength to body size and in this case women have only 5 per cent less strength when they have been training for the task.

Autosport magazine found the roles of women in Formula 1 enough of a worthwhile subject that they devoted an issue to it in August 2015, with Susie Wolff as guest editor. From a driver's perspective, she wrote,

it's all about performance – and in motorsport, performance is power. The stopwatch doesn't see gender, race, or any other factor; it just says whether you're quick or slow. And that's what you're judged on.[35]

Wolff continued,

I make no apology for having used gender as a USP in my career. Why should a woman deny her femininity just to conform with the expectations of the racing world? I'm a woman, I drive racing cars and if there's an advantage in terms of finding sponsorship or support, then I will make the most of it.

That's what racing is all about: finding competitive advantage and exploiting it. That can open new doors for me and other female racers, which is great. But then we have to stand or fall based on our ability.[35]

Unfortunately for Wolff and Carmen Jorda at Lotus F1, the only other female test driver in Formula 1, the big break to actually race on a Sunday afternoon or to acquire an all-important major sponsorship, has simply not yet happened.

There has however, off the track, been some improvement in female job prospects, not only in the more typical marketing and communications areas, but also in roles as engineers, mechanics and aerodynamicists, as well as, significantly, in senior management positions. The latter is most clearly exemplified by Claire Williams, Deputy Team Principal at Williams, and Monisha Kaltenborn, Team Principal at Sauber.

Kaltenborn told us:

I have experienced the same challenge as in any other male-dominated area. I firmly believe you have to work harder, you are criticised more, to come close to the recognition if you've done something right. That's OK because that's reality. You have to cope with that and you have to know that. Women are far from having it equal, we are not there. What we can do as women today, to work for this, to make sure that maybe the next generation will have it easier; that has to be your target. We don't do this for ourselves because we can't change the system. We can only be strong enough to have our position there and take all that harshness which comes across. Sometimes it's not even personal, it's just reality!

In an interview with a German newspaper, Claire Williams stated,

Formula One and motorsport are generally considered male-dominated, which is the external perception. But I think that 'dominates' is the wrong word – it's just simply that many men work here. No, it's not a man's world. 38 per cent of our viewers are female. If a woman could become a big-name brand in Formula One, that would be ground breaking. The PR effect would be enormous.[36]

Williams was asked if it wasn't discrimination, just why did it take so long for her to rise to her current position?

It was not because I was a girl. The only reason I had to work twice as hard is that I'm Frank's daughter. He did not want me in the company, he would not let it be said that it was down to nepotism. People should not say: look, Frank hands out jobs to his children. That would be wrong. I had to prove that I deserve my job.[36]

We asked Susie Wolff what organisations and women, themselves, had to do to make sure that women can achieve their full potential in whatever work they do. She replied:

Of course it is about being supportive and giving them chances, as women are, more often than not, the ones who won't push for a promotion or be vocal about how well they do they job. However, I believe it is up to us as individuals to achieve our full potential, not organisations. We must define our strengths, play to them. Know our weaknesses, work to improve them. Be confident enough to speak out and stand up for what we believe in. Ambitious women are sometimes wrongly labelled as 'bossy', but through the 'Lean In' campaign from Sheryl Sandberg, it does feel like things are slowly but surely changing. Onwards and upwards.

Formula 1 drivers

Our discussion about individuals in Formula 1 would not be complete without taking a look at the people who are the most visible representatives of the sport and the business – the drivers.

Damon Hill, former World Drivers' Champion, has written,

Drivers are special people when they're at the top of their game (and hell to be around when it's going badly). They glow; they exude some special gift, almost seeming to hold magical powers over us.[1]

Of course, as a former driver he might say that, but it must be stated that their images appear in advertisements, newsprint and often as items of television or social media news, beyond the sports section. Most drivers have enthusiastic followings that rival those of athletes participating in any sport, anywhere in the world. They are supported by their fellow countrymen for sure, but many transcend their own nationalities based on their public personas, whether real or created by the media.

According to Martin Brundle, another former Formula 1 driver and current television commentator:

Drivers, that's really all people want to know about. They want to know what the drivers look like, sound like, how they think, what they are like and what they do when they are not driving. You can offer the media all sorts of key personnel involved with the team, but actually the fans mainly want to know about the drivers.

The authors' experiences at workshops and speaking engagements since the publication of the first edition of this book in 2005 strongly bears this out.

As Sir Jackie Stewart told us:

While the driver doesn't have quite the authority today as he may have had during another period, at the end of the day I still believe that the driver is the captain of the ship. Whatever the CEO might think or the chief engineer might think or the technical director might think, at two o'clock in the afternoon it's only down to one man to interpret what he can get out of that vehicle's dynamics.

In today's Formula 1, given the engineering support that drivers receive from their teams and the electronics aids they employ, a controversy has arisen about whether the driver is as important as he used to be before there was a need to save fuel, save tyres and conserve energy in the batteries. Damon Hill, once again:

Man and machine. The car or the driver? I hear this all the time. But remember, the car does not build itself. It is a physical manifestation of the sum total of all our learning invested in a device designed to enable its driver to get 'there' first. It's a mean to an end, and the end is to put a man on the top of the podium. When we celebrate the driver we are acknowledging something deeply human … We put a man on a pedestal. Like a deity.[1]

In comparison to Sir Jackie's days, when drivers were well into their twenties when they started their careers, today it is a different story. According to Martin Brundle:

If you look at the new young stars they are in their late teens, or very early twenties, so the whole thing has moved forward three or four quite critical years. When I first raced in F1, I was twenty-four and was quite young at the time to be a Grand Prix driver. I know in the past there have been some exceptions, but generally speaking the driving age of these guys really getting the job done is just coming down and down and down.

Brundle continued:

Kids are starting at eight years old. By the time they're sixteen they've done literally hundreds of races. So they are experienced, have confidence and race craft, and they are so mature. Most will have had some media training along with a fitness regime and they are more ready for it; they're not as green as we were.

It has been estimated by Mercedes F1 Chief Toto Wolff that the cost of developing a young driver before he reaches Formula 1 can reach over €4.5–5 million, taking into account a typical progression through racing series such as karting, Formula 4/Formula Renault/Formula 3 and GP2. At that point he adds,

You are on the verge of getting into Formula One but you are not in there. You need another €2 million to €3 million to get the drive. So you are talking about €7 million to €8 million.[37]

Driver development has taken on a new meaning from Sir Jackie Stewart's day. He told us:

When I was coming into Formula 1 there was an enormous depth of experience and knowledge on the Formula 1 grid. As the young guy I had a great opportunity to learn from others. Today, the young drivers are full of exhilaration and seat-of-the-pants skills, but to succeed you have to have considerable knowledge, depth of knowledge, because first you get experience, then you get knowledge, then you get wisdom, and then you get maturity to go with your wisdom. There are not many that would fit into that last box. When young guys get into Formula 1 I think they genuinely think they know a lot. This is the only sport I know of where there's no coaches.

We asked Mark Webber about Sir Jackie's assertion. He replied:

You can teach someone up to a point and help them. I'm with Jackie to a degree, but when the lap times change so much due to technology also, it's very difficult.

Martin Brundle supported that view in terms of driver development:

There's another key factor and that is technology on the cars. Before, you needed experience to set a Formula 1 car up. Now you need data. It's a data-driven business and when a team turns up to a race, they have the track mapped to within a few centimetres on a computer software programme. They can run any number of set-ups on a software package with their CFD [Computational Fluid Dynamics] programmes and simulators. With the wind tunnels and aero testing they have packages that can change the aero balance by very small margins, along with corresponding suspension dynamics and weight distribution too. It's not like it used to be – educated trial and error backed up by experience.

The top drivers are rewarded handsomely having reached this level of competition. In 2015, drivers with reported salaries in the $20–40 million range included Alonso, Vettel, Hamilton and Raikkonen. In the $10–20 million range were Rosberg and Button, while at a still not-too-shabby salary of $1–4.5 million were Massa, Hulkenberg, Perez, Grosjean, Maldonado, Bottas and Ricciardo. Daniil Kvyat, a 17-year-old Russian driver who was driving in Formula 1 even before he received his regular driving licence in September 2015, was reportedly earning $820,000.[38]

In terms of personal net worth, the top ten all-time list was reported by *Wealth-X* in March 2015 as follows:[39]

Michael Schumacher	$780 million
Fernando Alonso	$220 million
Kimi Raikkonen	$180 million
Eddie Irvine	$180 million
Lewis Hamilton	$110 million
Jenson Button	$100 million
Alain Prost	$70 million
David Coulthard	$70 million
Sebastian Vettel	$45 million
Nico Rosberg	$30 million

Formula 1 drivers share most of the common characteristics that we have discussed to this point, such as passion, focus, desire to improve and attention to detail. But there are a few other traits that can be associated with them in particular:

• Competitive drive and being fast;
• Peak physical conditioning;
• Mental toughness to do their job under extreme pressure; and
• Ability to communicate effectively within the team and with partners.

Having a strong competitive drive and being fast

While competitive drive is a characteristic that defines all people in this sport, it is clear that the man sitting in the cockpit cannot succeed today without a work ethic that pushes his performance, as well as the performance of his teammates, to the limit. During his active days in Formula 1, Eddie Jordan discovered and nurtured the early careers of many successful drivers in what Jordan calls his 'University of Formula 1'. He summed up what he looked for in these young prospects:

*I have an old-fashioned way of doing this. I want to see if they have the ****ing fight for it; will they give their last ounce? I get up close and look into their eyes and say, 'Look at me and tell me you ***ing can instead of simply searching for it. Can you find it in yourself? Do you have the ***ing killer instinct, that cures or kills 'em?' I want to hear what they have to say, and very often the language can be very colourful.*

The late David Robertson, Business Manager for 2007 World Champion Kimi Raikkonen, explained his philosophy for what it takes to be a Championship-winning driver:

If you know the top stars, then you know what they're like, they have to have the 'head for what they do'. Their 'head' is all important. It's something that's in the kids' nature, you see the kids, they can't be beaten, they won't be beaten ... if he can do that, I can do that. They never at any time doubt themselves – these are the ones that have the chance to make it to the top.

And Mark Webber, former driver for Red Bull Racing, said in a May 2008 BBC Sports interview that he believes:

All Formula 1 drivers are talented, but the really great ones have an incredible feel for what they need to do, how to have the car on the limit ... It's not something you can usually see, but it's that 1 to 2 per cent difference.

Several writers have tried to describe what makes Formula 1 drivers different from all others, including amateur racing enthusiasts. Chris Partridge put it succinctly in a BBC Sport piece:

A racing driver has to push the car to the very limits, attacking corners to the point that the car is always sliding on the edge of adhesion – something that is not always obvious on television. They have to push the car into a state of instability – and feel comfortable with that – in situations which would hopefully never arise for ordinary road drivers. It's a much higher workload with many more subconscious corrections to the steering wheel and throttle.[40]

To give this more granularity, Partridge outlined the following five differences between pro and amateur drivers:

1 Courage in fast corners – taking corners in a higher gear
2 Articulating how the car behaved – putting the car on the limit
3 Discipline in driving – measured approach as he gets a feel
4 Braking on the limit – how late he hits the brakes
5 An eye for detail – picking their braking points

A driver's on-track skills are honed through countless experiences during testing and races as they work their way through the various racing levels up to Formula 1. While some drivers are natural talents, all need grooming because the skill requirements to drive in Formula 1 are a cut above any other car-racing formula.

Eddie Jordan told us:

The gap between all of the formulae and that of Formula 1 is so immense, it's huge, it's a chasm. With all the razzmatazz and all the bits and pieces and the gizmos on the car it is mind blowing what the driver has to do.

Suffice it to say, being able to drive a 600–760 horsepower Formula 1 car while dealing with all the technologies that Jordan refers to (including nowadays DRS and ERS systems), all the while maintaining control at the limit, takes fast reactions, exceptional coordination and strong nerve.

One often talks about drivers who are 'quick' or 'fast', and the teams see many young prospects who might be able, over time, to move up to Formula 1. McLaren's Team Principal, Ron Dennis, has said that speed is something that can be detected based on data, but it takes something more to develop drivers who can reach the top level:

Detecting speed is a science, as technology allows teams to study optimal sleep patterns, heart rates and the driving skills of cornering, braking and acceleration. But nurturing a fast young driver is, by contrast, an art.[41]

One thing that makes a top driver stand out is his racing intelligence. Drivers have a remarkable ability to memorise each turn and elevation on every one of the Formula 1 racing circuits. After driving for up to two hours, drivers can recall every gear change or other chassis or engine adjustment made at any given moment during a race. While making split-second decisions guiding their car around the track, drivers must also be thinking about race tactics, wear on their tyres, car handling and also dealing with unexpected situations. This capability is enhanced by the sophisticated driving simulators that all teams have or are able to access. Simulators are not only important for the drivers, but when used by test and back-up drivers they provide critical input to engineers as they develop upgrades to the car's components.

When Jenson Button achieved his first podium finish for the BAR-Honda team at the Malaysian Grand Prix in 2004, he revealed afterwards that he had suffered oil spikes during the early laps. This meant he had to repeatedly reset the oil pump during the race by pressing the pump button ten times in quick succession. Sometimes, he commented later, this was necessary more than once during a lap:

A driver makes thousands of decisions every single lap he's out there and he lives or dies by them, literally.[42]

Nothing has changed since he made that remark.

The top drivers take in a vast amount of data, compartmentalise it and then use the appropriate information when required. They retain everything and can bring forward remembered experiences and references to avoid problems and difficult circumstances. Being able to keep these memories on tap, ready for use, is a skill great drivers must develop.

Those hoping to become top-level Formula 1 drivers eventually learn the importance of continually upgrading their knowledge and skills.

Finland's Kimi Raikkonen, now driving for Ferrari, has remarked:

You never stop learning, I guess. I don't think you get much faster as you get more experienced, but you do get better. You learn to adapt to changing conditions. You learn to get the best out of your tyres as they degrade. And you learn to be more consistent. You learn to make fewer mistakes.[43]

Peak physical conditioning

It may not be obvious to those who do not follow the sport, but Formula 1 drivers must be highly conditioned athletes. A Formula 1 racing car can accelerate from 0 to 180 kph (110 mph) and back to 0 in less than six seconds. This can put a driver under 5G of body weight force under braking. Therefore, drivers must be as fit as fighter pilots. A driver has to contend with over twenty turns of the steering wheel each lap for around sixty laps, with each turn weighing up to 30 kg.

No longer are the days when drivers play hard into the night and then hop into their cars for races the next day. In the 1970s and 1980s, there were World Champions who smoked and drank considerably, but that would not be considered feasible or appropriate now in terms of the performance they must leave on the track or the image they must maintain for their sponsors. To be race-ready, all Formula 1 drivers today benefit from personal trainers, carefully crafted diets and scheduled rest and relaxation periods.

During a race, given the considerable levels of stress and heat in the cockpit, drivers can lose a large quantity of bodily fluids. This can be as much as 4 kg (8.8. lbs) over ninety minutes at the Malaysian Grand Prix, for example. Drivers are schooled in how to hydrate themselves correctly before a race and they also have the ability to drink fluids during a race through an electronically controlled tube fitted into their crash helmets.

Physically, drivers have become much more slender and leaner than, say, twenty years ago. Mansell, Hill, Cheever and Warwick, for example, were all tall, well-built men. Today, drivers are smaller, lighter and, certainly in terms of their well-developed cardiovascular systems, in much better condition to withstand the cumulative stresses of a twenty-one-race season.

Brad Spurgeon, who covers Formula 1 for what was in April 1996 called the *International Herald Tribune*, wrote in an article in which Erwin Göllner, a Formula 1 physiotherapist, had said that:

A race driver must be born with the sense of speed inside him, but he may not be born with the physical strength and condition necessary for driving a Formula 1 car. That must be developed through hard work and a program of exercise.[44]

One team that took conditioning of its drivers (and also other team members) to the next level was McLaren. In our second edition, we spoke with Aki Hintsa, Team Physician for McLaren-Mercedes (now retired from the sport) and the architect of the 'McLaren Lab Program'. He had experience with world-class athletes from many sporting fields, including track and field, where he has worked with some of the world's best. According to Hintsa:

It was not easy to build up the programme because the environment is very challenging in Formula 1. In track and field athletes are competing at the highest level, but Formula 1 is much more complicated. In both there are stress and health problems, but in the Formula 1 package comes jet lag given the constant travel, demanding nutritional issues and the constant pressure from the media and public interest. It is almost impossible for the drivers to live a normal life any more.

The McLaren Lab Training Program that Hintsa developed was a framework within which the team members can measure their physical and mental fitness and develop their overall physiological performance. Certainly, different teams take their own approaches to training that can build up the physical conditioning and capabilities of drivers and other team members. The McLaren Lab Program was unique in the systematic and consistent approach it took for measuring five elements of development, including cardiovascular fitness; biodynamical factors, e.g. musculoskeletal balance, flexibility and strength; nutrition; mental energy; and general health. Everything was measured and followed, goals were set for each individual, and follow-up was recorded with all other data so a complete picture of before, during and after could be seen and analysed.

Hintsa told us at the time:

We are following more than 150 different physiological and mental parameters; we have baseline tests and in all those tests we measure number and scales.

But along with top-notch physical conditioning, drivers need to have mental toughness to perform consistently in the highly pressured environment of Formula 1.

Mental toughness

In Brad Spurgeon's article referred to earlier in this chapter, the author wrote about another Formula 1 trainer at that time, Pierre Cometet. As an osteopath, a physiotherapist and an expert in ergonomics, Cometet worked closely with driver Ukyo Katayama, who drove for the Tyrrell team. Cometet was quoted as saying:

I've noticed that for many drivers, the higher they move up the hierarchy the more anxious they become, the more stressed out and nervous. This then becomes a major obstacle to continued success.

Susie Wolff from Williams is one of only two female Formula 1 test drivers. We asked her what mental preparation is needed to become a Formula 1 driver:

The biggest factor as you move up the motorsport ladder to F1 is coping with all the extra pressure. There is very little room for error and the expectations are high.

Then how do you deal with that pressure? She replied,

Fundamentally, you have to be the right character to cope with this, but each driver has their own individual way of coping. I believe in preparation and staying in the moment, not worrying or thinking about what could happen or what are the consequences of making mistakes.

Carlos Sainz, Jr., a young driver at Toro Rosso, told prolific F1 journalist James Allen,

The amount of mental work that you have to do is the toughest part. It is never ending and you can't have a five-minute rest and go off and relax as your mind cannot switch off in the paddock. Whenever you are in the paddock you are always switched on. It's very difficult to disconnect.[45]

He added,

[In F1] you need to be many things at the same time and it is not easy; you need to be a bit of a politician, a bit of a sportsman and you need to be correct, and most importantly, be yourself.

Another young driver, Marcus Ericsson at Sauber, talked how he had to learn the mental part of the game. He not only worked harder with his engineer, but also looked carefully at the 'non-driving' aspects of Formula 1, including fitness and also mental health.

Basically I changed my way at looking at the whole weekend. I count on professional help. I attend the Formula Medicine clinic in Italy, working on several areas.[46]

Formula Medicine is run by Dr Riccardo Ceccarelli, who has been working with F1 drivers for years. He stated,

Marcus is now more mentally mature. Drivers are now very young and take on huge responsibilities. Suddenly they realise not only that their future, but that of the team is in their hands. And I repeat, they are every young.[46]

Aki Hintsa, whom we mentioned earlier in the chapter, is famous for his holistic approach to assisting world-class athletes. While his influence on McLaren drivers has been documented, it may be less well known that he had a significant influence on four-time World Drivers' Champion Sebastian Vettel.[47]

Hintsa first noticed Vettel when he was a test driver for Sauber. In the autumn of 2006, they were on the same flight returning from a Grand Prix and had a chance to chat. As they live only 2 km from each other in Switzerland, Vettel also offered Hintsa a ride home from the airport, and their discussions continued.

They got to know each other further through playing squash and tennis and meeting for coffee when they were both at home. In spring 2007, Vettel was very keen for Hintsa to agree to work with him on a more formal basis. As McLaren's Team Physician, Hintsa was very cautious about how his working with someone from another team would appear in the very small and close-knit

Formula 1 world. However, in 2008, when Vettel was now driving with Toro Rosso, he persisted in his desire to work with Hintsa. So, Vettel asked Helmut Marko for permission to do so; while Hintsa promised to do the same at McLaren. Marko was suspicious but agreed. McLaren also agreed, with the caveat that Hintsa could work with him on any aspects of Vettel's development except physical training. It can be conjectured that perhaps McLaren had an eye on Vettel and thought this might be a way to bring him into their stable.

Vettel recorded that he appreciated that Hintsa did not lecture; rather they discussed, sometimes quite heatedly, about Hintsa's meaning of the CORE. Essentially, he was preparing Vettel to make sure he had his own identity; that is, it was he alone who must find the answers to such questions as who he is, what he wants and whether he controls his own life.

Furthermore, Vettel had to understand that he should not be copying anyone else. He would not succeed if he pretended to be anyone but himself.

Ultimately, both agreed that to become a Formula 1 Champion, Vettel needed to be *honest, passionate* and *himself*. Vettel's record speaks for itself.

The need for consistent results has been present in the sport since its inception, but the continual pressure on drivers due to heightened media attention has escalated in recent years to a fever pitch. As Martin Brundle says:

It's a twelve-hour day now, being a Grand Prix driver. The amount of meetings they are in regarding car set-up, tyre choice, engine parameters and race strategy is immense ... With media slots filling any voids, they are full-on through a GP weekend. Then as soon as they finish the race they'll be off testing somewhere or [at] a team media appearance. So with winter testing they are on a merry-go-round that doesn't stop year round.

We have had first-hand experience of this hectic schedule when we tried to organise interviews with drivers at Grand Prix and test dates. In addition to their team test or race driving commitments, they are being ferried between sessions with the media, sponsors, fans, celebrities and race authorities by harried minders. One of our interview time slots was lost just because the driver could not fit us in and still be able to eat lunch.

Given such demands on their time, it is amazing that most drivers remain level-headed and approachable (to the extent one can reach them). Martin Brundle replied to a hypothesis that today's drivers are so wealthy they tend to be arrogant:

I don't find Formula 1 drivers by and large arrogant at all. I find them down-to-earth people, which they are: they've two legs, two arms, just like other people. It's just that they happen to be good at driving racing cars. But they are under a lot of pressure; as the budgets get bigger the demands on them become difficult to handle while performing mentally and physically at the highest level. Imagine driving for a $400 million team consisting of 1,000 people and you are paid $20 million. That is an enormous opportunity and yet pressure for a 25-year-old to handle while also juggling the technical, commercial and media demands inevitably upon him.

Pressure on drivers can also build from within the team, and there is no better example than the McLaren-Mercedes team's experience in 2007. Two new drivers were paired up: two-time World Champion Fernando Alonso and rookie Formula 1 driver Lewis Hamilton. What unfolded was totally unpredicted. Hamilton's impact on the sport was immediate. During his first nine races he appeared on the podium nine times. As those who follow Formula 1 know, not only a close battle for the Drivers' Championship between these two and Ferrari's Kimi Raikkonen ensued, but also a rivalry that sometimes appeared quite bitter was played out in the media.

History repeated itself, at least where Hamilton is concerned, when during the 2014 and 2015 seasons he was battling for top position with his Mercedes teammate – and old friend as well as rival from lower Formula series – Nico Rosberg. The media had a field day analysing every move on the track, every word spoken and every non-verbal clue that seemed to emanate from the drivers.

Monisha Kaltenborn describes the dynamic of having one team, but two drivers competing with one another:

Having a healthy internal tension is very important and necessary for a team. I think the operative word is 'healthy', because the higher you go, the more the tension is between the drivers and the immediate teams surrounding the drivers. And if you're really quite high, you end up having two teams in one team. As long as they stimulate each other and have some healthy competition, it's alright. If it reaches a level where they are fighting so much against each other that the outcome of the team result is being affected negatively, then we have to stop that. So, we try to on the one side to encourage our drivers to be together, talk to each other, share things. On the other side, they're clearly told that you are also competitors, but the ultimate goal is the team support and the team. You do everything for both, but you also have to keep in mind [that] we cannot do it equally because in a race you will never be always parallel like this; one might be in front, one at the back and the team says we have fair rules, so who's in front gets the preference. So, from our side we try to be transparent. You can only try to handle it as fair as you can, but there has to be a heathy sense of competition between them as well.

Paolo Aversa at Cass Business School researched Formula 1 drivers in all races between 1981 and 2010. He wrote,

A typical mistake in assembling a team is to consider it is a mere sum of the quality of its individual parts. But team success is based on internal coordination and collaboration. Accordingly, when two talented professionals end up in the same organization, they can turn what looked like a promising partnership into a fight for internal supremacy.[48]

He continued,

A clash of egos is one obvious reason for the decline of individual and team performance . . . managers can either favour one of the employees – in order to avoid internal conflict – or refuse to side with either – thus promoting internal competition. The first (approach) tends to demotivate both team members as the favoured employee eases off their rivalry and the 'defeated' colleague loses their ambition by no longer being permitted to compete.

In the second case, where the team promotes internal conflict, the resulting antagonism often leads to the failure of intra-team collaboration, eventually triggering an aggressive duel to the detriment of one or both employees.

When two drivers enjoy similar status, teams might decide to split the available resources equally between the two stars, even when this decision doesn't maximize the team's likelihood of winning. Furthermore, the driver's battle to co-opt the team's best resources might slow down the internal resource allocation process.

Given the undercurrent of rivalry and tension in the Mercedes team, credit has to be given for their winning the Constructors' World Championship in 2014 and then defending that title in 2015 with four races still remaining in the season.

We had to ask Toto Wolff how they handled the situation. He started from an interesting perspective:

In Formula 1, one of the key parts is that if you think that the drivers are part of the team, you're wrong. They are contractors. They have been calibrated since a very early age – they are alone in a go-kart, and they need to beat everybody else, and it's just you – it's just themselves on the podium. You cannot change that calibration; it's how they function, which also makes them special. All the good ones have that opportunistic, egotistical, multi-character because you need to be . . . you're out there for yourself. I remember somebody important saying to me when I was young, the most important moment in a man's life is when you start to realise you're alone. And these guys are even more alone because they're out there alone in that car.

Former World Drivers' Champion Niki Lauda is Wolff's colleague at Mercedes, and he puts it bluntly,

There is no friendship out there. When you race you have to fight.[49]

He also said,

Sure, everyone drives selfish, what do you think these guys are there to do? That is the only way to win and the only way to win the championship.[50]

And,

We have two number one drivers – and they're passionate and committed. The rivalry drives us forward, we embrace it. They are born competitors – they used to race at eating cornflakes, for goodness sakes . . . People watch sports for emotions, authenticity and rivalry. We let our guys speak their minds and think it is right.[51]

So, how did Mercedes eventually find a path during the 2015 season to keep internal rivalry from destroying the team's to win a second consecutive Championship?

We set up an agreed set of 'rules of engagement' to better handle the inter-team battle . . . We as a team don't expect them to be nice; or let's say to play friends for the media. What we ask them is to be respectful of each other, to respect the rules of engagement.[52]

Ability to communicate

The driver's ability to communicate his views and insights is crucial. Much like the language divide that often exists between information technologists and commercial specialists, drivers and engineers have to get to know how each other speaks. Pat Symonds recalls:

We often laugh about a driver who'll come in and say, 'There's no grip at all out there.' Of course, the engineer says, 'Well, how did you get out of the garage, then?'

Symonds added:

You don't need a driver to be an engineer, but you do need him to be clear, logical and relatively verbose, without going on too much.

Internally, communication between driver and his support team is crucial. Feedback from drivers during test days about a new aerodynamic component, for example, provides them with the live, on-the-track performance knowledge that will validate the thousands of readings that have been taken in simulators and wind tunnels. On the test runs and qualifying laps that lead to race day, it is the driver's input that enables the all-important set-up of the car to be just right for when the five red lights go out to start the race.

James Key, Technical Director, talked about this in the perspective of having two young, less experienced in Formula 1 drivers at Toro Rosso during the 2015 season,

It certainly requires an extra effort on the part of our engineering team to derive more understanding from data when you have a couple of rookies ... In fact we had a sit down with the drivers and all the engineering team after the first nine races. That has led to us putting something in place with the aim of trying to improve and filter the understanding we are getting from the track to try and help us set development priorities from a driver comment perspective. During a race weekend, you very much live in the present in terms of track engineering and it's very easy to react to that weekend's problems. They might be very unique to that particular weekend. What you need to be able to do is filter that and say, well actually, the on-going situation is the car is tending to oversteer or it's got too much drag or whatever. That way, you can spot the underlying issues.[53]

External to the racing team, today's Formula 1 driver also needs to be what one might call 'sponsor-friendly', that is, schooled in the art of public relations and the business of marketing. They spend far more time touring around the world at the behest of their sponsors and performing public relations duties, in fact, than actually driving in racing competitions. An increasing number of drivers are masters at this task and they truly give superior value to their sponsors and other supporters. For many younger drivers this is a steep learning experience. In July 2008, Lewis Hamilton was asked whether he had realised the extent of the sponsorship side when he first got into Formula 1 the previous year. He replied:

When you are coming through the ranks, you have absolutely no comprehension of what it takes to be a top Formula 1 driver. You have no idea, because all you do until that point is train and race, train and race. Then you get here and it's all so new, and you really have to get on top of it . . . You just have to be on top of it the whole time.[54]

In considering the issue of finding the right people and placing them in the right roles, we can discern a further management lesson that can be drawn from Formula 1 into other areas. We summarise this as follows:

Lesson 8 At the edge, not over it

This may be an obvious statement, but conflict within an organisation can undo all of the strong efforts and goodwill that has been built to that point. Given the competitive nature of the individuals in Formula 1 and the fact that they operate within a media fishbowl, it is not uncommon that dirty laundry is aired in public. Whether it is an employee disgruntled because he was passed up for promotion who then shares insider information with a competitor, or two drivers on the same team who cannot seem to get along, their attitudes and actions most certainly impact the organisation's culture and eventually performance in a negative way.

Organisations that have a culture where people feel free to share their thoughts with peers and bosses without reprisal, where managers are in touch with their employees' aspirations and development needs and that foster teamwork as a guiding value are less prone to find themselves operating with internal conflict situations that get out of hand.

Plate 17 Nigel Mansell loses a wheel in the pit lane at Estoril in Portugal 1991, as a result of a misunderstood visual communication during a pit stop.
Source: Sporting Pictures

Plate 18 McLaren Honda pit stop.
Source: McLaren

Plate 19 Three-time World Drivers' Champion Niki Lauda (L) being interviewed by co-author Mark Jenkins

Plate 20 (L to R) Williams team's Pat Symonds, Executive Director of Engineering, driver Felipe Massa and Sir Frank Williams in discussion.
Source: Williams F1

Plate 21 Mercedes driver Lewis Hamilton seated in his car reviewing data prior to his next run.
Source: Mercedes AMG F1

Plate 22 Mercedes debrief session and celebration after winning their second consecutive World Constructors' Championship after the Russian Grand Prix 2015.
Source: Mercedes AMG F1

Plate 23 Williams pit crew in garage.
Source: Williams F1

Plate 24 McLaren Honda at the Singapore Grand Prix 2015 night race.
Source: McLaren

Plate 25 McLaren engineers at their pit wall controls reviewing telemetry data.
Source: McLaren

Plate 26 McLaren Honda motorhome.

Plate 27 (L to R) Mercedes' Technical Director Paddy Lowe being interviewed by co-authors Mark Jenkins and Ken Pasternak

Plate 28 Mercedes engineers review telemetry data.
Source: Mercedes AMG F1

Plate 29 Williams pit-stop crew in action.
Source: Williams F1

Plate 30 Williams garage at Brazilian Grand Prix 2015.
Source: Williams F1

Plate 31 Mercedes at Monaco Grand Prix 2015.
Source: Mercedes AMG F1

Plate 32 Co-author Richard West facilitates the Pit Stop Challenge in Melbourne, 2015

7 | *Formula 1: a team sport*

At the end of every Formula 1 race, the three top finishers stand on the podium facing the cheering crowds of team members and fans below. The winner stands in the middle on the highest pedestal, the second place finisher to his right on a lower platform and the third place finisher on his left on a still lower platform. The national flags of the drivers are raised behind them and the national anthem of the winning driver's country is played. This is followed by the national anthem of the winning team's country. After the trophies are awarded to the drivers and a representative from the winning team, champagne bottles (non-alcoholic in certain countries) are shaken and their contents sprayed at each other and the throng below although, understandably, several large swigs are also usually enjoyed.

Then a personality of some international or local renown steps in view to interview each of the drivers in turn on the international television feed. In recent times, this celebrity has varied between a former racing driver like Mario Andretti, Martin Brundle or David Coulthard; to a former F1 owner and now commentator such as Eddie Jordan; to former US Governor and movie celebrity Arnold Schwarzenegger. No matter who asks the first question about the race, before replying each driver will thank their team for the efforts they made that enabled them to reach the podium.

And it is right that they thank their teammates, both those at the track and the many more back in the factory working on the race weekend. Formula 1 drivers know they would not be flying around the circuit week after week without the extraordinary efforts of the entire team. While the driver is seemingly alone as he navigates the track, Formula 1 is a team sport and the skills of the best driver cannot guarantee victory without a well-coordinated and efficient team behind him.

Our research has determined that Formula 1 teams exhibit several key traits that foster the type of teamwork that is required to win races. Team members within their functional units:

- share a clear, common goal
- work at building trust between each other
- are willing to learn and collaborate
- communicate openly and often

Before discussing these characteristics, it is useful to clarify what we mean by a 'team' in the context of this business. Then we will examine, in detail, one crucial Formula 1 team activity that cuts equally across all of the competitors in this sport, no matter the competitiveness of their car: the pit stop, since all of the elements that symbolise effective teamwork are evident in how a Formula 1 team handles its pit stops – changing tyres and wheels and sometimes making adjustments to or even wholesale replacement of chassis parts – during a race.

By convention, the competitors in this business are known as *teams* – the Williams F1 *team*, the Mercedes F1 *team* and so on. When used in their full titles, they also carry sponsors names such as 'The Mercedes AMG Petronas F1 Team'.

Certainly, the use of this word to describe organisations participating in sports events is not uncommon. But even as the Formula 1 industry has evolved into a multi-billion-dollar business, the description of each of its participants as a *team* is significant, and the operative word '*team*' conveys something meaningful and powerful.

Unlike a working group, which tries to

achieve its performance challenge entirely through the combination of individual performances and where *no collective work or products or shared leadership is needed,*[55]

Formula 1 organisations are real teams. Each member of the team understands the others' capabilities and takes on complementary roles; they work together toward a common purpose, the achievement for which they hold themselves mutually accountable. They fully recognise that they can only achieve the levels of performance they require by sharing, supporting and learning together.

Having said all that, Toto Wolff at Mercedes expressed a different sense of the team in Formula 1:

What you see as a team, or what we commonly understand as a team, is a bunch of individuals put together and for the benefit of the team, they work together to try to extract the best possible result. In most sports teams, it's much easier than with us because if a football team wins, if a basketball team wins, or soccer team wins, the group of individuals enjoys that common achievement; they all win.

Maybe, but do not tell that to the Ferrari Scuderia mechanics when they began to see their drivers on the podium during the 2015 season after the dismal performance of the previous years. The hugs, kisses and even tears appeared to express a genuine, devoted belief in the concept of team.

A Formula 1 team is vitally dependent on the interwoven relationships between people working in different functional areas that include design, engineering, mechanics, testing, racing, marketing, finance and logistics. These separate disciplines become further inter-related through a growing number of complicated collaborations with partners outside their own organisations. Since Formula 1 organisations must operate as commercial businesses in a very competitive environment, they must also balance the internal coordination between innovation and control, between cash out and cash in.

In our second edition, Tony Purnell, the former CEO of Ford's Premier Performance Division that included the Jaguar Racing team at the time, told us:

Motor racing in particular, much like soccer, has got itself into a knot because it's certainly not a sport; it's a business with a sporting element.

This remains as true as ever. It is crucial that the activities within each of the business' distinct departments or disciplines, what we might call sub-teams, must come together throughout the year and, most significantly, at all of the races during the gruelling season.

Jackie Stewart has seen the Formula 1 business from perhaps more positions than almost anyone else in the industry. He has sat in the driver's seat as a triple World Champion, in the motorhome as team owner, in boardrooms as a motorsport advisor and in the broadcast booth bringing Formula 1 to television audiences around the world. According to Stewart, Formula 1 is:

entirely teamwork related, almost a dependency on teamwork.

In short, he described the key element on which a Formula 1 team succeeds or fails. He took the team reference further by referring to his associations in the sport as his *family*.

The people that work with us are not just employees. They're part of the family and you've got to build that family up.

The term *family* to describe a Formula 1 team is heard repeatedly in this industry. It conveys a sense that teamwork and working relationships are being taken to a deeper, more personal and meaningful level.

Raoul Pinnell of Shell experienced a culture clash between his concern for getting the contract negotiated – a more 'northern European' approach, as he put it – and Ferrari's Italian approach which focused more on relationships. But while enduring the initial discomfort of the experience, he was also introduced to the Ferrari way of doing business, where in Pinnell's words:

If you are one of the family, we will do things for you, and they expect that this will also work in reverse whether it is in the contract or not.

Perhaps this sense of family that one finds in most Formula 1 teams can be expected, given the constant pressure and tight deadlines under which they operate. Individuals exhibit remarkable commitment to their team and to each other. They are accustomed to pulling together in order to get the job done under difficult circumstances. This element of making it work under adverse conditions adds to the feeling that they are part of a *family*.

The Formula 1 pit stop

No demonstration of teamwork more fully represents the dedication and commitment required in this sport than that which is displayed by the pit-stop crew. Such is the dynamic of the activity that the authors frequently use the Pit Stop Challenge exercise as part of their client work to improve performance and communication within business teams. And as you will see in Chapter 10 on learning from Formula 1, the pit-stop process has had a significant impact in the medical profession and also improving collaboration among public transport crews.

Looking at the process from the start, the driver has the first critical task that – of bringing the car into an exact, pre-determined position in front of the garage. This enables the pit crew to maximise the efficiency of their efforts – the location of themselves, their equipment and the tyres – which in turn minimises the time of the pit stop. However, it is the twenty or so pit-crew members and their actions that are most visible. Their movements are first displayed and then replayed in slow motion, viewed by hundreds of millions on televisions around the world. The successful completion of the pit-stop task is absolutely crucial if a team wants to finish on the podium. Reflecting back to one of the pioneers of Formula 1 racing, Jackie Stewart said:

Enzo Ferrari knew as a racing driver that you had to have the pit stops working better because the time that was lost there could never be made up by the driver. Whatever time the driver could gain on the track, it wasn't as much as could be gained changing wheels or putting in fuel.

This message has been reinforced time and time again. With less passing occurring on the track than many Formula 1 fans would like to see, races are often won and lost by the team's pit-stop strategy and pit-lane turnaround, i.e. when to come in for new tyres and which compound to use, and by the ability of the driver and his pit team to perform adroitly and with speed.

The pit stop is clearly a very special part of a Formula 1 race. When we wrote the first edition of 'Performance at the Limit', competitive pit-stop times for changing four wheels and tyres were in the 5–7 seconds range, excluding time for refuelling which is no longer allowed. Today, we are seeing teams regularly performing pit stops of 2.5 seconds. The fastest recorded pit stop during a race was by the Red Bull Racing team at 1.923 seconds at the US Grand Prix in 2013.

A pit stop has been described as:

A preordained set of manoeuvres that is barely related to the rest of the weekend's efforts calling for complex activities where many discretionary, invisible, coordinated decisions are made in a split second.[56]

The pit stop in its basic form involves changing all four wheels and tyres. Taking a closer look at the pit stop reveals the teamwork required to accomplish it successfully. The pit-stop crew's performance in several ways also represents the many team interactions that enable an entire Formula 1 organisation to perform successfully.

A Formula 1 pit stop requires between twenty and twenty-three people working in a confined space, not much longer and wider than the car itself, in the pit lane in front of their team's garage. This is an extremely hostile environment, as other racing cars are racing on the other side of the safety wall at speeds of up to 320 kph (approximately

200 mph) only 15 metres away. In the pit lane, limiters installed on the car prohibit them from being driven faster than 80 kph (50 mph), still not so slow given the dimensions of the area and the fact that several cars may be driving though at the same time. Earplugs and radio headsets within fire-proof helmets are required because the noise from the engines, even with the hybrid V6 engines, can be deafening. Very often, competitor cars are pulling in or out of their pit area at the same time, passing a few centimetres away from the pit crew.

Until being notified by the senior racing team about a pit stop, the pit crew have been sitting in their chairs in the garage watching the race. They are wearing fire-retardant suits and underwear similar to those worn by the drivers, along with helmets and protective gloves. The driver is given a signal somewhere between one and three laps before being called up and the pit-stop crew are informed concurrently. The driver is given a final alert one lap before coming into the pit lane. He will hear in his earphones 'Box, Box, Box', and he signals back an acknowledgement by pressing the appropriate radio button on his steering wheel – this is received by the pit crew as an audible click. The crew are not permitted into the pit lane in front of the garage until 20–30 seconds before the driver steers the car into the pit lane entrance. All members of the team then take their carefully scripted positions in front of the garage door. The team members responsible for fitting the new wheels have them ready, having removed the electrical tyre-warmers which are essential for ensuring the tyres are fitted to the car in their optimum operating temperatures, and in position for fitting onto the car the moment it comes to a stop.

Prior to the race, in rehearsal with the drivers, a specific grid was marked with tape or paint markings on the ground. This is a target position for the driver to aim for that will maximise the team's efficiency by aligning the car with the new wheels and tyres and compressed air–operated wheel-nut guns.

While each of a team's two drivers will have dedicated engineers and mechanics, the pit crew is made up of individuals from both 'sides' of the garage, thereby they would be servicing not only the driver they support directly, but also the other team driver too. Positions in the pit crew are distributed to those who are best for those particular tasks. These are determined from some 1,500 to 2,000 practices the pit crew undertake during a season. These take place both at their factories and at the different circuits. Williams F1's Dickie Stanford has said that they might due up to 60 practice runs during a race weekend.[57]

Teams also watch videos of their practices and actual performance, much like other sports teams, to determine who should be in which position and to continually search for improvement.

With engines revving up to 15,000 rpm, the noise level is high, which makes voice communication within the confines of the helmets very difficult. Each member of the team must know his task, coordinate with others and be ready to communicate his intentions and actions clearly.

So, back to the driver, who has just pulled into the pit lane. He stops in front of a crew member holding a front car jack that is used for lifting the front of the car. The other members of the crew jump into action. As the cantilever action of the jack raises the front end of the car, another mechanic places a jack behind the car to raise the rear end in one motion. Three mechanics concentrate on each wheel and tyre assembly. The wheel nut is removed by one using a high-impact air hammer (or air gun). A second team member removes the spent wheel and tyre assembly as soon as the single, central wheel nut is off. He quickly, but carefully, places it to the side or holds it so that it cannot roll back and get in the way of the car or any other crew member. The third team member working on that corner puts the new wheel and tyre assembly onto the car. Finally, the wheel-gun man hammers the wheel nut back onto the threaded end of the stub axle.

This used to be done by clicking a switch on the gun to reverse the direction of the direction of the gun – clockwise to tighten the nut rather than counter-clockwise to loosen it. With advancing technology and looking for ways to increase speed while reducing potential error, wheel guns now automatically reverse their direction after the first action has taken place. This is a saving of a tenth of a second or two, but a saving nevertheless and a potential mechanical failure has been eliminated. At the other three corners of the car the exact same routine is being performed simultaneously. All of this in typically in the 2.5–3.5 seconds range.

If required, during this time other mechanics reach into the left and right air intake compartments beside the driver's seating position in order to make sure that no debris has been picked up from the track that could block the air-cooling system, while two other mechanics might stabilise the car.

In real time, all of these activities appear as a blur of movement. However, it is actually a carefully scripted and extremely well-rehearsed performance. When seen in slow motion, it appears very much like a ballet, as each team member performs his task in coordination with the others. The scene has been referred somewhat poetically as a place where:

task and process unite in a state of flow – a combination of head and heart.[56]

No words are spoken by the mechanics during all of these activities. It is too noisy and happening all too quickly. In the past, when a tyre change was completed the four crew members with air guns either raised their hands high into the air to signal that their tasks are completed or placed a coloured gloved hand flat over the top of the tyre surface to indicate they have finished. With a constant eye on reducing potential error (see the Nigel Mansell story in Chapter 9) and reducing even the time that it takes to raise one's arm, the crew member now simply presses a button on the gun to signify the task has been completed.

Unless there is a problem, only one person speaks during this very short period: the pit-stop team leader. He is responsible for ensuring that all the tasks have been completed as planned. Given the dynamics of this highly energised situation, he is also responsible for the safety of the entire pit-stop team and driver. This leader has been known in the past as the 'lollipop man', because until recently he stood at the front of the car with a round sign on a long pole. The sign said 'STOP' as the driver pulled into position. After the car was lifted off the ground, he would spin the lollipop sign around to show the words 'BRAKES – FIRST GEAR' written on the other side. This reminded the driver to engage the brake and to have the car in first gear so he can depart immediately upon the pit stop's completion. If the brakes are not engaged the rear wheels would spin, making the wheel and tyre change impossible. While this might appear to be an exaggerated, almost unnecessary gesture given the skill levels of Formula 1 drivers, it is important to recall that at this moment the driver is concentrating on the race situation and he might also be talking in his headset to team engineers who are monitoring the car's performance and to team management providing advice on race strategy.

The lollipop man takes full and final responsibility for the pit stop as he is the only one with a complete view of all the team members, including the driver, as they complete their tasks on the car. It was up to him to raise his lollipop at the right moment, signalling to the driver that he could accelerate back into the pit lane in order to re-enter the race circuit.

As with so many aspects of Formula 1 the lollipop man's equipment has changed, but his role is as important as ever. Today, almost all teams have switched to a system of automated lights. Sometimes they hang from overhead structures and sometimes they are affixed to the front jack assembly. In some cases, there is even a sensor on the front wheel jack that knows when the car has been lifted and dropped back down. In either case, the driver will not see a green light to pull away until the system has registered the 'go' signal from all for wheel gun operators.

The chief mechanic, formerly the lollipop man, still retains an overview of the entire operation. He has final say over release of the car. His judgment can be important, for example, in the case that a competitor car is approaching their location in the pit lane and by allowing his driver to pull away he could cause an accident. According to Nick Chester of Lotus F1:

The chief mechanic has an override, so he has to keep that pressed to keep the green light on. If anything goes wrong with the pit stop he lifts his thumb, a red light appears and the driver should stop, thus preventing an unsafe release.

An 'unsafe release', as it is called, could incur a stewards' penalty that adds additional time to the drivers final performance, or a 'drive through' penalty that requires him to pass through the pit lane at a reduced speed on one of his circuits around the track.

How far can F1 teams use technology to enhance the speed and accuracy of pit stops? There might be some limits, says Nick Chester:

There was some talk about having sensors on the car to check that the wheels were tight, strain gauges which would also feed a thumbs-up to the system. But so far they are not reliable enough to use as inputs so we rely on the mechanics signalling their wheels are tight via a switch on the pit guns.

The lollipop man or chief mechanic's responsibility is serious and critical. Things can go wrong.

During the past few years we have seen a number of pit-stop and pit-lane incidents that have even ended the races of drivers who were in the wrong place at the wrong time. In 2007, a driver departed too early from his standing position in front of the team garage, ignoring the fact that the lollipop was still down. In doing so, he pulled the refuelling hose (this all took place before F1 banned the refuelling of cars during the race) right off of the rig and took it with him a few hundred yards down the pit lane. That driver's Formula 1 career came to an abrupt end.

In 2008, at the Canadian Grand Prix in Montreal, Lewis Hamilton missed the red light at the end of the pit lane signalling the need to stop and wait for entrance onto the track. The outcome was a crash that ended his race (he drove into the back of a stationary Ferrari), the race of the potential lead driver, Kimi Raikkonen, whom he had hit, and eventually a third driver, Nico Rosberg, in his Williams, who ploughed into the back of Hamilton. Both of the 'guilty' parties were given a penalty at the start of the next race.

The pit-stop team accomplishes the changing of four wheels and tyre assemblies typically two or three times per race for each of their two cars, sometimes even four times, depending upon the race strategy and weather conditions.

How can they consistently maintain high performance in such a competitive, highly pressurised environment? What is it that enables these teams to perform successfully week after week? As indicated earlier in this chapter, these teams *share a clear, common goal*; they *work at building trust between each other*; they are *willing to learn and collaborate*; and they *communicate openly and often*.

Sharing a clear, common goal

For the pit-stop crew, a fast and error-free tyre change creates a clear and measurable goal. They know their previous times. They know the times of their competitors. The common purpose – to provide an advantage for their driver – is meaningful and can make a significant difference to the results of the race. Other functional areas of Formula 1 teams cannot as easily associate their efforts with making as direct an impact on the race. But their efforts to develop new designs, build new components and test them for their reliability give them clarity of purpose and direction. They know that in the end, it is the sum of all the activities that goes into the car and the race performance that will determine success for the whole team.

Toto Wolff told us about the following exercise that Mercedes F1 did to clarify the team's common goal, but also to build understanding of roles and responsibilities:

One of the things we did when Paddy (Lowe) and I were starting the 2014 season, was that we took the thirty most senior people on a two-day off-site, just to define the mission and the vision for ourselves. And we placed various skilled people into different areas – we put, for example, the race engineer in charge of marketing on the particular day; and the marketing guy in charge of race strategy so they could see the other side of things. Everybody then bought in so as you can see there's a lot of investment of time and resources into innovation, into education, into getting everybody aligned.

Building trust

According to Jackie Stewart, the one thing Formula 1 team leaders should never do is:

compromise their integrity. If you do the right thing you'll always be given credit. It may not come out and you may not hear everybody talk about it, but it's the respect you get for going about your business in an honourable fashion. It's trust ... you can't buy it.

Trusting the leader and trusting each other is the glue that binds a team into an effective working unit. It enables open communication and creates an environment for dealing with conflict. It extends from top down, bottom up and throughout the organisation. Stewart once again:

Being able to respect the people you are working with, to depend on them, to trust them, to have dependency and trust in somebody that you know is extremely important.

Effective teams work hard at building trust among team members, getting them to focus on their common goals and aspirations.

When Team Physician at McLaren, Aki Hintsa described an annual gathering that took place in Finland before the start of the season.

We have the drivers, engineers and mechanics together when we all play together, football for example, and we all do fitness tests and have daily routines and training with the drivers. The drivers can see these guys keep pushing hard, trying their best to improve; and the others can see that the drivers are hard workers, real athletes. There develops an understanding that without high-performance teamwork, the drivers will not be able to perform at the optimum level.

In the most effective Formula 1 teams, roles are clearly defined and individuals know how their jobs inter-relate with others. In order to achieve the speed and consistency discussed earlier, the pit-stop crews, as we have seen, carefully plan out their individual and then coordinated

actions beforehand. They review videos of their performance and practice with slow-motion rehearsals. The team looks at every aspect of the
pit-stop activity. They consider whether better positioning of themselves
or their tools, refinement of the equipment being used or even changing
personnel can save fractions of a second. Among these teams there exists
a constant thirst for new and better ways to improve. No one is willing to
stand on the laurels of past performance.

We were told by a former pit-stop crew chief and Sporting Director
at Minardi, John Walton, that they also learn by practising mistakes.

*We practise getting it wrong. Anything you can think of that may possibly go
wrong we try to see how to deal with it. Say there's no power on the gun,
a nut flies off down the road, the driver stalls the car and you have to restart,
or a wing is knocked off in an accident. We practise them all.*

Recognising that Formula 1 teams work closely with partners who
provide technical and other support, Mike O'Driscoll acknowledged
the challenge by emphasising the importance of focusing on the people
involved.

*You've got to remember that when you bring in partners, they themselves
have networks of companies that they work with, so you need to have
a joined-up strategy. You also have to be aware that when you bring in
a new partner they need to be compatible with your existing partners and
are going to work in a harmonious way. It is important amongst the people
here at Williams and it's equally important amongst our partners.*

Communicate openly and often

Constant team practice and discussion about performance provide
opportunities for continual review of actions (input) while maintaining
a clear focus on the goals (output). It also provides chances for open
sharing of views and the retention of useful knowledge gained from
experience.

When he was Team Principal at Ferrari, Jean Todt, currently
the President of the FIA, the governing body of motorsport,
echoed the words of many team leaders when he said:

*Communication is the key thing in a company because you have to be seen
and you have to explain to people. You have to enable people to participate in
what you do.*

Or, as Jackie Stewart put it,

Communication. Total communication. No hiding behind closed doors. No telling lies. Total openness. Total frankness. Total integrity. That's what's required.

We asked Monisha Kaltenborn how her vision and views and those of Peter Sauber, the team's founder, get driven through the organisation. She replied:

First of all, we have a very straightforward structure – we are two owners, one being myself who is actively involved in the operation side. It's very easy for me to talk to Peter Sauber. We have a mutual agreement on whatever way we want to go and then it's me instructing it into the structure. We have a management committee where these ideas are given, the direction we want to go, what we want to do; then it goes further down to the departments. It is equally important is to have regular touch with your employees, all of them. So, it's not just me to the next level and they to the next level. We have regular team briefings where we invite the entire team and whatever has to be said is said there, good or bad. We also have done it so that I went through the entire company having meetings where I'd invite a limited group. We'd go through the whole company, mixing the departments so everybody gets a chance to learn and ask questions. We do it as a breakfast and they have a chance to talk directly to me and ask whatever they want to. It's a dialogue actually, it's not a question and answer.

Perhaps no Team Principal has had a more difficult job to communicate an optimistic future than Eric Boullier, Racing Director at McLaren-Honda. The team's under-performance in 2014 and 2015 as it struggled to field a competitive car with their power-unit partner, Honda, is regular media news. We asked Boullier how he was able to keep short-term motivation when they are clearly focused on getting back to McLaren's greatness in the medium and longer term. He said,

It's a question of communicating with people, explaining what we're doing and where we want to go. We all want to win – no one more fervently than I. But in these trying circumstances I sometimes need to sit down on my own for ten minutes to reflect. The key for me is to be transparent – no bullshit!

Toto Wolff said,

There is a lot of communication within the team, and we have a culture of ruthlessly exploring our weaknesses and mistakes without blaming, without pointing fingers at one another.[58]

8 | Partnerships (sponsorship)

Across a range of businesses via the authors' speaking and training commitments, the questions '*Does a Formula 1 Team make money?*' and '*What does a sponsor or partner get out of an association with F1?*' frequently arise. To answer them fully, one has to really understand the way the commercial platform works within the sport and, more importantly, the team.

In Chapter 1, we explained cash flows to the teams in terms of their share of the overall revenues Formula 1 generates. However, within the teams their own commercial and licensing and rights departments are now highly specialised in terms of their function and accountability.

Sponsorship today is a global business in its own right. Wherever one works, relaxes, reads, tweets, uses LinkedIn, browses or indulges, it is impossible not to be bombarded with various commercial messages when travelling, sitting at home in the front of the TV or now even on an aeroplane, using the internet or attending a sporting or leisure event, for sponsorship is all around us in our daily lives.

In motor racing, sponsorship has continued unabated from the trend set in the 1960s when Bruce McLaren's team's association with Reynolds Aluminium and Sir Jack Brabham benefitted from Repco's support. There was, however, very little real commercialisation of the sport. It was Colin Chapman of Lotus who was the first to recognise the true value of his racing cars appearing on television and in front of large crowds, and hence team title sponsors began to appear.

Chapman's Lotus, with the famous Gold Leaf Team Lotus title, was one of the first really 'corporate' deals, and this was to set the scene for Formula 1's appeal to a range of sectors and commercial companies' investments since. Around that time, one Bernard Charles Ecclestone was taking his first steps towards becoming the ring master of what is now a multi-billion-dollar business, and a highly profitable one at that, for both the rights holders and the teams.

The phrases 'sponsorship' and 'partnership' frequently become blurred. In the very early years of racing, 'patronage' rather than sponsorship was a better description of the money that was spent on racing. Wealthy team owners such as Rob Walker (of the Walkers Scotch whisky empire) supported their cars and drivers from private funds or family-owned dynasties, and it was not until the emergence of the 'Chapman era' that sponsorship became the holy grail for team owners.

Let us now look more closely at what these two terms mean, starting with sponsorship.

Sponsorship in Formula 1 has become an essential part of a team's budgeting strategy. Each team has its own brand values, and it is an important part of the internal commercial department of each team to evaluate and recognise what these values are in order to match them with potential sponsors to best financial effect – put simply, the sponsors have the money the teams want and each individual team has a set of brand values that will benefit individual brands and services who are looking for sales and publicity. The rest is down to skilled negotiation.

Many of the teams also have associations with external sponsorship search agencies and skilled sponsorship individuals who also seek out companies and brands wishing to associate themselves with Formula 1 (FOM Corporate) and/or the individual teams. These agencies mainly work on a fee or a 'fee and finder's percentage' basis.

Companies associating themselves with FOM and circuit signage rights and/or the individual teams do so for a variety of reasons. They include a desire to build or enhance an existing brand via television exposure and/or selected programmes aimed at influencing key markets, consumers and political decision makers.

Currently, examples of corporate sponsors using F1 in a global sense are DHL (also the Official Logistics Partner of Formula 1), Emirates Airlines, Rolex Watches and UBS bank. Their corporate logos are clearly laid out in prominent positions from circuit to circuit. In addition, certain companies take race name rights such as Shell at the Belgian Grand Prix or Emirates at others.

Team sponsors currently include Martini, Shell, Santander,Blackberry, Petronas and Red Bull. In some cases, these arrangements have been extended to embrace a further technology partnership and, in the case of Red Bull, outright team ownership. Brand names can also be seen on cars such as PDSV or Banco do Brazil, but these are frequently associated with drivers who bring with them substantial sums of money to enable young drivers to gain a seat in Formula 1. Irrespective of this, this additional revenue equals cash flow for the teams, for the raw material of Grand Prix racing is money.

These corporate brands are among the names frequently seen by the public on television as each race is shown via live and deferred broadcast, and this 'televisual presence' links each company with one of the most glamorous and expensive sports in the world. Every campaign is carefully crafted by each organisation's staff and respective agencies to promote their products and services to bespoke audiences and attendees. These are not just simple circuit advertising deals or team-branding associations where logos appear on cars, track bridges and on circuit trackside hoardings, but carefully designed and delivered marketing programmes that encompass global TV branding and a range of other benefits.

For the corporate circuit sponsors, they will link their circuit branding into advertising campaigns, consumer competitions and loyalty programmes, as well as guest access to exclusive hospitality programmes using The Formula 1 Paddock Club™ where the finest levels of race viewing, seating, catering and VIP services are combined. At the highest levels, guests will be further accredited by FOM and selected guests taken on tours of the F1 Paddock area and even out onto the starting grid just prior to the start of the race. The teams also utilise the Paddock Club in addition to their own paddock-side HQ's to entertain.

In terms of team sponsorship, this comes at a variety of levels and offers a much wider range of marketing options. In simple terms, a potential sponsor has to decide what level they wish to expose themselves to and to what level of audience prior to entering into discussions with a team. This decision will be made based on a number of criteria, such as the amount of desired television visibility (certain areas of the car give greater TV visibility but carry much higher investment costs). Is hospitality a requirement? Will the sponsor be operating a VIP programme at race weekends, are team factory visits, use of display cars, driver appearances and direct product endorsements required? A shopping list is a must before entering into negotiations with a team.

Some of the great success stories of recent years in F1 sponsorship terms are associations such as Vodafone with McLaren, Rothmans and

RBS and now Martini with Williams, Marlboro with McLaren and Ferrari and ING Bank with Renault.

These were/are organisations and brands that effectively wanted to create 'team ownership' in terms of visual identity. With investments running into hundreds of millions of dollars when taking into account the team 'fee' over a period of years, along with the exploitation budgets for advertising, hospitality, competitions, VIPs, staffing and in-house promotion, these deals are really reserved for the high-stakes players. It is commonplace to advise an activation spend of a further two to three dollars per actual dollar spent on the sponsorship fee to the team to make the programme effective.

A current example of a team title deal is Williams Martini Racing. Both the Williams team and Martini are iconic global brands.

Both have long associations with Formula 1, they are associated with success and sophistication, global reach and wealth and success. This is an example of how 'brand matching' can achieve the best results and how once certain levels of investment are obtained, the team gives actual naming rights as part of the sponsorship package.

Past iconic sponsorships such as John Player Special Lotus, Rothmans Williams Renault, Canon Williams Honda, Marlboro McLaren Honda and today's Mercedes AMG Petronas Formula 1 Team illustrate how naming rights play a major part in the contractual arrangements of the top teams and brands.

The branding of the team, the racing cars, the team's road transporters, garage interiors and even the race wear of the drivers and team members are carefully planned and researched. Every space on the car carries a team 'rate card' value linked to TV exposure. The rear wings, upper engine cover and the side-facing radiator pods of the racing cars carry the highest opportunity for achieving visibility on TV. Lesser areas such as the nose cone, wing mirrors, the front and rear side–facing wing end plates and even the impact structure surrounding the driver's cockpit area are considered for branding.

Within these spaces, sponsors will sometimes add specific brand names or change the brands represented under their ownership in deference to individual country market preferences.

The real key to a sponsor's investment is to drill down into the requirements of the brand, products or services they are marketing and then create a bespoke package of identity, rights and benefits to suit those particular requirements.

In many sponsors' cases, full television visibility is not the primary concern and therefore a sponsorship programme where a small amount of on-car branding is required to create the association is sufficient, but greater access to Grand Prix attendances, access to tours in the F1 Paddock, visits to the team's factory and appearances by senior team members, engineers and marketing staff are called for. This would be referred to as secondary sponsorship.

In reality, there are few deals a team will decline provided the levels of investment are commensurate with the marketplace, their own rate card and international legal agreements such as those in place with the World Health Organisation in relation to tobacco. Underlying many cash-rich team title and secondary sponsorship programmes are, however, a range of deals where suppliers provide, relatively speaking, lower levels of cash, but higher levels of expertise and services or equipment in return for the use of the team's name and image in endorsements and advertising.

This then leads to the partnerships within a team which can range from the supply of materials, technology, expertise, equipment and even the supply of mineral water for the team's motorhome HQs. 'Official suppliers', 'technology partners' and 'innovation partners' are often-used terms in relation to these purpose-built programmes for partnership programmes.

In the case of the Williams team, they have one of the finest conference facilities in the UK, which houses a very large collection of their racing cars that have won so many races and titles over the years for the marque.

Such was the branding requirement of RBS (Bank) in their more successful times, that even the conference centre was renamed 'The RBS Williams Conference Centre'. Catering for team sponsors and external parties alike, branding a conference centre in the grounds of the team which at that time carried headline title sponsorship for RBS was a stroke of marketing genius as it carried the RBS name across all areas of the racing team and into other organisations' corporate days, as this provided potential B2B and B2C opportunities.

The science of sponsorship in Formula 1 began to change rapidly in the late 1980s. The combination of Ayrton Senna and Alain Prost in the Marlboro McLaren Honda MP4/4 dominated the 1988 season and won fifteen out of sixteen races. In doing so, Team Principal Ron Dennis, now Chairman of the McLaren Group and Team Principal of the racing branch of the group, engineered new levels of corporate branding and quality in the way that the team was turned out both on track and in its public persona.

This attracted many new sponsors both on track and away from the racing in the team's HQ in Woking. Even the factory furniture programme at that time was provided via a sponsorship deal though a German furniture systems manufacturing company called Voko. The marble flooring came from Italian specialist Mirage Ceramica, and a range of other organisations provided services and materials to benefit from the McLaren association, even through to the audio visual equipment in the presentation theatre. All of these services were provided in return for these associations, effectively saving cash off the bottom line of the business model for the team.

There are, therefore, clearly many 'layers' to team sponsorship. As already mentioned, team title and secondary sponsorships are where the real cash lies for the team – today these are referred to as 'corporate partners' more than 'sponsors' – but in today's economically challenged, post–global financial crisis world, finding title sponsors with the right amount of cash has become a major challenge for the teams.

Ron Dennis, Chairman of the McLaren Group and Team Principal for McLaren Honda, recently commented that team title sponsorship was dead, perhaps a thing of the past, such were the levels of investment required by top teams today.

Title sponsorship doesn't exist any more as a concept. If you look at what title sponsorship would normally be, it would be somewhere between 40–50 per cent of your budget. Where the budgets are for a competitive team, no company will come in and give you that kind of money. Therefore what you do is you cut it up into bite-sized pieces, so you get a range of companies with similar philosophies to join you on the car. Do we have room for bigger brands on our cars? Yes we do.[59]

While at the time of writing McLaren does not have a title sponsor, Dennis continued:

But the reality is that we put ourselves in a position where the technology side of our business is providing different dynamics [of revenue].[59]

Zak Brown, Chairman of sports marketing company CMI, sees it from a slightly different perspective, one where the problem is more about the costs of F1 than the availability of title sponsors:

I think the costs of Formula 1 now are far greater than the overall commercial value for a title sponsor to pay these budgets, and that's because the costs have outpaced the commercial value of the sport. In previous years, a title sponsor would cover 50 per cent of your budget; it's now a $300 million budget for a team, the commercial value of the car to a title sponsor is only worth $75 million and therefore your title sponsors are only going to pay 50 per cent of your fee.

Kevin Eason, F1 correspondent of the *Times*, also sees this as an end of an era:

There aren't any Vodafones around any more willing to throw in 20/30 million quid [pounds sterling] a year – they've all disappeared. The financial model now is to some extent broken, so there is the reliance now on partners so here you've got McLaren reliant on Honda, Red Bull are reliant on [Dietrich] Mateschitz. I think that's one of the reasons why it's in such a muddle. You just can't get people to put a sticker on the car, spend 20 million quid and then bugger off out of the way so that you can get on and go racing. The partners now want something for their money.

It is an interesting comment when one looks at both the variety of companies currently backing McLaren's F1 programme, as well as Zak Brown's comments that an F1 team title sponsorship is now too much money for a single company to contemplate in the context of the team's expenditure versus sponsorship investment model. However, one of the ways that the F1 teams have dealt with this is to broaden the offering they make to sponsors. Zak Brown again:

There are more sponsors in Formula 1 today then there were ten years ago. Just in sheer numbers of companies. What's happened is teams have assets beyond the race car, McLaren being the best example. They have the whole factory and facility with something that sponsors commercialised so they have sponsors that you know rarely if at all go to the Formula 1 track because they're buying other assets that have been built up out of these Formula 1 teams.

Honda is clearly a headline deal via its engine supply programme for the team, which represents a solid revival of the engine–team partnership that brought so much success in years gone by. However, today McLaren's 'portfolio' is much broader; Table 6 illustrates the large variety of companies associated with this iconic racing team across a very wide range of products and services.

Table 6 *McLaren Honda partners 2015*

Type of Partner	Company	Business
Corporate Partner	Johnnie Walker	Drinks
	TAG Heuer	Time pieces
	Segafredo	Coffee
	Hilton	Hotels
	CNN	Media
	Norton Rose Fulbright	Global legal practice
Technology Partner	Mobil 1	Lubricants
	SAP	Software and Technology solutions
	Esso	Fuels
	Pirelli	Tyres
	Akebono	Brake calipers
Innovation Partner	KPMG	Audit and Tax specialists
Official Suppliers	Enkei	Wheels
	Repucom	Sports Evaluation
	Kenwood	Communications, Audo, Car Electronics
	Mazak Machine Tools	Advanced Manufacturing machines and Tooling
	Sparco	Racing Overalls and Clothing
	Sikkens	Paints
	Maxi Nutrtion	Health
	ASICS	Sports Shoes

A model partnership

As can be seen from the wide range of companies associated with McLaren, it takes a great deal of input from a wide range of companies to assist a team in its quest for winning. The team's internal marketing and media departments are not only charged with sourcing these commercial arrangements, but servicing and supporting them as well. The old adage *'it's better to keep a partner than have to search for a new one'* is very true, and one organisation that has anchored its roots in a relationship that gives great benefits is Shell. Its association with Ferrari is a model example of how to link two organisations together.

Shell has a long and illustrious relationship with motor sport at all levels, from rallying to sports car racing to Formula 1. Shell and Ferrari have a very special relationship and it is a partnership that dates back to 1929, when Enzo Ferrari formed his team in Modena, Italy, and Shell was his lubricants and fuels partner of choice.

While Shell had breaks in its sponsorship history, in the mid-1980s it came back as a sponsor of the McLaren team and benefitted from a period of unqualified success due to being associated with the team during its period of virtual domination of Formula 1 in the Lauda/Prost/Senna/Berger era.

As one of the world's leading petrochemical companies, Shell understands the need to link its racing heritage with its road consumers, and it has done this to a level that it is rightly proud of, namely its current relationship with Ferrari.

Towards the end of the company's relationship with the McLaren team, it began to evaluate its need to link brands successfully and to do so looked back into its motor sport history. It had its envious previous experience of the Ferrari brand, and by recreating a partnership in 1996 that has grown and prospered, it successfully linked together the two companies to a point where all Shell service station staff now wear Ferrari-branded clothing and carry a heavy Ferrari presence 'in store'.

Shell is a company of some 92,000 employees in some 70 countries and territories and has a global service station network of some 43,000 stations where it retails a range of fuels including V-Power, a fuel directly developed out of its relationship with the Ferrari team. The partnership is now one of the most successful in Formula 1 history, having together amassed twelve Drivers' World Championship titles and ten World Constructors' Championships.

Clearly, technical partnerships are about quantifiable returns for all parties. Shell have contributed greatly to lubricant and fuel technologies for their teams over the years, and Ferrari are reaping the rewards of this today.

On 6 September 2015 at Ferrari's traditional home at Monza, Shell signed a new five-year sponsorship agreement with Ferrari.

Both parties were delighted with the arrangement and for Formula 1, this cements yet a further endorsement of the power of its brand when two like-minded organisations work in collaboration.

As Maurizio Arrivabene, Ferrari Managing Director, explained:

Signing this contract is a further step forward in terms of stability and we are happy to have extended our collaboration with Shell. Historically, engines are the cornerstone of our company and that means all the work we do with Shell starts from our history as an engine builder. This season, the collaboration with Shell contributed to our wins in Malaysia and Hungary; proof not only of professional dedication but also the result of great teamwork.[60]

John Abbott, Shell's Downstream Director, added:

Of course, fuel and motor oil are just two of the many parts that need to come together for a Formula One car to cross the finish line first. As our relationship with the most successful team in Formula One evolves, we are determined to help bring success to the Scuderia, and develop even better fuels and lubricants for our millions of customers.[60]

It is hard to find a sector that is not or has not been involved in a commercial partnership with either the teams or as part of the larger commercial picture of FOM. At all levels of the F1 business, it is possible to see such relationships, even down to the relationship of TATA Communications, who are the official web hosting and content delivery network providers of Formula1.com, the official website of Formula 1.

Launched in 2012 and still running today, it is easy to see how TATA have linked their services with Formula 1 to provide an exciting communications medium for their global business aspirations and how F1 has benefitted from their skills and services, as the following extract of a press release from their launch shows:

Tata Communications announces global technology association with Formula 1™

Thursday, 23 February 2012

Mumbai (BSE) & New York (NYSE) – 23 February 2012 – Tata Communications, a leading provider of The New World of Communications, today announces a multi-year technology service and marketing agreement with Formula One Management. The agreement will see Tata Communications delivering world-class connectivity to all 20 Formula 1™ race locations over its global network, the largest in the world. It will also provide hosting and content delivery services to Formula1.com, which is accessed by tens of millions of fans around the globe.

The innovative deal positions Tata Communications corporately as **A Technology Supplier of Formula 1™** with category exclusive designations as **Official Connectivity Provider of Formula 1™ and Official Web Hosting and Content DeliveryNetwork Provider of Formula1.com**

Formula One group businesses and race locations will now be connected to the Tata Global Network ('TGN'), supported by secure MPLS connectivity. Formula One Management's IT infrastructure and Formula1.com will be co-located and hosted in Tata Communications' world-class data centres.

Vinod Kumar, Managing Director and CEO of Tata Communications, says, 'Formula 1 requires fast and secure connectivity, because even a split second of downtime can have huge repercussions for its business, brand and reputation. This delivery is at the heart of our organisation and working with one of the world's most highly technical and innovative organisations is an exciting opportunity for Tata Communications. The collaboration leverages our technology leadership and vision for emerging markets and represents a tremendous opportunity for growth and innovation for both companies.'

Bernie Ecclestone, CEO of Formula One group, says, 'I'm pleased to welcome Tata Communications into the Formula 1 family and I hope this is the start of a long and successful relationship. Connectivity and content delivery are critical issues for Formula 1 and working with the best in the business is a priority for us. This is a collaboration that will help us stay at the technological cutting edge in these categories.'

Tata Communications' capabilities in video and content delivery networks ('CDN') will enable uninterrupted, high-quality connectivity to the multi-media portal on Formula1.com. The (TGN) has Trans-Atlantic and Trans-Pacific data transfer capacity of one terabit per second. This capacity will ensure Tata Communications is able to fully support Formula1.com during race weekends, when the site gets on average four million unique visits per weekend, peaking at seven million over some events. Tata Communications' infrastructure will enable the sport's official website to instantly scale up to cope with these significant and sometimes unpredictable traffic spikes.

Tata Communications will also provide Formula1.com with a new Managed Security Suite and will apply an additional layer of managed security monitoring to ensure an increased level of protection to Formula One Management's IT infrastructure.

9 | *Winning culture*

We don't blame people but we are brutally honest in assessing the problem and trying to solve it, but we don't point fingers at anybody. That is so important and it's not always easy to have that philosophy.

Toto Wolff, Mercedes Benz AMG F1.

The management thinker Peter Drucker is attributed with the quote: '*Culture eats strategy for breakfast*': you can do what you like in terms of strategy, but if you don't have the right culture you're wasting your time. The ability to build a winning culture is one of the critical tasks of any leader in any organisation, but in F1 it is fundamental to sustained success. Of course, every individual in every team wants to win the next Grand Prix and the World Championship, but they can only do so if those leading the organisation are able to create and sustain a winning culture. From our look into the world of F1, there are four critical elements to such a culture: 1) constant communication, 2) a no-blame philosophy (as described by Toto Wolff above), which is in reality a 3) one-team mindset framed within a 4) long-term perspective.

Constant communication

We have already discussed the importance of open and constant communication in building effective teams. Likewise, we have addressed the power of review and learning in driving innovation. These behaviours underpin an all-important continual focus on communicating with everyone in the organisation. This is best exemplified by looking at 2014 and 2015 World Champions Mercedes AMG F1's activities on the Monday morning following a race on Sunday, as summarised by Technical Director Paddy Lowe:

I chair two meetings on the Monday after a race. The first we would call a debrief, which is with the senior management, about thirty or so

180

individuals, and we're going through a quick summary of how the weekend went, what were the key issues, what points need to be taken forward, focused on for the next event. Then we have also a full staff briefing where every employee is invited [note – at Brackley this involves 820 employees]. In that twenty minutes you've given a brief account of the weekend, we have a glass of champagne if we won the race, so it's not all about work, it's also about celebration. And again, it's just giving the full company a picture of where we're at and where we're trying to head next.

No-blame philosophy

We first referred to the no-blame culture in the first edition of *Performance at the Limit*, which was published in 2005. There we defined one of the business lessons from Formula 1 as '*Isolate the problem, not the person: the no-blame culture.*' This came from an interview with Dickie Stanford, then Team Manager with Williams F1. He was describing a situation where a pit stop involving Nigel Mansell at the 1991 Portuguese Grand Prix at Estoril went horribly wrong, as can be seen in Plate 17.

Mansell had been leading the race by a significant margin and came in to make a scheduled pit stop on lap 29. Unfortunately, as is graphically shown in Plate 17, this resulted in him losing his rear right wheel in the pit lane. The team then fitted a new rear right wheel, but as they had provided assistance in the pit lane (which the sporting regulations count as part of the race track) he was disqualified from the race, and, in the words of commentator Simon Taylor 'this marked the end of his championship hopes for that year'. So what would the natural reaction be in most organisations for such a failure? You look to blame someone or some department of course. The tendency to blame is a natural reaction, not least because we divert the focus away from us, making us feel better about ourselves. So how does an organisational culture negate or counter a natural tendency to blame? Dickie Stanford takes up the story:

We had a wheel-nut failure. So you go back. You talk to the person or the people who were actually using the equipment and we tried to redesign the problem right there. Then we looked at our overall procedures during the pit stop. With the significance of the incident behind us we decided there were a lot of loopholes that we had missed, so we totally rescheduled the way we did a pit stop, from the equipment to personnel. We put in different procedures so the car couldn't go without everybody signalling according to a new approach.

In those days everybody put their hand up when the wheel was finished, so you had three people putting their hands up at each corner of the car. You got a group of people all squashed within a 5 feet area and it's such a rush when you've all twenty-three putting their hands up. One person is controlling it and he can't see every one of those twenty-three people. We realised that we only need the guy who does the last job on the wheel to signal to say that he's finished. The lollipop man needs only to be able to see the last four men on the wheels, the jack men and the refuelling man.

Individuals doing certain jobs on the car now wear different coloured gloves, so the lollipop man is looking for colours rather than actual people. When the wheels are finished he's looking for four yellow hands because everyone else's gloves in the pit stop are dark. He is looking for four fluorescent yellow hands, two jack men signalling to him thumbs up that everything is finished and then the refuelling man. We even tried putting the refuelling man in yellow overalls to make him more visible so we could see him, because the fuel always takes longer than the wheels, but the sponsor's influence put an end to that.

What appeared at first to have been a human error – the wheel nut not being securely fitted – was in fact caused by a failure of the wheel nut; the person fitting the wheel nut was attempting to replace the faulty nut with a new one, but the car had been released before it could be fitted. The system for signalling the release of the car – everyone raising their arm – was flawed and ambiguous, so they improved the system to ensure that it couldn't happen again. In a blame culture the individual would have been blamed and removed from the process, making it just a matter of time before it happened again. A no-blame culture maximises your opportunity to learn from every opportunity (see Chapter 4). Dickie Stanford's comment below helped us to crystallise the concept of the no-blame culture:

We don't hang anyone out to dry. You don't just point a finger at someone and say they're to blame. That doesn't help because all you do is create bad feeling. You try to isolate the problem, not the person.

It was interesting that these ideas came from Williams from their experience during the mid-nineties, as a recent article by their new Race Director, Rob Smedley, indicates that the quest for a no-blame philosophy is a constant one:

Perhaps Williams was a bit guilty in the past, and it's not the only team, of having a bit of a blame culture on the technical side. Pat [Symonds, Chief

Technical Officer] and I both have the same core value that you absolutely must not have a blame culture. When you have a blame culture, people spend 60–90 per cent of the effort covering what they have done rather than doing anything positive and understanding the problem, making the car go quicker or making operations slicker.

Smedley also suggests how leaders can begin to build a no-blame philosophy – by taking the responsibility themselves:

[I]f you actually say to people, 'look, that's my job. The buck stops with me, it's actually my fault', no matter who made the call, the situation is diffused very quickly. We're not looking for people to sack or for scapegoats, meaning people end up focusing on something positive.[61]

A further dimension of the no-blame philosophy relates to how it extends to the relationship with partners. Every F1 car is an alliance of different technical partners working together, and it is interesting to see how well they are able to collaborate, especially how they cope when things go wrong. At the 2015 Formula 1 Shell Belgian Grand Prix at Spa, Sebastian Vettel suffered a failure of one of his Pirelli tyres which led him to describe the situation regarding tyre failures as 'unacceptable' in an interview with the media. However, his boss, Ferrari Team Principal Maurizio Arrivabene, was more careful in his comments, and refused to get drawn into a battle of words across the media:

I don't want to open any kind of fight. I don't want to start a story going back and forwards.[62]

In contrast, the relationship between Red Bull Racing and their power-unit supplier, Renault, appeared to have broken down irretrievably during 2015, with RBR owner Dietrich Mateschitz making an unprecedented attack on Renault:

Beside taking our time and money they have destroyed our enjoyment and motivation – because no driver and no chassis in this world can compensate for this horsepower deficit.[63]

This led to a similarly unprecedented response from Renault CEO Carlos Ghosn:

So you are in the game that when you perform very well you are never mentioned, and when there is a problem with the team you are the first guy to be pointed [at] ... I think it's a question of sportsmanship. We are expecting, that when we are in a sport working with other people, we win together and we lose together.[64]

Perhaps unsurprisingly, towards the end of 2015 they were looking at ways to end their working relationship.

A non-F1 example of this is featured in Alastair Campbell's book *Winning*,[65] which describes how Willie Walsh, then CEO of British Airways, handled the crisis related to the opening of London Heathrow's Terminal 5 in 2008. Terminal 5 had been positioned as BA's flagship terminal and much was expected from its opening in March 2008. However, it soon became apparent that there were major issues with the baggage handling systems and BA had to cancel thirty-four flights and suspend the entire baggage handling system. Since Terminal 5 was effectively a joint venture between the British Airports Authority (BAA) and British Airways, it would have been very easy for Walsh to apportion blame on BAA, but his response to the first question from a journalist, '*Who's fault was this?*' was '*Mine, this was my decision to do this, I take responsibility and now I'm taking responsibility for fixing it.*' Leadership behaviours go a long way to sustaining or destroying the no-blame philosophy.

One-team mindset

The term 'silo' or 'stovepipes' are probably familiar to many in organisations. They refer to situations where vertical structures are created that focus on the performance of individual components of the system as opposed to the whole system. This can mean that the customer experience is poor, not because of any particular incompetence, but because the organisation does not operate in a joined up way to make the experience seamless. Similarly, government policy and healthcare stove-piping refers to situations where information is not shared across the organisation, and therefore overall objectives and patient-care standards are not met because there is no focus on the overall picture.

The one-team mindset is therefore the basis on which an organisation moves away from a silo or stovepipe mindset to something which considers the overall focus from the perspective of the whole organisation working as one team. In F1, probably the best example of the one-team mindset was that which Ferrari developed during the period of their unsurpassed dominance from 1999 to 2004. But the journey to achieve this was a long one, and John Barnard, Technical Director during the 1980s, was one of the first to try and shift the culture away from one which was based on silos, and also one where the engine department was the most important silo:

The first time at Ferrari I was overall technically in charge and that was my position in charge of the engine and everything. Obviously I couldn't be in day-to-day charge of the engine because a) I wasn't based there, I was based in Britain, and b) with a thing that big you have to work through managers so you have to be interfacing through one or two people but what I had to get into their head was that the engine had to be part of the package, you couldn't just let the engine designer say, 'Well, I'm going to hang the water pumps out here, I don't want to hang it on the chassis like that, I want to do it', so you have to then dictate to the engine people how you want the package to work.

This problem was that even if Ferrari produced a great engine, if it was developed purely as an engine it would compromise other aspects of the design such as the aerodynamics or the chassis, and therefore meant that overall performance was undermined. After Barnard, this concept was taken forward by his successor as Technical Director, Ross Brawn, who, as noted earlier, described the one-team mindset as a form of innovation – the integration of the whole:

Ferrari doesn't have an individual feature, perhaps it never has had, but our innovation is an integration of the whole. Our efforts have always been to make everything as good as it can be, but to work together as a complete package.

The fact that Ferrari, unlike most of the UK-based F1 teams, also designed and built its own engines was a potential source of advantage, not in terms of producing the best engine, but in terms of getting the whole package to work together:

It's only really within Ferrari or a team that's doing the whole package where I think you can achieve the ultimate, otherwise you're working at a distance, and however willing the partners are it's not as good as the fact that Paolo's [Martinelli, Engine Director] office is thirty metres from mine and the same people are all working together to achieve the objective of the car. A Ferrari is a Ferrari, it's not an engine, it's not a chassis, it's not an aero package, it's a Ferrari.

Ross Brawn was also very clear that this is not question of organisational structure or location, it's a way of thinking:

It's a state of mind that you just enter into the job without looking for, well, 'excuses' is the wrong word, but I'm just as unhappy if we've got problems with the engine as I am if we've got problems with the car and Paolo's the same, it's never, 'Well, that's his problem, I'm doing my bit alright.'

Long-term perspective

Formula 1 is famed for its incredibly short time scales, as famously described by Flavio Briatore, in that it really is equivalent to having a year-end statement but every two weeks:

Every two weeks you present your balance sheet. Every two weeks people are judging if you have done a good or a bad job.

But in the context of a winning culture, a long-term perspective is key, as once a team gets fixated totally on the short term they lose the ability to stand back and focus on the long term, on Championships rather than each individual race, a problem that was not lost on F1 driver Mark Webber when reflecting on his career:

I once read something by Stirling Moss saying that his first aim was always to win whatever race he was in, and that's why he never won a championship. I could relate to that: back then [in Mark's early career] I was never concerned with trying to build up for a championship. But time showed that to be a strategy that didn't really work in terms of trying to put championships together.[14]

Toto Wolff also believes that Mercedes Benz needs to take a longer-term perspective, particularly if it is to outperform some of the great achievements of other teams in F1:

We compare ourselves to the best and if you look at the best, you must admit that we haven't even won the second Championship or the second year [statement made in July 2015] – Red Bull did it four times in a row and before that, Ferrari as the clear benchmark did it five or six times in a row. So there is no reason in here to believe that we are any better or that we are great – we've beaten some records, we've won more races than anybody else before, but also because there are more races. So if you are completely honest, there have been many more great people out there first. And this is important to remind yourself all the time.

The turnaround at Ferrari during 2015 has been partly attributed to the influence of Technical Director James Allison, who joined from Lotus in mid-2013. Ferrari endured a fairly torrid year in 2014 with one of their worst performances since before the Schumacher era, but in 2015 they have been the closest challenger to Mercedes. Allison says his main influence so far has been to end a culture of short-term thinking and ease the pressure on the design team by bringing a long-term mindset to Ferrari's technical department.

[I'm here] to make sure pressure has been taken off people to deliver things for next week but to work with a slightly long time scale in mind – which frees up your hand to do a good job. It's hard to do anything in a two to three month timescale. You need to build a programme over months and years rather than weeks.[66]

In considering the role of building a winning culture in organisations, we can discern a further number of management lessons that can be drawn from Formula 1 into other areas. We summarise these as follows:

Lesson 9 Maintain open and constant communication

During our research, one concept was voiced by virtually all the individuals we interviewed: the importance of maintaining an open flow of communication involving everyone in the organisation. This communication takes place both formally and informally, on a small and large scale, in person and virtually.

Lesson 10 Isolate the problem not the person: the no-blame philosophy

Here we pick up on Williams F1's Dickie Stanford's comment that when something has gone wrong, the focus must be put on resolving the problem in a systemic sense, rather than blaming the person. This is difficult to achieve in practice. In many instances, when a team falls into difficult times it goes through a period of blame to explain the failure. It is the ability to break out of this blame culture which often leads to a period of further success. This can be stimulated by improved performance, but to be sustained it has to be underpinned by a work environment that allows failures to be shared and openly discussed by all.

Lesson 11 Be realistic about what can be achieved

Continual change is necessary in order to keep pace with competitors' strategic actions and customers' ever-changing demands. However, change fatigue is not an unusual problem in organisations today. One of the important lessons that can be drawn from the recent success of Ferrari is that change in organisations has to take place within realistic constraints, otherwise the development process may fall apart. Setting high but realistic goals and keeping everyone apprised of progress against those goals is a key factor in driving the change process forward.

Lesson 12 Never believe you can keep winning

The *Icarus Paradox*[67] considers the problem of success blinding the organisation to future threats. In the case of Ferrari, the solution against this appears to be to refuse to believe that you are inherently capable of being consistently successful. Always assume each win is your last victory and, therefore, you will continually search for those extra tenths of seconds that will sustain you at the top. There is not a better time to challenge one's processes and methods, or business strategy for that matter, than when leading the industry. The really hard part is maintaining the pressure and urgency to do so while retaining the energy and motivation that is so important for the team. That is one reason why Ferrari was able to build such a formidable record in 1999–2004.

While vying for a second Constructors' Championship in 2015, which they eventually did achieve, Toto Wolff, Head of Mercedes Motorsport, was well aware that his team could not ride on the successes of the past. He told us,

Complacency is a danger. I had a discussion with one of our top guys on the days after Melbourne [Australian GP 2015, where Mercedes finished 1–2] and he said, 'You know what, it is bizarre, I come to my office and we've all seen the race and we are all very happy, but it is not the same wow factor as we had last year.' How should we tackle that? We have a system in place how to tackle that, but as a matter of fact, the next race in Malaysia we got a slap! We lost against Ferrari! And somehow this came as a wake-up call that if you just give up a millimetre, or if you are not hungry any more, you will lose. I think that plays a crucial role. If you look at the teams in the past where they've been very successful over a couple of years, it is important to maintain the same hunger with the same group of people. Of course, you have to keep that group of people together – that's why this system works very well; we have nobody leaving us within the top performer group; but that is going to bite us one day if we are not proactive.

10 | *Learning from F1 teams*

Formula 1 teams have built up experience and expertise working in a fast-paced, ever-changing business environment. They have come to realise, initially through informal channels and more recently through carefully thought-out business strategies, that they can apply these competencies to other industries. In doing so, they are creating cash-generating business activities that smooth out the potential cyclicality of their business and support their primary objective of 'going racing'. Some of the teams have even created separate business entities to leverage these capabilities, such as McLaren Applied Technologies and Williams Advanced Engineering.

Ferrari and Great Ormond Street Hospital

Perhaps the most well-known example of knowledge transfer from Formula 1 to other industries is the case of Ferrari and Great Ormond Street Hospital (GOSH) in the United Kingdom. The story begins in the mid-1990s in the city of Bristol, where there were very high mortality rates for surgery in congenital heart disease, which prompted a contentious public inquiry. In a subsequent study of the situation, a key finding was that that the patient's journey from the operating room to the intensive care unit (ICU) was high risk.[68]

Moving the story forward to a Sunday in 2003, after a particularly tough day in the operating theatre, Dr Allan Goldman and surgeon Martin Elliot were watching a Formula 1 race on television. Both were racing fans, and they noticed striking similarities between the interchange of tasks at a racing pit stop and patient handovers at their hospital. But while a twenty-member crew could switch a car's tyres, adjust its front wing, clean the air vents and send the car roaring off in seven seconds (a fast pit stop for that period), hospital handovers seemed downright clunky by comparison. They clearly saw the F1 pit stop as analogous to the team effort of surgeons, anaesthetists, nurses and Intensive Care Unit (ICU) staff in transferring the patient, equipment and information safely and quickly from the operating room to ICU.

In fact, the *Wall Street Journal* reported two years later, in 2005, a study that *'found that nearly 70% of preventable hospital mishaps occurred because of communication problems, and other studies have shown that at least half of such breakdowns occur during handoffs'*.[69]

Back in 2003, the two doctors invited members of McLaren F1 to provide insights into pit-stop activities and movements. Armed with videos and slides, the racing team described how they used a human-factors expert to study the way their pit crews performed. They also explained how their system for recording errors stressed the small ones that might go unnoticed, not the big ones that everyone knew about.

After employing their own human-factors expert, the hospital contacted the Ferrari F1 team, which invited a team of doctors from the hospital to attend their practice sessions at the British Grand Prix in order to get a closer look at pit stops. GOSH doctors then visited and observed the pit crew at Ferrari's headquarters in Maranello, Italy. There they noted the value of process mapping, process description and working out specific tasks for each individual. Following their trip, the GOSH team videotaped the handover in the surgery unit and sent it to be reviewed by Ferrari. From the analysis a new handover protocol was developed with more sophisticated procedures and better choreographed teamwork.

The GOSH researchers also noted the important role of the lollipop man, the one who waves the F1 car into position from the pit lane and oversees the whole pit stop (still in use at that time, although it has since been replaced by the light system today). Under the new handover process, the anaesthetist was given overall responsibility for coordinating the team until it was transferred to the intensive care personnel at the termination of the handover. The lead surgeon and the anaesthetist were charged with the responsibility of periodically stepping back to look at the big picture and to make safety checks of the handover.

After the changes, the average number of technical errors per handover fell by 42 per cent and 'information handover omissions' fell by 49 per cent. It also took slightly less time to execute each handover, though, unlike the Ferrari team, the doctors were not trying to speed up their process.

The Great Ormond Street Hospital demonstrates the value derived from a deep understanding of how an F1 team, nowadays changing four tyres in 2.5 seconds, can offer consequent insights into attaining smooth teamwork, more effective communication, better process management and an all-important attention to detail.

Dr Goldman and co-author Richard West have since jointly presented updates on this story to a number of medical and pharmaceutical conferences drawing on Dr Goldman's surgical and West's Formula 1 experiences. Together, they cover parallel activities from these two worlds that relate to communication, integration of resources, and strategic planning and review. After their appearance at the the Association for Perioperative Practice (AfPP) Nurses Conference in the United Kingdom, Diane Gilmour, President of the AfPP said:

Richard and Allan's presentation emphasised leadership, teamwork and the ability to change. This created a buzz for all attendees and enabled team working to become an underlying theme in many sessions that followed.

Other organisations have also benefited from pit-stop analyses, including the Royal Air Force in the United Kingdom. They must be on alert 24/7, their crews and aircraft in a permanent state of readiness. In the mid-2000s they faced significant budget cuts, but were still expected to maintain readiness even with these reductions. They achieved that mission, in part, by looking at how pit-stop crews and F1 mechanics working in the garage positioned their kit, tools and test equipment in pre-determined positions, thus making their movements more efficient and less time consuming.

Another example comes from Air Asia, a Malaysian no-frills, budget airline founded by Tony Fernandez. Fernandez was, incidentally, also the founder of the Caterham F1 team, which began racing in 2010 as Lotus Racing and then raced in 2011 as Team Lotus before the team was then sold in 2014. The budget airline business is based on large volumes and low prices. A critical factor for success therefore is getting planes in the air as soon as possible where they can produce revenue. Viewing the plane turnaround processes while on the ground as if it was a pit stop, Air Asia developed cabin-cleaning, plane-refuelling and passenger-loading processes that emphasised speed and agility without sacrificing attention to detail.

As with the Great Ormond Street Hospital story, other areas of the medical profession benefits and will continue to benefit greatly from Formula 1 expertise. The transferable learnings go beyond what can be gleaned from observing and replicating pit stops. Brad Hollinger is Chairman and CEO of Vibra Healthcare, a provider of acute rehabilitation and long-term acute care hospitalisation across the United States. Since 2015, Hollinger has also been a shareholder in Williams F1. Apart from being a lifelong racing enthusiast, as a successful businessman he sees what Formula 1 has to offer his field:

I see some very exciting opportunities for us coming from Williams Applied Technologies. We face many challenges to improve efficiency and reduce costs in the healthcare business in the USA. The capabilities and knowledge found within F1 racing teams can be applied to help streamline processes, improve collection of patient information remotely, and create software applications tailored to our specific needs.

McLaren Applied Technologies

Using its remote sensors and telemetry expertise from F1 experiences, McLaren Applied Technologies (MAT) is helping doctors at Oxford University Hospitals in the United Kingdom to monitor patients' progress after treatment. According to Dr Caroline Hargrove, Director of Performance at MAT, in a BBC.com interview:

We put sensors on people and, we get much better objective feel for the level of activity, its intensity and how well they sleep. That gives us a much better picture of how well that person is.[70]

Such granular monitoring is routine in F1 racing cars, but not for patients. She also noted that,

pre-operative monitoring combined together with post-operative monitoring could help to reduce the guess work in medicine.

MAT has also taken medical application beyond monitoring of patients. They are providing Oxford University Hospitals with decision support, based on F1 racing experience using data analysis techniques that might maximise patients' opportunities for positive treatment outcomes. According to Fred Hamdy, Head of Nuffield Department of Surgical Sciences at Oxford,

Applying McLaren's simulator to medical situations is going to be a complete paradigm shift in how we implement new techniques.

Further in the medical profession, Dr Robert L. Masson, an internationally recognised neurosurgeon specialising in spinal injury and sports spine medicine, applies the metaphor of high-performance race-car driving to his surgical procedures and his teaching. His 'Racing Paradigm' is having a major impact on the performance successes of surgeons across the USA. In his own words,

I passionately believe that the motorsports metaphor is ideal for the performance effort in health care.

Aki Hintsa, whose contribution to fitness of Formula 1 drivers was described earlier, retired from the sport in 2014; but his philosophy and approaches developed through his association with World Champion drivers such as Mika Häkkinen, Kimi Räikkönen, Lewis Hamilton and Sebastian Vettel continue to be espoused in the paddock through personal coaches and trainers who he has trained. In 2015, Hintsa's company, Performance Management, merged with HeiaHeia.com, a technology company that offers a digital all-in-one social platform for individual and corporate wellness. Companies such as PepsiCo, IKEA and the United Kingdom's National Health Service have adopted the company's well-being software.

F1 technologies and expertise are being applied in many other contexts as well.

GlaxoSmithKline, the health and pharmaceutical product conglomerate, struggled with the thirty-nine-minute changeover of its toothpaste manufacturing line when switching between brands such as AquaFresh and Sensodyne. After analysis by MAT, that changeover time was reduced to fifteen minutes. This change theoretically enabled GSK to fill an additional 6.7 million tubes of toothpaste every year. In practice, the company has used the time savings to switch production streams more often and more easily, as dictated by demand.

MAT is also working with a consortium of companies to improve efficiency at Heathrow Airport Limited. The group, which also includes NATS, Siemens Postal, Parcel and Airport Logistics and AVTECH Sweden AB, won a four-year contract that will deliver enhanced capacity-management capabilities throughout the UK's busiest airport. The real-time software employed is based on the technology used by race strategists in the McLaren Formula 1 team. It is able to assess multiple factors that can affect efficiency, including stand reallocation, taxiway closures, schedule delays and weather conditions. These data feeds will be monitored and analysed simultaneously to provide instantaneous decision-making support. According to MAT's Dr Caroline Hargrove, newfound efficiencies brought a 19 per cent increase in capacity at Heathrow.

Williams Advanced Engineering

Shifting to the consumer space, Williams Advanced Engineering (WAE) has collaborated with a UK start-up, Aerofoil Energy, to develop new aerodynamic device that can significantly reduce the energy consumed by refrigerators in supermarkets and convenience stores. Energy consumption makes up a significant percentage of a supermarket's operational costs, with energy-hungry refrigerators that keep produce cool the largest consumer of power. Open-fronted multi-deck refrigerators that line the aisles of supermarkets consume excessive energy, with some of the cold air used to cool produce spilling out into the aisles, resulting in increased energy consumption and 'cold aisle syndrome' which can be unpleasant for shoppers.

Aerofoils are carefully designed and engineered profiles that control the direction of air flow. These are essential in Formula 1 car design. Aerofoil Energy and WAE are developing a new aerofoil system that can be retrofitted and attached onto each refrigerator shelf to keep more of the cool air inside the refrigerator cabinet. This technology will result in significant energy savings for supermarkets and convenience stores, with corresponding benefits for their carbon footprint. The technology will also make the shopping experience more pleasant.

A number of supermarkets are evaluating the aerofoil technology, and the results are promising. Sainsbury's, the UK's second-largest supermarket chain, has been testing the product at a number of its stores. Sainsbury's operates 1,100 stores and uses 1 per cent of the UK's energy in total. As part of its 20x20 Sustainability Plan, Sainsbury's has committed to reducing its absolute operational carbon emissions by 30 per cent by 2020, and this technology can play a key role in achieving this target.

WAE is also working with Hanergy Solar Power UK, the entity in charge of Commercial Solar Developments and Innovative Renewable Technologies Developments for the United Kingdom. Hanergy will start to utilise Williams Advanced Engineering's extensive experience in different forms of energy-storage technology in two clean-energy projects based on the development of advanced energy-storage technologies to optimise solar-power generation. Finding a reliable way to store and reuse energy is seen as crucial in unlocking the true potential of renewable energy sources for both commercial and residential use.

It should be noted that WAE is also drawing upon the battery systems used in Williams' Formula One cars to create new battery and battery management systems that are capable of powering a fully electric racing car in the new Formula E electric car series. As one might expect where speed and motion are involved, F1 technology has a contribution to make.

The British bike manufacturer Brompton is using Formula 1 technology to produce its own pedal-electric bikes. Once considered bulky and heavy and only for the lazy or unfit, electric bikes are catching on among commuters as they allow faster travel for less effort. About 854,000 electric bikes were sold in Europe in 2012, with sales in Germany making up almost half the total. In China, they are already a big business. Working with WAE, Brompton is developing a lightweight electric bike that, like F1 power units, would be capable of using F1 kinetic energy recovery system technology, which works by using waste energy created by braking and transforming it into electrical energy when the driver needs extra power to accelerate.

Sauber Motorsport

In recent years, Sauber Motorsport has also used expertise acquired in its F1 racing experience to participate in important revenue-generating commercial projects to support the cash flow needs of this private F1 racing team. Monisha Kaltenborn, Team Principal of Sauber Motorsport AG, told us,

We use the infrastructure we have to provide engineering services for other motorsport areas or even areas outside motorsport. So, for example, on the aerodynamic services side we use our wind tunnel to provide aerodynamics services related with CFD [computational fluid dynamics] services because you have that very close link today. We also develop software which we sell [and] offer various consultancies from set-up services, mechanical engineering consultancies and other specific areas.

In one specific case, Sauber is assisting SwissBob, a company responsible for building a monobob, a new racing series for junior athletes under the auspices of the International Bobsleigh & Skeleton Federation. Monisha Kaltenborn commented,

Formula One and bobsleigh racing have a great deal in common, such as the aerodynamics of the bob, the physical principles underpinning the development of the chassis and the process engineering involved in the construction of the monocoque, which is new to bobsleigh.

Lifeline fire suppression systems

Formula 1 technology also has a role to play where safety is concerned. Peter Digby of Xtrac reminded us of Lifeline, a producer of fire suppression systems,

However, I am aware that some companies have made the successful transition of racing technology transfer such as Lifeline, the fire extinguisher, fire suppression system which has been used in racing cars for many, many years. Authorities realised they needed to protect troops in Afghanistan by installing their equipment on military vehicles.

According to Lifeline, they are the leading manufacturer of on-board fire suppression systems to the motorsport industry (including Formula 1, Le Mans series and IndyCar). This experience, they say, has made them ideally placed to supply the defence market in order to meet exacting military requirements.

We, the authors, have our own experience applying Formula 1 team management concepts and business lessons to industries that have included telecommunications, banking, professional and public services, manufacturing, production, air traffic control and airports, mining and many others. We have worked as a trio, in pairs and also solo, running seminars and delivering speaking engagements that have brought insights from *Performance at the Limit* to business executives and their teams around the world.

Further examples of learning from F1

In addition to roles within the finance, mining, aviation and shipping sectors, Richard West has been working with Metro Trains Melbourne, Australia. The city's metropolitan rail service, Metro operates 203 six--carriage trains across 830 km of track, transporting 415,000 customers each day utilising 15 lines and 218 stations and providing services seven days a week. Andrew Lezala, Chief Executive Officer at Metro Trains Melbourne, said:

We are using Performance at the Limit *in a programme aimed at focusing the employees on performance, safety and continuous-improvement methodology. The Pit Stop Challenge, where team members actually change the tyres on a resident Formula 1 car, has been a key component of this experience. Less than one year into the programme, we are already noticing a marked improvement in staff engagement in processes such as the development of core working teams. In a short time, we have cleared a backlog of work going back some two-and-a-half years, freeing up a further 100 hours of maintenance hours per week, which is now being used on further service and examination work enabling us to run a safer and more efficient network.*

Feedback from staff who have experienced the programme attest to the value added, as various respondents explained:

We are doing more work than before but we are not working any harder ... Teams are the best thing we've ever done – everyone's lifted their game ... Should have done this years ago ... There is more trust and understanding – both ways ... Everyone's more involved and making more of an effort.

In a previous position with London Underground, Lezala contracted West to use PATL principles and the Pit Stop Challenge where, as a result, track teams established new records in track-sleeper replacement programmes, increasing the original three to four sleeper replacements per night to a total of thirty-two replacements per night. This resulted in a productivity saving to the business of £64 million in one year.

Among various applications of PATL lessons, Ken Pasternak has used Formula 1 case studies and related exercises in senior management workshops, whose purpose has included aligning the top leadership team with the organisation's vision, mission and values, as well as examining ways to work more effectively together. In one case, that of a Middle Eastern bank, the CEO bought miniature models of

Ferraris several weeks after the seminar to remind his direct reports of the transformation process Ferrari went through that parallels many of the challenges the bank was attempting to overcome.

Mark Jenkins has worked with a wide range of organisations, using Formula 1 to stimulate ideas and initiatives around the themes outlined in this book. Recently, a senior manager of a global organisation remarked how he had visited a plant in Austria where Mark had given a presentation several years earlier, and one of the managers he was talking to explained that he had to leave their meeting to go to the weekly Monday morning 'race meeting'. This was a gathering where the plant's management presented a review of last week's performance and outlined the priorities going forward for the following week, involving everyone in the factory – several hundred employees. This idea had come directly from the F1 presentation, and is a great example of how the Formula 1 debrief was being applied in practice to improve organisational performance.

In many executive development programmes, F1 can be a powerful learning tool, as illustrated by the following comments from delegates:

Lots of learning here! ... Contingency – don't rest on laurels or become complacent ... Review lessons from successes ... Foster culture of team and all components are equally important ... Very powerful ... Loads of metaphors to externalise internal debate ... Often helps remove bias and emotion to externalise it by looking at a very different context.

But it's not just the obvious technology and commercial firms that learn from F1. In public sector organisations there is much to gain from an F1 approach to dealing with regulation:

Regulation is often seen as a barrier to innovation but F1 is one of the most innovative industries. Perhaps the public sector could move from its position of 'learned helplessness' in the face of increasing regulation and learn from F1's approach.

One delegate from a housing association in the UK made the following comment when asked what the highlights of the programme were for them:

Formula 1 – I didn't think this would be as interesting and transferable as it was, the one-team mindset and the no-blame philosophy were the real takeaways for me.

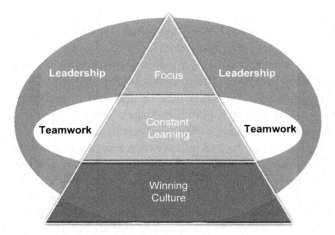

Figure 18 The F1 Performance Pyramid

Using the Performance Pyramid

The F1 Performance Pyramid, outlined in Chapter 2 and reproduced here, is a powerful framework for considering a number of key questions arising from the Formula 1 context and the implications for all organisations.

Do you have a clear focus?

The basis of success in F1 is that everyone in the organisation has a clear sense of what they are trying to achieve. If such clarity does not exist then it is difficult, if not impossible, to provide the clarity of decisions and the focus on learning needed to perform at the highest level. As Figure 18 shows, this is the responsibility of leaders and the leadership team to help create the clarity and focus of purpose. Sir Frank Williams' question '*Will it make the car go faster?*' demonstrates how clarity of purpose can help to both endorse and challenge organisational decisions and investments being made. A clear focus helps to provide an agenda for decisions and resources and it also helps to define where the organisation should *not* spend time and effort: an effective focus makes it just as clear as to what you will not do as it does for what you will do.

An alternative way of framing this question is to ask *'What does winning look like for you?'* This question helps to establish whether there is some level of agreement as to what the organisation is actually looking to achieve, or whether there are many diverse views on this. When one of the authors posed this question to a group of eight senior managers of a financial services company, they wrote down eight different answers – if they do not have a shared view of what the organisation is trying to achieve, what chance do their teams have?

Do you learn from every learning opportunity?

Formula 1 has clearly defined learning events, whether these are a practice session, qualifying, the race, a season or the introduction of a new car. The challenge in other organisations is to work out what is a learning event for you? When are the points at which you can effectively review? As we have discussed, F1 is data driven and therefore every learning opportunity is supported by data so that the discussion is focused on interpretation and next steps, rather than debating or working out what has actually just happened. Therefore, clarifying the points at which you have the data to sensibly review in a timely manner is critical – not too frequent so that you have no chance to really extract the learnings and put them into practice, but not too slow so that you lose the advantage over the competition. These could be a quarterly sales period, a new product introduction, the delivery of a module on a course, a one-day conference or a weekly production performance from a manufacturing plant. Once you are clear on the points at which learning can usefully occur, you need to define the review process and make sure that this is focused on the basic debrief/review structure as outlined by Christian Horner:

After each Grand Prix there will be a debrief with the whole factory talking about the events of the weekend: What we did well, what we didn't do so well, what are the targets for the short term and what changes we are going to make.

Do you have a winning culture?

As outlined in Chapter 9, a winning culture can be characterised by four aspects:

- routine *constant communication* with everyone in the organisation (as exemplified by Christian Horner above);
- a *no-blame philosophy* – where individuals are supported by their peers and their superiors when mistakes happen in a way that enables a climate of honest reflection in order to improve performance, rather than a dysfunctional blame culture where everyone focuses on blaming their colleagues or other departments or partners, rather than trying to openly discover where the real problem lies. Without the no-blame philosophy, mistakes will always be repeated and performance will never truly improve;
- a *one-team mindset* – everyone is working for one team, not their individual departments or elements. Everyone understands what the one team is and, although they need to focus and deliver on their part of the jigsaw puzzle, they also understand that it all must fit together to deliver the ultimate performance;
- *long-term perspective* – are you driven by the tyranny of the short term? If you only focus on the next race you will never be a champion. You need to focus on the longer term (as well as delivering in the short term) as this will give you the perspective and vision as to how it will all come together.

Do you have the leaders and the teams to make this sustainable?

The pyramid aligns the challenge of leadership with providing focus and enacting the winning culture. Leaders therefore need a strategic perspective and need to be able communicate what this means to all stakeholders inside and outside the organisation; perhaps most importantly, in a way which is not about soundbites and PowerPoints but through actions and stories that capture the essence of the organisation. Think about Frank Williams only signing cheques to make the car go faster. Leaders at all levels need to be thinking of the focus of the organisation and demonstrating constant communication, a no-blame philosophy, a one-team mindset and a long-term perspective. Is this how people become leaders in your organisation? If not, you may not have the leadership capability to deliver the high performance that is needed.

So perhaps a subset to these questions could be, do your leaders:

1 Have a clear focus for the organisation, one which they constantly communicate to all stakeholders?
2 Demonstrate a no-blame philosophy by consistently taking responsibility for mistakes and errors themselves?
3 Repeatedly underline that there is only one team, whether or not they are responsible for a distinct part of the organisation?
4 Maintain a long-term perspective and avoid short-term panics to deliver short-term results?

Teams must be based around a constant learning approach. They have to have a clear focus, but above all they have to work in a way that allows them to learn and improve. If your teams don't develop and learn, neither will the organisation. So a further subset here could be, do your teams:

1 Have a clear understanding of their focus and overall objective?
2 Recognise the key points and stages when learning can be achieved through review?
3 Always act as one team, but also recognise that they are part of a bigger single team?

Management lessons from Formula 1 motor racing

In the first and second editions of this book, we distilled twelve lessons from Formula 1 that might be applicable in part or in whole to organisations in other industries. Since then, we have had opportunities to discuss and test these concepts during our speaking and teaching engagements, with a large number of businesses representing different industries and countries. Our judgement is that they are as well-received, germane and as much on-target today as when they were first written.

These lessons are the underpinning of our performance framework shown in Figure 5. In the framework we explain organisational performance as a function of individuals, teams and partners coming together; and by integrating, innovating and transforming these elements in changing competitive situations, sustainable performance can be achieved.

These lessons are not instant panaceas that every organisation should necessarily adopt, but they do offer insights that will help business leaders who are trying to galvanise their organisations into becoming more performance-focused, flexible, innovative and, above all, more competitive.

Lesson 1 Focus, focus, focus

The rigour of a nineteen- or twenty-race season puts a heightened premium on getting the right job done at the right time. It seems quite a basic concept, given the industry's often changing regulatory constraints, the budgetary limitations under which many teams operate and very tight deadlines that must be met. Formula 1 teams must focus on the tasks at hand in order to be on the grid with an improved car, week after week. Even in this context, we have seen examples of where successful teams have lost their focus, lost their edge and ultimately paid a very high price: perhaps most famously through McLaren's departure into high-performance, limited-edition road cars in the early 1990s (the McLaren F1). Likewise, drivers who are facing great demands on their time have to learn to focus on what truly matters, which in the end is performance on the track.

Lesson 2 One team – alignment of goals between individuals, teams and partners

There are two parts to the issue of alignment. One is commonality of goals towards which teams and sub-teams in the organisation are striving. The other is the connection between individuals' actions and the end result. Perhaps this is best illustrated in the way that Frank Williams constantly asks the question when signing cheques: '*How will it make the car go faster?*' against which all can measure the value of their specific contributions on a day-to-day basis. From the Formula 1 team partner's perspective, the question may be different: '*Will it help us sell more products?*' It is the continual alignment of these factors that helps to optimise business processes in Formula 1 teams.

Lesson 3 Build the organisation around informal processes, networks and relationships

Across all of the teams we found a common emphasis on building from the expertise and relationships of the people within the organisation and the partners allied to the business. This approach enables the structure to emerge from these relationships, rather than imposing a 'theoretical' organisation which is populated by rigid, specified roles and job descriptions that do not relate to the pressurised world that Formula 1 teams inhabit.

Perhaps we could criticise those teams who do not have ready-to-hand organisational charts or detailed job descriptions. Clearly these are important aspects of modern organisational life. But in a situation where there is real commitment and passion from employees, the lack of such management tools illustrates how the organisation becomes 'empowered' by removing layers of potentially needless bureaucracy.

In reality, we know that organisation charts rarely reflect how people in the business actually work together or relate to one another in terms of getting tasks completed. The Formula 1 organisation is an emergent structure that is designed to optimise and facilitate the potential of individuals and their relationships, rather than determining and micro-managing such interactions. The conclusion that we reach is that it is only through effectively supporting these interactions and relationships that performance can be truly optimised.

In business management there is a mantra that structure drives strategy, which in turn drives performance. In Formula 1, people and their relationships drive the structure, which in turn drives performance. Perhaps surprisingly given its strong technology orientation, Formula 1 is a very people-driven business.

Lesson 4 Leaders exist at all levels of the organisation

Due to the fast pace of this industry, employees throughout Formula 1 teams are empowered to make decisions, drive processes and take risks. We have witnessed people at all levels within Formula 1 organisations stepping up to be accountable and to lead their colleagues when it is their time to take responsibility.

This means that the more senior roles are concerned with problem-solving and connecting up different parts of the organisation, rather than coaching or directing. At times this can be problematic, particularly where big egos are not in short supply, but the lesson here is to recognise that in the most successful teams people are prepared to put their heads above the parapet and lead their project or initiative. Also, in these contexts, the drivers are not prima donnas but real catalysts for the team, encouraging everyone to play their part to achieve performance at the limit.

Lesson 5 Make quick decisions and learn from the results

Seeing the opportunity, being decisive and then learning from the result of one's actions is central to continual improvement of performance in this fast-paced environment. These ideas fit closely with the concept of the learning organisation, where continual experimentation and learning provide the basis from which firms move forward. Formula 1 teams have to continually learn from their mistakes otherwise they soon fall off the pace and lose the interest of their sponsors.

But for it to work, it also requires a culture where individuals are not constrained from trying something, and where failure does not undermine their position or credibility in the organisation.

Lesson 6 The real gains come at the boundaries

The real performance gains occur at the margins, at the boundaries between the various interfaces, whether these are component areas of the car, between partner organisations or between different teams and sub-teams. These are the gains that are particularly difficult to achieve and sustain, but they are the ones that will make the difference in performance if all other areas are working effectively. When teams are operating at the top of their game, their focus moves from building up particular specialist competences to integrating the whole system and ensuring that it operates to the maximum. In order to deliver the best racing package, barriers between functional departments must be eliminated so that communication between and across them can be clear, constant and directed towards achieving their common goals.

Lesson 7 Measure everything

Formula 1 is first and foremost an engineering-based industry. In that context, the delivery of the key product, a fast Formula 1 car, is entirely contingent on design, manufacture and refinement, using the latest in software, telemetry and computer capacity to measure everything. Measurement comes into play at the factory, in the pit lane, on the track and also, as we have seen, in the physiological readings of the drivers. Like all people in business, Formula 1 teams have to determine what useful information can be drawn out of the massive amount of data that is captured. They must apply reasonable thinking to utilise that information, to make strategic and tactical decisions. In turn, those decisions need to evolve, usually very quickly, into actionable tasks. Once delivered, the impacts of those tasks are measured, and the process starts over again. Recording of input and measurement of output goes beyond the teams themselves, and is the primary process by which sponsors determine whether their investment in the sport provides the returns they are seeking.

When a business is using scorecards of some sort or re-engineering techniques, it is embracing a model of measurement, evaluation and action in the organisation, just as Formula 1 teams do.

Lesson 8 At the edge, not over it

This may be an obvious statement, but conflict within an organisation can undo all of the strong efforts and goodwill that has been built to that point. Given the competitive nature of the individuals in Formula 1 and the fact that they operate within a media fishbowl, it is not uncommon that dirty laundry is aired in public. Whether it is an employee disgruntled because he was passed up for promotion who then shares insider information with a competitor, or two drivers on the same team who cannot seem to get along, their attitudes and actions most certainly impact the organisation's culture and eventually performance in a negative way.

Organisations that have a culture where people feel free to share their thoughts with peers and bosses without reprisal, where managers are in touch with their employees' aspirations and development needs and that foster teamwork as a guiding value are less prone to find themselves operating with internal conflict situations that get out of hand.

Lesson 9 Maintain open and constant communication

During our research, one concept was voiced by virtually all the individuals we interviewed: the importance of maintaining an open flow of communication involving everyone in the organisation. This communication takes place both formally and informally, on a small and large scale, in person and virtually.

Lesson 10 Isolate the problem not the person: the no-blame philosophy

Here we pick up on Williams F1's Dickie Stanford's comment that when something has gone wrong, the focus must be put on resolving the problem in a systemic sense, rather than blaming the person. This is difficult to achieve in practice. In many instances, when a team falls into difficult times it goes through a period of blame to explain the failure. It is the ability to break out of this blame culture which often leads to a period of further success. This can be stimulated by improved performance, but to be sustained it has to be underpinned by a work environment that allows failures to be shared and openly discussed by all.

Lesson 11 Be realistic about what can be achieved

Continual change is necessary in order to keep pace with competitors' strategic actions and customers' ever-changing demands. However, change fatigue is not an unusual problem in organisations today. One of the important lessons that can be drawn from the recent success of Ferrari is that change in organisations has to take place within realistic constraints, otherwise the development process may fall apart. Setting high but realistic goals and keeping everyone apprised of progress against those goals is a key factor in driving the change process forward.

Lesson 12 Never believe you can keep winning

The *Icarus Paradox*[67] considers the problem of success blinding the organisation to future threats. In the case of Ferrari, the solution to this problem appears to be to refuse to believe that you are inherently capable of being consistently successful. Always assume each win is your last victory and, therefore, you will continually search for those extra tenths of seconds that will sustain you at the top. There is not a better time to challenge one's processes and methods, or business strategy for that matter, than when leading the industry. The really hard part is maintaining the pressure and urgency to do so while retaining the energy and motivation that is so important for the team. That is one reason why Ferrari has been able to build such a formidable record in recent years.

Appendix A: Grand Prix Champions 1950–2015

Year	Drivers' Cup	Car/Engine	Constructors' Cup
1950	Giuseppe Farina	Alfa Romeo	
1951	Juan Manuel Fangio	Alfa Romeo	
1952	Alberto Ascari	Ferrari	
1953	Alberto Ascari	Ferrari	
1954	Juan Manuel Fangio	Maserati	
1955	Juan Manuel Fangio	Mercedes-Benz	
1956	Juan Manuel Fangio	Lancia-Ferrari	
1957	Juan Manuel Fangio	Maserati	
1958	Mike Hawthorn	Ferrari	Vanwall
1959	Jack Brabham	Cooper/Climax	Cooper/Climax
1960	Jack Brabham	Cooper/Climax	Cooper/Climax
1961	Phil Hill	Ferrari	Ferrari
1962	Graham Hill	BRM	BRM
1963	Jim Clark	Lotus/Climax	Lotus/Climax
1964	John Surtees	Ferrari	Ferrari
1965	Jim Clark	Lotus/Climax	Lotus/Climax
1966	Jack Brabham	Brabham/Repco	Brabham/Repco
1967	Denny Hulme	Brabham/Repco	Brabham/Repco
1968	Graham Hill	Lotus/Ford	Lotus/Ford
1969	Jackie Stewart	Matra/Ford	Matra/Ford
1970	Jochen Rindt	Lotus/Ford	Lotus/Ford
1971	Jackie Stewart	Tyrrell/Ford	Tyrrell/Ford
1972	Emerson Fittipaldi	Lotus/Ford	Lotus/Ford
1973	Jackie Stewart	Tyrrell/Ford	Lotus/Ford
1974	Emerson Fittipaldi	McLaren/Ford	McLaren/Ford
1975	Niki Lauda	Ferrari	Ferrari
1976	James Hunt	McLaren/Ford	Ferrari
1977	Niki Lauda	Ferrari	Ferrari
1978	Mario Andretti	Lotus/Ford	Lotus/Ford
1979	Jody Scheckter	Ferrari	Ferrari

(*cont.*)

Year	Drivers' Cup	Car/Engine	Constructors' Cup
1980	Alan Jones	Williams/Ford	Williams/Ford
1981	Nelson Piquet	Brabham/Ford	Williams/Ford
1982	Keke Rosberg	Williams/Ford	Ferrari
1983	Nelson Piquet	Brabham/BMW	Ferrari
1984	Niki Lauda	McLaren/Porsche	McLaren/Porsche
1985	Alain Prost	McLaren/Porsche	McLaren/Porsche
1986	Alain Prost	McLaren/Porsche	Williams/Honda
1987	Nelson Piquet	Williams/Honda	Williams/Honda
1988	Ayrton Senna	McLaren/Honda	McLaren/Honda
1989	Alain Prost	McLaren/Honda	McLaren/Honda
1990	Ayrton Senna	McLaren/Honda	McLaren/Honda
1991	Ayrton Senna	McLaren/Honda	McLaren/Honda
1992	Nigel Mansell	Williams/Renault	Williams/Renault
1993	Alain Prost	Williams/Renault	Williams/Renault
1994	Michael Schumacher	Benetton/Ford	Williams/Renault
1995	Michael Schumacher	Benetton/Renault	Benetton/Renault
1996	Damon Hill	Williams/Renault	Williams/Renault
1997	Jacques Villeneuve	Williams/Renault	Williams/Renault
1998	Mika Hakkinen	McLaren/Mercedes	McLaren/Mercedes
1999	Mika Hakkinen	McLaren/Mercedes	Ferrari
2000	Michael Schumacher	Ferrari	Ferrari
2001	Michael Schumacher	Ferrari	Ferrari
2002	Michael Schumacher	Ferrari	Ferrari
2003	Michael Schumacher	Ferrari	Ferrari
2004	Michael Schumacher	Ferrari	Ferrari
2005	Fernando Alonso	Renault	Renault
2006	Fernando Alonso	Renault	Renault
2007	Kimi Raikkonen	Ferrari	Ferrari
2008	Lewis Hamilton	McLaren/Mercedes	Ferrari
2009	Jenson Button	Brawn/Mercedes	Brawn/Mercedes
2010	Sebastian Vettel	Red Bull/Renault	Red Bull/Renault
2011	Sebastian Vettel	Red Bull/Renault	Red Bull/Renault
2012	Sebastian Vettel	Red Bull/Renault	Red Bull/Renault
2013	Sebastian Vettel	Red Bull/Renault	Red Bull/Renault
2014	Lewis Hamilton	Mercedes	Mercedes
2015	Lewis Hamilton	Mercedes	Mercedes

Note: The Constructors' Championship is based on the cumulative points gained by a team during the season. Currently each team is limited to entering two cars and drivers per race.

Appendix B: Grand Prix Graveyard 1950–2015

	Team	First year	Final year	Formula 1 races
1	AGS	1986	1991	48
2	Alfa Romeo	1950	1985	112
3	Arrows	1977	2002	382
4	ATS	1977	1984	99
5	BAR	1999	2005	117
6	Benetton	1986	2001	260
7	BMW Sauber	2006	2009	70
8	Brabham	1962	1992	394
9	BRM	1951	1977	197
10	Brawn	2009	2009	17
11	Caterham	2012	2014	56
12	Cooper	1950	1969	129
13	Dallara	1988	1992	78
14	Eagle	1966	1969	26
15	Ensign	1973	1982	99
16	Fittipaldi	1975	1982	104
17	Forti	1995	1996	23
18	Gordini	1950	1956	40
19	Hesketh	1974	1978	52
20	Hispania	2010	2011	22
21	Honda(1)	1964	1968	35
22	Honda (2)	2006	2008	53
23	HRT	2011	2012	36
24	Jaguar	2000	2004	85
25	Jordan	1991	2004	250
26	Lancia	1954	1955	4
27	Larrousse	1992	1994	48
28	Ligier	1976	1996	326
29	Lola	1962	1997	139

(*cont.*)

	Team	First year	Final year	Formula 1 races
30	Lotus	1958	1994	491
31	Lotus (2)	2010	2012	38
32	March	1970	1992	230
33	Maserati	1950	1960	69
34	Matra	1967	1972	60
35	Mercedes	1954	1955	12
36	Midland	2005	2006	18
37	Minardi	1985	2005	340
38	Onyx	1989	1990	26
39	Osella	1980	1990	132
40	Pacific	1994	1995	22
41	Parnelli	1974	1976	16
42	Penske	1974	1976	30
43	Porsche	1958	1964	31
44	Prost	1997	2001	83
45	Renault	1977	1985	123
46	Renault (2)	2002	2011	180
47	Rial	1988	1989	20
48	Shadow	1973	1980	104
49	Simtex	1994	1995	21
50	Spyker	2007	2007	17
51	Stewart	1997	1999	49
52	Super Aguri	2006	2008	39
53	Surtees	1970	1978	118
54	Talbot	1950	1951	13
55	Tecno	1972	1973	11
56	Theodore	1978	1983	34
57	Toyota	2002	2009	140
58	Tyrrell	1970	1998	418
59	Vanwall	1954	1960	28
60	Wolf	1977	1979	47
61	Zakspeed	1985	1989	54

(Adapted from Collings (2002), *The Piranha Club*. Virgin Books, p.278.)

Appendix C: Interview respondents (contributing to this and previous editions)

	Name	Organisation	Position at time of interview/s
1	Sir John Allison	Jaguar Racing	Operations Director
2	Chris Aylett	Motorsport Industry Association (MIA)	Chief Executive Officer
3	John Barnard	McLaren (1981–1986) Ferrari (1986–1990; 1992–1997) Benetton (1991) Arrows (1997)	Former Technical Director
4	Eric Boullier	McLaren	Director of Racing
5	Ross Brawn	Ferrari	Technical Director
		Honda Racing F1	Team Principal
6	Zak Brown	CSM Sports and Entertainment	Chief Executive Officer
7	Flavio Briatore	Renault F1 Team	Managing Director
8	Martin Brundle	Sky F1	Former F1 driver and commentator
9	Alex Burns	Williams F1	Chief Operating Officer
10	Nick Chester	Lotus	Technical Director
11	Luca Colajanni	Ferrari	Motorsport Press Officer
12	Isabelle M. Conner	ING	Chief Marketing Officer
13	Andy Cowell	Mercedes AMG HPP	Managing Director
14	Peter Digby	Xtrac Limited	Chairman
15	Stefano Domenicali	Ferrari	General Director

(*cont.*)

	Name	Organisation	Position at time of interview/s
16	Kevin Eason	The Times	F1 journalist
17	Bernie Ecclestone	Formula One Administration	President
18	Paul Edwards	Edwards Hospitality Services	Managing Director
19	Bernard Ferguson	Cosworth Racing	Commercial Director
20	Scott Garrett	Williams F1	Head of Marketing
21	Sir Patrick Head	Williams F1	Director of Engineering
22	Aki Hintsa MD	McLaren-Mercedes	Team Physician
23	John Hogan		Freelance Marketing Consultant
24	Brad Hollinger	Vibra Healthcare	Chairman and Chief Executive Officer
25	Christian Horner	Red Bull Racing	Team Principal
26	John Howett	Toyota F1	President
27	Eddie Jordan	Jordan F1	Founder and Chief Executive Officer
28	Paul Jordan	Minardi	Commercial Director
29	Monisha Kaltenborn	Sauber	Team Principal
30	Heikki Kovalainen	McLaren-Mercedes	F1 driver
31	Niki Lauda	Mercedes AMG F1	Non-Executive Chairman
32	Graeme Lowdon	Manor/Marussia F1	President and Sporting Director
33	Paddy Lowe	Mercedes AMG F1	Executive Director (Technical)
34	Paolo Martinelli	Ferrari	Engine Director
35	John Mardle	Renault	Operations Director
36	Felipe Massa	Ferrari	F1 driver
37	Allan McNish	BBC	Former F1 driver and commentator
38	Max Mosley	FIA	President
39	Mike O'Driscoll	Williams F1	Group Chief Executive Officer

(*cont.*)

	Name	Organisation	Position at time of interview/s
40	Ian Phillips	Force India	Director of Business Affairs
41	Raoul Pinnelll	Shell	Chairman, International Brands
42	Tony Purnell	FIA	Technical Consultant to FIA and former CEO of Ford's Premier. Performance Division
43	David Richards	BAR	Team Principal,
44	David Robertson	Formula Management Ltd	Business Manager for Kimi Raikkonen and Jenson Button
45	Nico Rosberg	WilliamsF1	F1 driver
46	Joe Saward		F1 journalist
47	Dickie Stanford	WilliamsF1	Test Team Manager
48	Sir Jackie Stewart	Jaguar Racing (2000–2004)	Director, Jaguar Racing
		Stewart Grand Prix (1996–1999)	Owner and Team Principal
49	Paul Stoddart	Minardi	Owner and Team Principal
50	Pat Symonds	Renault F1 Team (2002–2009)	Executive Director of Engineering
		Williams F1 (2013–)	Chief Technical Officer
51	Jean Todt	Ferrari	Chief Executive Officer
52	David Tremayne		F1 journalist
53	John Walton	Minardi	Sporting Director
54	Mark Webber	Red Bull Racing	F1 driver

(*cont.*)

	Name	Organisation	Position at time of interview/s
55	Charlie Whiting	FIA	Director of Formula 1
56	Clare Williams	Williams F1	Deputy Team Principal
57	Sir Frank Williams	Williams F1	Team Principal
58	Susie Wolff	Williams F1	Reserve F1 driver 2015
59	Toto Wolff	Mercedes AMG F1	Head of Mercedes-Benz Motorsport
60	Jim Wright	Toro Rosso	Head of Sponsorship
61	Hiroshi Yasukawa	Bridgestone	Director of Motorsport

Further to the above, we have also utilised transcripts from a series of research interviews conducted by the first author to explore the nature of performance in Formula 1:

Gordon Murray	Brabham (1972–1986) McLaren (1987–1989)	Former Technical Director
Ken Tyrrell	Tyrrell	Founder and Team Principal
Derek Gardner	Tyrrell (1971–1977)	Former Technical Director
David Williams	Williams F1 (1992–1998)	General Manager

Appendix D: FIA regulatory process

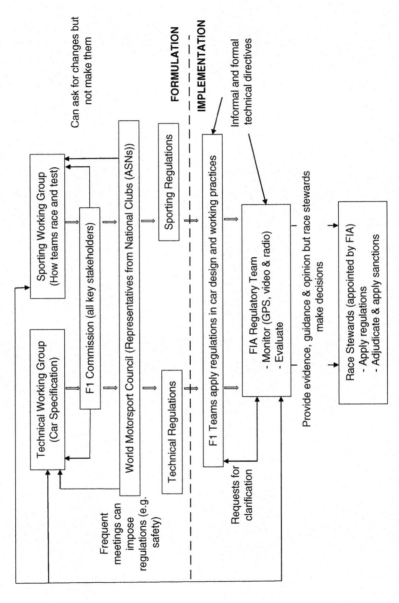

Figure 19 FIA regulatory process

References

1. *F1 Racing* (2015). March.
2. Autosport.com: http://forix.autosport.com/cmake.php?l=0&c=0.
3. *F1 Racing* (2015). July.
4. Autosport.com, 2 October 2015.
5. F1i.com, 16 October 2015.
6. Totalsportek.com, 'Formula 1 Prize Money 2015', 17 September 2015.
7. Repucom, January 2015.
8. Motorsport.com, 'Why the Singapore GP Is a Success Story', 16 September 2015.
9. Collins, J. C. and Porras, J. I. (1994). *Built to Last: Successful Habits of Visionary Companies*. New York: Harper Business.
10. Pitstop.com, 14 December 2015.
11. Pitpass.com, 11 July 2015.
12. Skysports.com, 25 May 2015.
13. Motorsport.com, 29 April 2015.
14. Webber, M. (2015). *Aussie Grit: My Formula One Journey*. London: Pan Macmillan. p.249.
15. Shenkar, O. (2010). *Copycats: How Smart Companies Use Imitation to Gain a Strategic Edge*. Boston, MA: Harvard Business Review Press.
16. Mosley, M. (2015). *Formula One and Beyond: The Autobiography*. London: Simon & Schuster. p.340.
17. Robson, G. (1999). *Cosworth: The Search for Power*. Yeovil, Somerset: Haynes Publishing.
18. Henry, N. and Pinch, S. (2002). 'Spatializing Knowledge: Placing the Knowledge Community of Motorsport Valley'. In Huff, A.S. and Jenkins, M. (Eds.). *Mapping Strategic Knowledge*. London: Sage. pp.136–169.
19. Lovell, T. (2003). *Bernie's Game*. London: Metro Publishing.
20. *F1 Racing Magazine* (2001). 'Ferrari's Nigel Stepney: The Man Who Can', April. pp.69–71.
21. Collings, T. (2002). *The Piranha Club*. London: Virgin Books.
22. Ramirez, J. (2005). *Jo Ramirez: Memoirs of a Racing Man*. Yeovil, Somerset: Haynes Publishing. p.87.

23. Hamilton, M. (2002). *Ken Tyrrell: The Authorised Biography*. London: Harper Collins. p.293.
24. *Autosport* (1980). 'Seasonal Survey', December.
25. *Autosport* (1992). 13 February. p.5.
26. *Autosport* (1992). 'The Man Who's Rebuilding Ferrari', 10 September. pp.28–30.
27. *Autosport* (1998). 'The Day the Magic Died', 13 August. pp.32–37.
28. Pitpass.com, 30 September 2015.
29. Motorsport.com, 7 January 2015.
30. Formula1.com, 9 September 2015.
31. *Financial Times* (2008). 'The Business of Sport: Formula One', 23 May. pp.40–41.
32. *F1 Magazine* (2004). July. p.48.
33. Autosport.com, 25 November 2014.
34. Hotten, R. (1998). *Formula 1: The Business of Winning*. London: Orion Business.
35. *Autosport* (2015). 6 August. p.16.
36. F1i.com, 16 August 2015.
37. Raconteur.net, 16 July 2015.
38. *Business Book* (2015). 3 June.
39. Wealthx.com, 'Wealth-X Reveals: The Top 10 Wealthiest Formula One Drivers of All Time', 17 March 2015.
40. BBC.com, 30 September 2010.
41. *International Herald Tribune* (2008). 'The Art (and Science) of Making a Formula One Champion', 6 June.
42. Spurgeon, B. *International Herald Tribune*, 27 April 1996.
43. *F1 Racing* (2004). February. p.43.
44. *Autosport* (2002). 'Seats of Power', M. Hughs, 28 November, p.39.
45. Jamesallenf1.com, 29 August 2015.
46. Grandprix.com, 10 September 2015.
47. Saari, O. (2015). *Aki Hintsa: Voittamisen Anatomia*. Helsinki: WSOY.
48. Cityam.com, 'Business Lessons from Formula 1; Have You Overloaded on Talent?' 15 September 2014.
49. Grandprix.com, 12 April 2015.
50. Pitpass.com, 12 April 2015.
51. Mercedes Twitter feed as reported in pitpass.com, 12 April 2015.
52. Grandprix.com, 22 July 2015.
53. F1i.com, 5 August 2015.
54. *F1 Racing* (2008). 'Britain Expects', July. p.78.
55. Katzenbach, J.R. and Smith, D.K. (1994). *The Wisdom of Teams: Creating the High Performance Organization*. London: Harper Business.

56. Gilson, C., Pratt, M., Roberts, K., and Weymes, E. (2000). *Peak Performance: Inspirational Business Lessons from the World's Top Sports Organizations*. New York: Texere.
57. Paddockeye.com, 24 April 2015.
58. Autosport.com, 7 August 2015.
59. Autosport.com, 12 February 2015.
60. Formula1.ferrari.com, 10 September 2015.
61. Autosport.com, 'Williams: Eliminating Blame Culture Key', E. Straw, 21 August 2014.
62. Autosport.com, 'Ferrari Denied Strategy Risked Tyres', B. Anderson and M. Beer, 23 August 2015.
63. Autosport.com, 15 June 2015.
64. Autosport.com, 'Renault Renegotiating Deal with Red Bull', D. Rencken and L. Baretto, 15 September 2015.
65. Campbell, A. (2015). *Winning*. London: Hutchinson. p.342.
66. Autosport.com, 'Allison Changing Ferrari Design Focus', L. Baretto and M. Beer, 7 April 2015.
67. Miller, D. (1990). *The Icarus Paradox*. New York: Harper Business.
68. Excerpted from Sower, V. E., Duffy, J. A., and Kohers, G. *Benchmarking for Hospitals: Achieving Best-in-Class Performance Without Having to Reinvent the Wheel*, chapter 10, and Wall Street Journal, 14 November 2006.
69. Wsj.com, 'A Hospital Races to Learn Lessons of Ferrari Pit Stop', 14 November 2006.
70. BBC.com, 28 March 2015.

Index

Lightning Source UK Ltd.
Milton Keynes UK
UKOW06n0326260817

308017UK00001B/1/P

9 781107 136120